One of Us

Sex, Violence, Injustice
Resilience, Love, Hope

Sandi Giver

A PEACE CORPS WRITERS BOOK

ONE OF US: SEX, VIOLENCE, INJUSTICE. RESILIENCE, LOVE, HOPE

A Peace Corps Writers Book

An imprint of Peace Corps Worldwide

Copyright © 2016 by Sandi Giver

Printed in the United States of America
by Peace Corps Writers of Oakland, California.

For more information, contact peacecorpsworldwide@gmail.com.

Peace Corps Writers and the Peace Corps Writers colophon
are trademarks of PeaceCorpsWorldwide.org.

ISBN 978-1-935925-69-9

Library of Congress Control Number: 2016959785

First Peace Corps Writers Edition, November 2016

What started as a statement to the Naval Criminal Investigative Service became a testimony of inspiration and empowerment.

For this reason, this book is dedicated to all of us.

Acknowledgement

Living through the events that inspired One of Us was a challenge. Writing in a raw and genuine way about my experience and the interactions that followed was also. Thank you to the following individuals who without their support and contributions this book would not have been written:

Peace Corps/Uganda staff including Medical Officers Liz and Anni, Safety and Security Coordinator Fred, Country Director Ted and Program Manager Shiphrah.

Washington, DC, based staff Kelly, Ed, Claudia and Richard.

Most of all, thank you to Security Specialist David, my advocate, road trip trial buddy, and the calm within the storm.

Friends and family members who supported me throughout the journey. Thank you for your love, letting me slowly, slowly heal and gain strength. Especially Kat for being an awesome friend in Uganda as well as in the states. I miss your face.

Everyone for the conversations that we have had in regards to the reality of sexual assault.

Spencer for our content-editing book club nights. Claiborne for his writing insights and review. Bethany for her on point review. Mike, Sandi, and Shelley for feedback.

Helen for the first copy edit and ridding the book of my Ugandan English.

Erika for being able to turn a conversation about meanings and ideas into a solid book cover.

Sarah for your work as the official copy-editor and your patience as I slowly worked through the revisions within sections that still bring up strong emotions.

Fellow Uganda Peace Corps Volunteer Nick for sharing your knowledge about Peace Corps Writers.

Frank with your honesty about the book layout and the need for better maps. Also, for being a cartographer and making a new map.

Josh for stepping up to the challenge of the internal graphic design work and Carrie for utilizing all of your experience formatting books.

I would like to thank the following people for being the greatest, kindest, most generous, encouraging people for backing One of Us:

Alexis, Allison A., Allison L., Amelia, Andrew and Caroline, Aubri, Becky, Ben Y., Benny, Brian, Candace, Cathy, Claiborne, Dave C., Dave H., David F., David N., Deborah, Dona, Erin, Ginger, Glenn, Haley, Helen, James, Janelle, Jenny, Jesse, Jessica, Joey, John, Jose, Kelly, Laura and Reid, Liz, Lori, Lynette, Mary, Ryan, Stephen, Susan, M.S., Sarah H., Sarah L., Sean, Stephen, Vasu, and the anonymous individuals.

Introduction

Sexual exploitation knows no bounds. Its injustices do not happen to specific people, committed by one type of assailant, with precise variables leading to the same crime. Sexual predators may use a demeanor that gets them close to their victims that goes unnoticed by others around them. Individuals we would never label as a predator by their appearance traumatize our friends and family members. While a few of these perpetrators are held accountable, the majority are not. This is not a women's issue that only affects females. Men have also come forward with stories of abuse. The impact of sexual assault goes beyond the primary victim to impact those around them. This is a human rights violation that we have the power to stop.

Nearly every time I turn on the news, there is another story of sexual assault—on high school and college campuses in Steubenville High School and Penn State, gang rapes in India, military sexual assaults all over the world, even incidents committed in the streets of my community are covered on the nightly news. They are stories of a victim, an assailant and whatever snippet of information the news source believes will improve ratings.

I fought back tears reading the comments following an Associated Press article released in over 220 news sources on my own story of rape and sexual assault. I sought legal justice in hopes that my attacker would be held accountable for his actions—so that his hands would no longer be able to traumatize other women. The press pitted the Peace Corps against the U.S. military since I was a volunteer serving in-country and he was an American Navy sailor supporting Navy SEALs in Uganda. I was not prepared for the malicious comments made by strangers drawing their own conclusions after reading a one-page article that could never depict that night or the year and a half that it took to get to trial.

One of the commenters said the newspaper articles from the first day of trial did not provide enough information to make a conclusion. Another said that because the newspapers revealed the alleged perpetrator's name the alleged victim's name should also have to be published. As the victim, I intimately know details of that that night. As the victim, I am not ashamed of my behavior so I will gladly provide my name:

My name is Sandi Giver and this is the story of my sexual assault. I started writing this after the Naval Criminal Investigative Service (NCIS) took my statement. I started because I knew I would have to recount every detail in my testimony, and continued writing as a way to release my tormented thoughts and my internal challenges. After having several conversations trying to understand sexual assault and learning about so many misconceptions, I felt the need to share my story— not only to help others find comfort in the fact that they are not alone in their struggles but to also bring about awareness and positive change.

Most of this book was written within days of the actual events. Dialogue is quoted as it was spoken, and as it stood out in my mind days after the events. This story is as accurate as possible. I struggled typing the words, but by doing so fortified my resilience for standing for truth and justice. And I found accepting individuals who supported me along the way in the Peace Corps, the military, with fellow survivors, and in the few friends and family members with whom I shared that portion of my treacherous journey.

We must educate ourselves about the impact of sexual assault, to be cognizant of the signs of sexual predators, and learn how to support our friends and family members who have experienced this kind of injustice. Within our communities, it is essential we have a system to raise a generation with healthy sexuality and to be law-abiding citizens. We must train our first responders to be trauma-informed and victim-centered, to have fair and just trials that truly deliver legal justice, and provide social service resources for victims. As a society, we need to start believing victims rather than blaming them. The cultural norm should be that we treat each other with dignity rather than tolerate sexual violence, and that we keep institutions and agencies accountable.

Please read what follows with a contemplative mind. Challenge your current conceptions of sexual assault, and become aware of the reality that survivors like me live through. If we acknowledge the reality of sexual assault, we can take action and change the status quo. I hope that in our lifetime, sexual assault will no longer be tolerated.

I am one of us. This is my story.

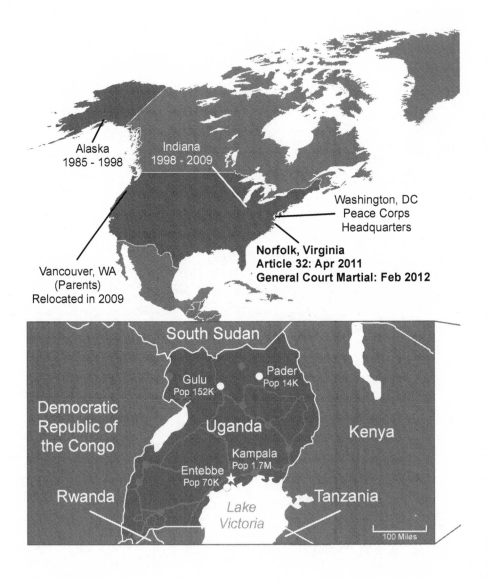

Alaska
1985 - 1998

Indiana
1998 - 2009

Washington, DC
Peace Corps
Headquarters

Norfolk, Virginia
Article 32: Apr 2011
General Court Martial: Feb 2012

Vancouver, WA
(Parents)
Relocated in 2009

South Sudan

Pader
Pop 14K

Gulu
Pop 152K

Democratic
Republic of
the Congo

Uganda

Kenya

Kampala
Pop 1.7M

Entebbe
Pop 70K

Rwanda

Tanzania

Lake
Victoria

100 Miles

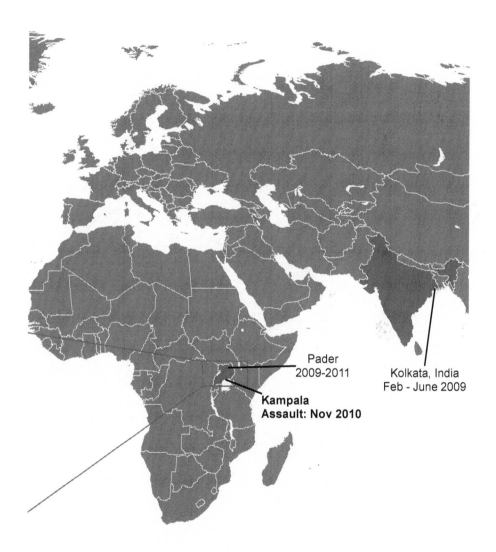

Pader
2009-2011

Kolkata, India
Feb - June 2009

**Kampala
Assault: Nov 2010**

Timeline

The Assault
Come On, Let's Go Already! - 11/5/2010

Report Filed with Peace Corps
It Hasn't Been Quite 72 Hours - 11/8/2010

Interview with NCIS Agents
Life as an Episode of NCIS - 11/12/2010

Article 32 (Military Pre-trial)
When You Choose to Prosecute a Rapist
4/21/2011

The Virginian-Pilot News Article
A Game of Telephone - 5/8/2011

First Proposed Trial Start Date
8/15/2011

Second Proposed Trial Start Date
9/3/2011

Google Search Warrant Approved
Confidential? Think Again.- 10/19/2011

Second Victim
And the Plot Thickens - 11/9/2011

Rape Trauma Expert
Pillow Talk- 11/16/2011

Third Proposed Trial Start Date
11/14/2011

Fourth Proposed Trial Start Date
12/5/2011

General Court Martial
A Peace Corps Trial Begins - 2/27/2012

Associated Press News Article
The Public Speaks - 2/28/2012

Contents

In allowing convicted rapists to be buried with full honors, the military continues to perpetuate the culture of impunity that allows soldiers to commit sexual violence with little worry of being brought to justice... It is sadly ironic that even though rape and sexual violence are now considered war crimes, our own military persists in practices that perpetuate those crimes. Unfortunately, this is merely one more example of the misogyny implicit in military culture. Women's bodies and lives have always been considered the spoils of war. The military's continuing disregard and disrespect for the safety of women's lives even within their own ranks, and in disregard of international law, should give us pause to wonder just whose freedom we are protecting.

—Lucinda Marshall, Los Angeles Times, January 30, 2008

Come On, Let's Go Already!
If We Don't Go Now, We Are Never Going To Leave!
6:30 p.m., Friday, November 5, 2010
Kampala, Uganda

I live in an African village called Pader. I used to live in a thatch-roof hut where I bathed under the stars and peed in a latrine—a cement slab with an oval opening over a deep hole in the ground. Now I live in a compound with a living room/cooking area, bedroom and a bathroom. No running water, but I heat up water before taking a bucket bath, stand in a basin like a giant Tupperware and pour water over my head, then dump the grey wastewater into the toilet to flush. Compared to a pit latrine, this is pretty spectacular.

I have been in Uganda since August 2009 as a Youth Development/Health Specialist as a Peace Corps volunteer (PCV). I love it. My partner organization is a girls' school for formerly abducted child soldiers and sex slaves, child mothers, orphans and vulnerable children due to the 21-plus years of insurgency caused by the Lord's Resistance Army. Thankfully, the official language at the school is English although there are 60-plus languages in Uganda. The cultural differences can be tough, but I like to think I am strong enough to take on a good old-fashioned challenge.

But enough of the challenge. This weekend, I am out of the village of Pader and headed to the Big City to relax. The mid-service training at the one-year point of being in-country as a volunteer is here. Time to join the other PCVs in solidarity.

I travel to Kampala a couple of days before the training to see people I hadn't seen in a long time. I hugged my fellow PCV Bridgette[1] when I saw her for the first time in two months. This is the first time we have to spend quality time together in seven months. We decide on Indian for dinner at the restaurant with outside seating on the roof. The greenery and Ugandan sunset soften the fact that my friend is not ecstatic about being back after a month spent with her family in the U.S.

"Sandi, do not go to the States. You are surrounded by friends and family who love you and do not judge you. Coming back to country is hard," she says.

Bridgette and I were first roommates at staging in the States. Staging is a day or two of orientation before being sent to your country of service. Since then, we've traveled this volunteer journey together. During training, we supported each other every day as we learned to survive in a new country without electricity or running water. Once we swore in as official volunteers, moving to our different sites, we had to learn to cope with isolation while trying to figure out what values we would bring to our new communities.

Personally, I love being a volunteer in a remote village. I enjoy learning and experiencing a culture unlike my own. Having to figure out the complexities of working in Africa is frustrating at times, yet rewarding and fulfilling at others. I have been extremely busy with a few projects in the works that help students deal with the psychosocial effects of living in a post-conflict area, as well as an income-generating activity utilizing international partners and the local economy for financial sustainability. I am well immersed in my community and I like being here.

Over a glass of wine, we chat about Bridgette's sister's wedding, village life and Peace Corps drama. At this point in service, I want to be around others and I need to converse easily about things only a fellow American would understand. I was glad fellow PCVs were in Kampala since I did not feel like spending the night in the hostel alone.

Bridgette and I have had our ups and downs, like many friendships. Living far apart rather than being able to quickly go to brunch to talk things out made friendships a little more difficult. Large group gatherings help us reconnect with the others in our small, forced Peace Corps community. Bridgette and I continue our conversation as we leave dinner. The sky is dark but clear as we walk 20 minutes back to our hostel.

Our hostel is a favorite of volunteers. Occasionally volunteers would come into Kampala to take care of medical needs or business. Out of the 150 volunteers in-country, a small handful are typically around trying to take advantage of the night life and entertainment.

Bridgette and I are tired after long journeys over rough roads. I'd taken an overnight bus and gotten four hours of sleep the night before. Neither of us has

---

1 The names of volunteers, the accused and his associates and some staff have been changed.

energy to be overly social so we agree that watching a movie in the room sounds better than going out. That is, until we stop at Gwen and Crystal's room to say hello.

Gwen and Crystal are two more volunteers in our training group of 43. During training, I was not close to either one of them, but we were friendly in social situations. I liked Gwen's carefree attitude and she always knew how to have fun. Crystal and I both grew up in Alaska but that's all I really knew about her.

At first, Bridgette and I lethargically sit on one of the beds helping Crystal choose which outfit to wear. Somehow, between Bridgette's embassy friends calling and the other two individuals in the room, we decide to push through the fatigue and take on the night. Flat irons are heated and makeup is applied.

When living in a village where a bucket is used for bathing, looking cute is the least of your concerns. Kampala, land of hot running water and feeling clean, reminds us of life before the Peace Corps. After washing up and looking halfway like we did on a ladies night in the States, we are confident women.

We take a few photos as we finish putting on lip gloss. Since I know we will be dancing, I choose to not wear my glasses for the night. They have grown loose and fall off if I turn my head too quickly. I can see perfectly fine up close and won't be wandering around without the others, so I think nothing of it.

I don't want my phone stolen (again) and the other three are bringing theirs so I leave mine in the room. I place my glasses and phone next to the bed where I know they will be safe when I return. I stick some cash in the side of my bra and leave everything else at the hostel.

We finally leave just before 11 p.m., after Gwen keeps saying, "If we don't go now, we are never going to leave." While riding in a taxi to a nightclub, we sing "Lean on Me" by Bill Withers at the top of our lungs. I, of course, sing as loud and off-key as I can to make the ride as ridiculous as possible.

Although Africa has the stereotypical village life, with thatch-roof huts and toddlers running around naked, the continent is full of cultural and economic diversity. There is money in Africa, but just a few people control these financial resources. People own mansions with swimming pools on hills with a staff to clean and secure the grounds. Uganda has a lot to offer tourists, including gorilla trek excursions, rafting the Nile and safaris. The country is so beautiful and easy to live in that I have met Europeans who retired next to resorts in Jinja near the source of the Nile. In America, $15 cocktail drinks at fancy clubs are maybe five bucks and at far more impressive locations. In Uganda, the average American can live like royalty.

Tonight, we are enjoying the nightlife that Uganda has to offer. Our first stop is Iguana, known as the young hip place to dance in Kampala, which is owned and run by Germans. There are quite a few German 18- to 20-year-olds doing their one year of service here, either volunteering at orphanages or helping with small-business plans. As the night continues, the place gets packed with expats and locals.

Our group of four chats with Bridgette's embassy friends. One of the guys buys us a round of drinks. I have not planned on drinking since tomorrow night we are celebrating Laura's birthday, another PCV. I tend to get horrible hangovers so I don't drink too often. I accept the beer the embassy guy buys but resolve to not drink any more. After a couple of hours, I am happy to leave Iguana. The drunken crowd is growing and men's hands are wandering.

We walk 10 minutes down the hill, rushing past the security guards and down the stairs to the expat land of the Irish pub of Bubbles O'Leary. The usual types of people are present: the 60-year-old man with the beautiful 20-year-old Ugandan woman wrapped in his arms, random businessmen and women and a few regulars watching rugby. While scoping out the place, the other three order drinks and I get a Fanta pop.

We dance and dance. Crystal goes crazy when certain songs are played, stomping her foot and pumping her fist. She is hilarious.

I glance to my right, toward the bar, and see a guy resembling an ex. Tall, blonde and handsome. My desire for international work made it impossible to commit to a man who was unable to live overseas due to a health issue.

Handsome and Friend walk onto the dance floor behind us. Friend's chest tattoo is peeking out of his button-up shirt. I find the stories behind tattoo placement and design intriguing. We talk but the loud music makes it difficult.

Nate is tall, blonde and handsome, and his friend Dominik has a similar muscular physique.

"I like my tattoos because they look good on me," Dominik says egotistically. Conversation is lost as the song changes and the four ladies regroup to dance.

Bridgette is flustered and irritated after an unpleasant conversation with an acquaintance. I suggest we leave and find a new place to hang out.

Just as we are heading out, Nate and Dominik come over to talk. Nate is from Alabama, I can hear the South in his voice. He is a "picture taker" for children's social studies textbooks. Dominik is from Reynoldsburg, Ohio, now working in construction a couple hours north of Kampala. They do not know each other well: They met at the hotel they are staying at in Kampala. They say they will only be around for the weekend.

Bridgette comes over and somehow Nate amazingly gets her to talk to him. At first, Bridgette does her usual brush-off—one-word answers to his questions. Nate even gets her to smile and before long they exchange phone numbers. I let Dominik in on the breakthrough while watching their facial expressions.

Dominik seems like a decent guy. I had lived in Indiana for 11 years and he was from Ohio; it's as if we have been long-time neighbors who found each other halfway across the world. Somehow, there is a sense of familiarity and comfort talking to someone relatable. I miss home and he can relate to the Midwest. We make small talk, chat about life in this crazy country, what work brought us here, joke about life overseas. Having a normal conversation away from the village and laughing is a feel good.

We are about to leave when Gwen and Crystal invite the men to join us. Nate declines but Dominik excitedly agrees to continue the night with four women. His demeanor becomes more of a ladies' man as we leave. Meeting new people and enjoying the nightlife in Kampala is the social norm in the expat community.

In the taxi, I take the front seat, the other ladies sit in the middle, and Dominik is in the very back, also known as the trunk of a hatchback car. The conversations are comical in an American way, yet rather vulgar and embarrassing as the Ugandan driver is listening in.

The topic of how female Peace Corps volunteers are sexually frustrated is blurted out.

"I heard that there are 'unmet needs with the ladies' in Peace Corps! I don't understand since I would totally take care of all of your bedroom needs. Aren't there guys who could take care of you?"

"The quality guys are taken by girls back home and the single ones are not doable!" they say in unison. It is interesting to hear them say that since Gwen has an expat boyfriend from Egypt, Crystal has previously dated another volunteer during training and Bridgette has made out with the male volunteer conveniently located near her village.

"I could satisfy each one of your needs tonight!" Dominik responds.

"Driver, I am so sorry about this conversation they are having!" I say. "It is not good for them to be talking like this!" I chat with the driver as the four of them continue to make sexual innuendos, egging Dominik on.

"I love Uganda!" he says, smiling ear to ear as he got out of the taxi.

Dominik offers to pay but he is fidgeting with his money and the driver tries charging him more than we had agreed on. I have exact change and hand over the proposed 15,000 Ugandan shillings, equivalent to about $7.50.

"Why did you pay?" Dominik asks.

"Because you were taking too long and he was going to overcharge you," I say matter-of-factly.

He hadn't been in country long enough to know how to work the taxi system. I also wanted him to see that I can take care of myself and didn't want to feel indebted to him in any way.

Although I make a very small amount by Western standards (around $250 a month), I live well in Uganda and live within my means.

We are now inside a more traditional African club when Dominik offers to buy us all drinks. Since I had just paid for the taxi, requesting a bottle of water does not seem like a big deal. Once we reach the back of the club, loud music makes conversations hard to hear once again.

As we stand in a circle, I am next to Dominik and Bridgette. I can't really dance but find it humorous to play around. Africans can dance and move their hips as if they learned in the womb. One of the more traditional African songs comes on and I jokingly danced with Dominik for the first line of a chorus. After a moment I return to watching the crowd.

A guy comes over and starts talking nonsense. I sometimes play the role of protector and caretaker. I feel responsible for Dominik because I initially approached him about his tattoos. The others invited him to come along with us but they are drinking and I feel a little responsible for their well-being too. I am the sober "mom" of the group. Between keeping an eye on the crowd and not being able to hear over the music, I am not paying attention to the conversations.

"Sandi, are you a squirter?"

"A what?"

"A squirter," they say again with giggles. Two of them confidently say they are. I turn back to watching the Ugandans dance. I look back at the group a few minutes later and see Dominik's shirt is pulled up around his chest and the other three rubbing his six-pack abs.

A few moments later when I turn back to the group, Dominik's penis is out of his pants and Crystal has unzipped the fly of her jeans. I stand there, mouth agape, wondering what the heck was going on. Apparently, the sexual conversations kept going and Dominik said he would do any of us right then, right there.

I look around quickly hoping no one else is seeing this ridiculous display. Before this, the night seemed mostly harmless, with a slight edge to it. Now, Crystal is toying with the open zipper of her jeans giving this badass expression and shifting her weight from hip to hip as if saying she is game to counter his own.

"I'm serious," he says as he pushes Crystal against the wooden support beam as if about to make good on his promise. Thankfully they stop. Crystal zips her pants and Dominik puts away his dick.

I'm overwhelmed with anxiety and leave to find the restroom. When I find it, it's repulsive and women are squatting in their short dresses and peeing on some sort of platform. I go back to the group.

As I approach Bridgette, Gwen and Crystal, they are discussing who should go home with Dominik.

"Sandi, how long has it been since you got off?" one of them asks me point blank. Before traveling and living in India with a different organization and then the Peace Corps in Uganda, I had purposefully chosen not to get involved with anyone I would be leaving behind. The others are amazed at how long it has been.

"Oh, honey, you need this the most," Bridgette exclaims with pity in her voice, hand on my shoulder.

I am in a dancing mood, not a hook-up mood. Because they saw me dance with Dominik for 10 seconds, and now they know how long it has been, they agree I should go home with him.

I decline.

I personally wasn't looking for a one-night stand—they aren't my thing. We've been hanging out with Dominik so he is not a complete stranger. He's definitely willing and available, but that doesn't make me want to sleep with him.

I can see the pity in Bridgette's face as she puts her hand on my shoulder and gives me the look. The dear-you-have-contracted-the-problem-of-being-the-least-sexually-active-of-this-group-of-females-and-we-are-here-to-help-cure-your-dry-spell look with one eyebrow angled.

Anxiety starts to bubble up inside me as I stand there utterly bewildered. My gut is saying I should get out of this situation and I want to. The others think it's funny as they keep badgering me to go home with him. Gwen senses how uncomfortable I feel. She comes over to whisper in my ear.

"You don't have to go all the way. Go, make out. See what happens. Relax and have a good night and then we'll see you in the morning."

Maybe I am overreacting and taking this all too seriously. Gwen's comment has me second guessing my own judgment. So, sure, why not? The ladies head to the front of the club leaving Dominik and me behind. I talk about how ridiculous the night has been and how random Uganda can be.

Dominik inches closer.

He kisses me.

He puts his arms around me.

He slides one hand down over my jeans. To my crotch.

"No, no, no. That is not OK. In Uganda, white women get bad reputations from things like that," I remind him and gently push him away.

I am tired of random men groping me. As a traveler in countries where women are seen as sex objects with inferior status, being a tall American blonde with blue eyes has not been easy. I was once wearing a top where the bottom was very loose and covered my jean pockets and an Indian guy decided to go under the shirt from behind me and grab my crotch while I was walking away. When I turned around and pulled my hand back to slap him, his friends apologized and I settled for only giving him a dirty look. I should have slapped him.

I'm not generally violent. In previous jobs, I'd been trained to stay calm in intense situations with violent, mentally handicapped individuals. I am trained to keep my cool and show no emotion, never lashing out at a client.

An eye for an eye is not usually how I play, but I wonder how many other times that same Indian guy had gotten away with violating other women. Dominik sliding his hand down instantly reminds me of this and I do not want the men in the club to think this is any way to treat any woman.

I am not so sure about Dominik.

Decent enough but a little intense.

Maybe the others are still around and I can leave with them. He hesitantly follows as I walked to the front to check. I am relieved to see the ladies sitting at a picnic table 10 feet from the exit.

Rather than taking separate taxis, we all leave together. First stop, Dominik's hotel. "Have fuuuun!!" cheer the other ladies as my foot meets the pavement.

"Are you OK, Sandi?" Gwen attempts.

I only nod in response.

I've been on my own since I was 19 and I've been able to manage.

Dominik takes my hand as he led the way into his hotel, which caters to foreigners. The main gate is closed so we walk around the wall, passing a security guard. We go through glass doors entering the large lobby.

I do not quite know what to expect from the night, but you never do in Uganda. You roll with the punches and take on the challenges as they come. With Dominik, his joining the ladies night was definitely not planned but that was OK. My last time even kissing a guy had been over a year ago. I would prefer to be with someone where we had a deep connection and we passionately kiss the night away. At 25 years old and single, I'll have to do with hopefully a good make-out session and nothing complicated. I've done this before and things didn't get out of control so I don't see why this time would be any different.

We make it to the elevator and he starts to kiss me and then grabs my long hair and pulls. It is not a gentle hair grab, but rather uninhibited.

Once out of the elevator, Dominik says how he has a roommate named Todd who should still be out. I hope Todd isn't there.

I keep thinking about how awkward walking into the room is going to be. The second-floor hallway never seems to end as we silently pass by doors on the right and large windows and seating on the left.

The door to room 123 opens and I see Todd lying on the larger bed, closer to the window straight ahead. Dominik's bed is the twin closer to the hallway. There is a closet to the sharp left, a flat-screen TV on a stand across from the beds, a large bathroom to the back left of the room and a chair next to the windows.

"Go to the bathroom," he commands without hesitating.

I look behind me as he closes the hotel room door.

The time is 3:15 a.m.

• • •

At 10:34 a.m., the door finally opens and I am able to leave. He gives me a halfhearted hug, a "good riddance" hug for me. I was taught to be a polite young lady so I muster enough energy to play nice while leaving.

I am numb inside.

Something very, very wrong just happened.

Whatever that was, it's now over. I made it. I don't like this feeling inside and I never want to relive those hours in that room.

I turn and walk down the halls of his hotel without feeling a thing. Empty. As empty as I can be after leaving that stale room. There are mirrors in the stairwell and I glance at my face as I bounce down the stairs. Sure, the reflections show my hair messy and pulled back but there are no physical bruises or marks. I am physically sore and feel like collapsing, but I am still breathing and the soreness will pass.

No one will ever be able to tell what I lived through. I can't think straight enough to verbalize it cohesively.

Empty.

Disgusting.

No one will ever know by looking at my glazed-over eyes what has just happened to me.

I am still Sandi.
I am still alive.
A piece of me is dead.

Walk of Shame, Walk of Shame
The Incident, November 6, 2010
Kampala, Uganda

I walked out of the hotel and took a deep breath, filling my lungs with the polluted air of Kampala. The air that surrounded me in Dominik's hotel room was gone. I was free. I could take a real shower soon. I wanted to scrub with soap and hot water to try to rid myself of the feel of his body against mine. Exhausted, I turned left down the sidewalk and started the trek back to my hostel. I didn't want to see anyone. I couldn't stop the images running through my mind.

Every year, Peace Corps/Uganda gets two new training classes—so at any given moment there are several PCVs in the capital city. As I numbly put one foot in front of the other, I looked up to see another volunteer. I was in the training class of August 2009 and she was in the training class the next August. Holly was on her way to the post office with gifts she had bought to send home to her family back in the States. I had no desire to talk to anyone about anything, but I stopped on the sidewalk anyways and talked to her about her family. It felt odd to talk to her about something so normal when I was coming back from Dominik's hotel room, but then again, I would never tell her about him or anything that happened.

As we were talking, Bridgette, Gwen, and Crystal walked toward us on the hill. They were wearing outfits over swimsuits. Their eyes lit up as they recognized me from a distance and all began to chant and clap their hands.

"Walk of shame, walk of shame, walk of shame!" they screamed.

I felt humiliated and wanted to disappear. With Holly present, I did not want to go into details. My head lowered and shoulders bent forward. Here I was, with a new volunteer and the ladies in front dripping with anticipation to hear about the "passionate" night with Dominik. This was not how I wanted this morning to be.

"So, how did it go?" they said simultaneously with grins that stretched from ear to ear.

"Wait, are you just now walking back from being with a guy?" Holly asked.

Perfect. I did not want this in the Peace Corps rumor mill and now they were bringing this up in front of someone I hardly know, much less trust.

"It was...OK..." I said as vaguely as possible. This was neither the time nor place. Maybe if I gave them pseudo answers they would drop the topic.

"Was he good? Was it a night of passion? Did you get off?"

"No, not really. It was not a great night," I said hurriedly. Maybe if I said it quickly enough this would be over soon. I told them how uncomfortable it was having Todd in listening distance. Then I mentioned how Dominik was rough and started to choke me.

"That's kinky," replied Crystal, looking down at her toes.

Wait.

What?

My chest tightened at this haunting comment. I looked up to see Crystal standing there with a look that said she wished she had gone, that she would have been into aggression and choking. Rather than friends who were concerned about my well-being or health, I got "That's kinky."

I was confused and slightly upset. I shut down. I did not feel like being belittled by the same women who pushed me on Dominik to begin with.

I wanted to be alone.

Silent.

Holly left to mail her package. The others were on their way to brunch and told me I would feel better after eating something.

I thought about that.

Maybe the void I felt in the middle of my body was not the hollowness of my soul but the physical emptiness of my stomach.

I reluctantly followed them to brunch and sat quietly eating a bagel. Afterward they decided to go swimming at the pool. Dominik's hotel pool. They planned to use his name if anyone asked.

This was not right. They asked if I wanted to go use the pool at Dominik's hotel. There was absolutely no way I was going back there. I could feel the irritation swelling from the fact that my initial attempt to tell them what happened was dismissed so easily. I quietly began to divulge more.

"The first thing he said to me was, 'Suck my dick.'"

"Really? There wasn't any foreplay? I told him to go down on you first," Bridgette said, confused.

"No, and then he didn't want to wear a condom. He reluctantly put one on but then later purposefully had it come off inside me twice. He started to choke me after I told him to stop."

"He didn't wear a condom!?"

No.

I continued to mumble about what happened and I could feel my blood getting hotter and my eyes begin to swell. I could not cry in front of them.

Gwen pulled me aside to say she was there for me, but what did that even mean?

"Are you still going to his hotel to use the pool?" I asked.

"Yes."

I didn't like this. I didn't like that they were going but there was nothing I could do. Why were they going to his hotel after what I just said? There was a public pool closer to our hostel but it charged $5 to swim. I thought to myself, If they were going, at least maybe they could get my earrings if they ran into Dominik.

"I left my earrings on the nightstand beside his bed. If you happen to see Dominik, can you ask him for them?"

Once we reached the street, I turned left toward our hostel and the others turned right to Dominik's hotel.

I walked alone back to our hostel. Upon entering the room with two beds, I saw my site mate Katherine. I changed into shorts and a tank top before crawling under the covers. I didn't have enough energy to shower at this point. I needed sleep and to forget the last 12 hours.

"Are you OK?" Katherine asked as she sat down on the edge of my bed.

"Yeah, I am fine. I am just really tired."

I could not go into details at this point. I was on the verge of bawling and I didn't want anyone around to see. Katherine's boyfriend was waiting for her anyways. She left and I fell into a dreamless sleep. When I finally woke up, I showered. Shortly afterward, the ladies came back to the room sunburned and smiling. I sat on the bed as they prepared the cake for Laura's birthday.

They told me they hung out with Dominik at the pool and how fun he was. Gwen left early and the other two women went up to his room and watched TV. All I could think was how they sat on the same bed where he had pinned my neck to the mattress no less than 12 hours earlier. Bridgette, with her degrading demeanor, mentioned how Dominik said I had been wet the whole time. Did he mention he spat in his hand to use as lubricant? Did she think I enjoyed his hand around my throat after I told him to stop? Why was she talking about how fun he was? Was she siding with this guy she had just met?

They must have mentioned how I said he choked me.

His response?

"I thought girls were into that!"

He never asked me if I was into that.

I told him to stop.

I tried to get up.

How did he perceive that as an invitation to place his hand around my throat? Even when I did get away, he waited until I turned around, my back to him, to put my neck in the crook of his arm and force me under the running water of the shower as I gagged and choked.

Girls Just Wanna Have Fun

Day 1: Sunday, November 7, 2010
Kampala, Uganda

I was wide awake, sharing the same mattress with Birthday Gal Laura. Saturday night had been a good birthday night. Right when we climbed into the taxi, "Girls Just Wanna Have Fun" blasted on the radio. Eight 20-something females sang away as the driver took us to Bubbles. The mood was set and the rest of the night was fun and carefree.

Now, Laura was still feeling the alcohol flowing in her blood from the night before as she peeled her arm off my face. At least six people slept in the three beds. Originally, I was supposed to be sharing with Bridgette in the room with Katherine, but when no one answered my knock at 4:30 a.m., I thought they were passed out and incapable of letting me in. Turns out, they hadn't gotten back yet.

After a few hours at Bubbles the night before, Laura and half the group went to another dance club, and I stayed behind with the others. Apparently, they ran into Dominik and Nate. Friday night, Crystal, Bridgette and Gwen had joked about how Dominik should be Laura's sexy birthday present. Today, the still half-drunk people in the room were talking about him. I sat listening silently. "Dominik was good-looking, but I think he took a little too much to heart being my birthday present. He wouldn't leave me alone," Laura said.

The consensus was that no one really liked his arrogant personality and they spoke of him with slight distaste.

Once the conversation moved to other topics, I walked across the hall to find my stuff. Bridgette was up and getting ready for the day. She was happy and glowing. Something good must have happened.

It seemed that Nate had gotten through to her. She was pitter-patting like Thumper and could not stop talking about him. She quickly regaled me with tales of how last night went.

"I am not going to sleep with you," she told him.

"Do you at least kiss guys?" he asked.

"Yes," she answered.

"Can I kiss you?" he proffered.

I was glad that she was happy but found her leading statement—I am not going to sleep with you—peculiar. Bridgette needed to be up front in telling Nate, "Hey, my friend Slutty Sandi slept with your friend Horny Dominik last night. Don't get your hopes up because I am better than that and I am not a whore like her." Maybe I was overreacting, or maybe it was the look she had on her face combined with the finger in the air, the head shaking back and forth and the disgusted voice.

Bridgette was the first person in the Peace Corps I ever shared a room with, at staging in the States. We had had late-night conversations about our dysfunctional families and had plenty of heart-to-hearts. Bridgette and I had a similar history, but different values.

Months before, after a week of sharing a room during an in-service training, I had gotten frustrated with how Bridgette disagreed with everything anyone had to say and made it known in a haughty fashion. I grew tired of her negativity toward men and host country nationals and the superiority that wafted off of her when she talked about people. I saw others get uncomfortable as she complained about how thin or attractive she had been back in the States. As Peace Corps volunteers, we all had to learn coping mechanisms to face the challenges of village life. But Bridgette's way of dealing with it seemed harmful to her psychological health.

I couldn't handle being her cheerleader anymore or feeling awful about myself after being around her. I didn't want to give up on the friendship though. So after the conference, I sent her an email explaining my view on different conversations, how they had made me feel and how we could improve our friendship. I had asked that she help me understand what had happened in her perspective and how to improve. She was cold and refused to answer any texts.

Because of this falling out, we didn't share a hotel room at the All-Volunteer Conference in September but, the last night before leaving, we had a short awkward chat. I got excited about a few new shirts I had found and showed them to her in my room. There, she said she had missed me and wanted to hang out again. Since this was the Peace Corps, with a limited amount of people in the volunteer community, I decided to give Bridgette a second shot.

Three days in and I was starting to regret my choice and think she was the black plague. Arrogant comments such as, "I am not going to sleep with you," from Bridgette were starting to get under my skin. Trying to be polite and play nice with others, I stayed quiet.

Oh, Bridgette. It was never my idea to elect one of us to go home with Dominik. Bridgette was the one who said I needed it the most. I had declined. She was always saying how great of a friend she was, yet I couldn't see it.

She kept repeating her story of Nate and her kiss throughout the day to our friends. Every time, I felt a little more upset, a little more judged and questioned why I stayed around. This was someone I had considered one of my closest friends in Uganda. But now I felt I couldn't trust her.

Bridgette kept talking about Nate while we walked to the movie theater to check showtimes. Just as we started up to the second floor, my heart stopped as

I saw Dominik walking toward us. I quietly said, "Hello," and looked away. After a couple of minutes of Bridgette talking to him and me staring off in the distance, refusing to look at him, we finally started back up the ramp.

"That was weird," said Bridgette.

"What do you mean?"

"He was fun yesterday. Today, there was something odd in the way he was acting."

"Probably because I was standing there," I responded.

"No, I don't think that was it. He didn't seem like himself," she said.

Maybe yesterday at the pool he never thought he would see me again?

Deep breath. Bridgette kept talking about her adventures with Nate and Dominik. After finding the movie times and traveling to our mid-service training, I would need to get away from her voice. Apathy and irritation toward Bridgette increased to full force.

Originally when I came down to Kampala for mid-service training, I thought I would be spending my free time cheerfully talking to other volunteers, hearing exciting news of what they were doing at their sites. I thought I would be cutting people's hair in the evenings, videotaping people as they answered questions about their Peace Corps experience and enjoying being out of the village.

I was out of the village, but I was definitely not enjoying it. I felt sick and just wanted to hibernate in my bed.

It Hasn't Been Quite 72 Hours
Day 2: Monday, November 8, 2010
Outside Kampala

Mid-service—a time of refreshment when volunteers re-connect with medical and managerial Peace Corps staff. Each session is specifically designed to prepare volunteers for facing Peace Corps life after a year of living at their sites. Sessions on complexities and frustrations of the workplace, cross-cultural issues, new income-generating ideas and medical care are fit into a tight schedule.

Chuck, one of the volunteers, talked about how he had previously thought forgetting his malaria prophylaxis was not a big deal. That was, until he got malaria. The nurses talked about the latest immunizations and shots we were about to receive. They set up a separate area at the end of the day for anyone who wanted one-on-one medical attention.

Another volunteer, Chad, spoke about HIV/AIDS in his village. In Uganda, polygamy is practiced, where one man will have five wives in the same location or spread out among various villages. They coined the term "sexual network" to indicate when married or committed people slept around with people who weren't their spouse (called a "side dish"). When the husband was not home or was with wife number four, it was common for the other women to get bored and lonely and find comfort with another man. If one husband has five wives, and those five wives each have one boyfriend but the boyfriend has another five women he's sleeping with, it becomes a very risky game of HIV roulette.

In America, serial monogamy is the norm: We think that most people have one partner at a time, or at least don't have multiple wives at the same time. If people get tested between partners, they can pinpoint the source of a new sexually transmitted infection, enabling people to take better precautions in spreading disease. In Uganda, the dialogue is more complicated when sexual partners aren't always consecutive and polygamy is, for the most part, accepted. (Although, there are happily married one-husband/one-wife couples as well.)

All of this made me think. During the course of Friday night and Saturday morning, Dominik had boasted he had been having sex since he was 15, would have sex as a job if he could, was proud that he had never gotten a woman pregnant and that he had just slept with a woman the weekend before and she did not have any problems with getting off. That is two women in one week's time. It takes up to three months for STD tests to show positive. Dominik forced me to have sex with him without a condom. My mind ran wild with the possible diseases that could be in my body at that very moment. I started getting nervous in my chair. At break, I looked for Gwen and saw her standing in the back of the room.

"Gwen, do you think I should talk to the PCMO? After Friday night, I am starting to feel sick about the whole thing and how he did not wear a condom."

I asked if I should talk to the nurse about being put on post-exposure prophylaxis, PEP, which needs to be started within 72 hours of possible exposure. PEP is the use of antiretroviral drugs after a single high-risk event to stop HIV from making copies of itself and spreading through the body.[2]

As much as my numb mind could, I was freaking out inside. I would be an idiot to have access to medical care that will give me something to decrease the likelihood of HIV and not take it.

"Do what you think should be done," Gwen said in her carefree way.

Not quite the answer I was looking for. OK. I decided to grow a pair of ovaries and talk to a nurse. I sat in the conference room for the last person in line to leave, thinking of what words to use to explain the situation.

Finally, I walked through the glass doors and sat in the chair at the end of the table. Susan was to my left.

"It hasn't been quite 72 hours," I said quietly with my head staring at the wood grains in the table.

"What do you mean? Seventy-two hours since what?"

"It has not been 72 hours since the incident."

"Sandi, can you please tell me what happened."

And I did. I told her the truth.

"This shouldn't have happened," I told her as I could feel my eyes start to water. "I tried to make him wear a condom. I didn't want to have unprotected sex. I told him to stop. I tried to push his hips away but he kept going. This shouldn't have happened."

"Sandi, were you raped?"

Rape? Rape. I knew what had happened was wrong but hadn't used that word in my head. When I had told the three women the basics of what happened, they didn't even flinch. They never mentioned the words assault or bad or wrong. They seemed excited by it.

Rape. I hate that word. The word itself sounds like you should be vomiting while saying it. That's what happens to weak women who can't defend themselves or when situations are inescapable. Rape is what happens to women who are too drunk and pass out around despicable men. Rape is what happens when guns or knives are present. If you admit to being raped, you admit to being a statistic.

Dominik sexually assaulted me. I was raped.

---

2 Centers for Disease Control and Prevention, http://www.cdc.gov/hiv/basics/pep.html

To me this did not add up. I should have never been raped. I used the buddy system and went out with a group of fellow female volunteers. I had very little to drink at the beginning of the night and felt very much in control. I didn't go out with the intention of a one-night stand and, even when the opportunity presented itself, I declined. But then I was the extremely tired idiot who believed my friend when she said it would be harmless, that we could make out and see what happens. I was the idiot who soberly put herself in the vulnerable position. Had I not cared about the condom, had he respected my one demand of wearing a condom, this may have been different. If all the variables had been on separate nights, this may not have happened. Too many variables colliding made it possible for his hand to be around my throat as he raped me.

"I guess," still not fully able to comprehend it.

I still did not want to say the words out loud. This was overwhelming. To speak to someone who was aware enough of sexual assault issues, who knew how to respond, had taken Saturday, Sunday, to now Monday at 5 p.m.

"Sandi, I am so sorry. I have to tell the country director. In cases like this, he has to be informed."[3]

Although I could see reason in that, I did not want Ted, the country director, to know. He knew me as the volunteer in the North. After this, he would know me as that volunteer who got raped. I wanted to be put on PEP. I wanted to be healthy. I wanted this to go away.

We talked about what would happen next as I sat there feeling smaller and smaller in the chair. We would have to do a rape kit and go to an outside medical facility to do that. Peace Corps nurses would be able to start me on all the meds. I would need to meet with Ted as well. They gave me five minutes to grab my purse and then a vehicle would take us all into town.

This was not how I expected to spend my mid-service. When I went upstairs to the room, Bridgette was on the bed watching TV on my laptop. I told her how I was leaving with the nurses and how this incident was getting a lot more complicated. She had Nate's number in her phone and offered to call to see if he knew how to get a hold of Dominik. Bridgette was not overly excited about calling him but she grudgingly did.

Nate answered and Bridgette told him how we were trying to reach Dominik. She said a little about "forced sex without a condom and HIV testing or something." I was not paying attention since I needed to leave and I had a million thoughts running through my brain. At the end of the conversation, Nate said he would call back with information. He didn't.

I left with the nurses for the 35-minute drive to the Peace Corps office. When we reached the office, I made my way to Ted's office. As usual, he was looking at his computer screen as I knocked on the door. I tried to smile as I entered but it didn't reach my eyes. I sat in the chair across from him on the other side of his desk.

---

3 Since September 2012, the Peace Corps now has two reporting options: restricted and standard. Under the restricted reporting option, only a limited number of staff are informed of the assault to provide direct services to the volunteer.

I liked Ted. He knew how to get things done and was very matter of fact. We had spent a lot of time working together on different projects. He reminded me of a stern yet devoted father, although he didn't actually have any children of his own. He played by the rules and expected others to be smart.

And I was not overly smart with this incident. I felt bad that I was sitting there about to complicate his life. This was definitely not in my plan.

"Sandi, I am sorry this happened."

I had to tell him the basic events of the night. Ted had already been in contact with the American embassy, the regional security officer and the Peace Corps Office of Safety and Security, and was covering all the bases he knew to cover. I knew with him, we would be working together on the more legal side of the situation in Uganda.

I didn't know much about Dominik, just that he mentioned he was doing construction north of the capital, that he had been there just over a week; he was staying at Golf Course Hotel over the weekend and then leaving. I didn't know how long he was staying in Uganda. I was disappointed in myself for knowing so little information about such a complex situation. I did know his last name, which was helpful and could help get the process started.

Ted asked if I wanted to press charges. Honestly, I was more worried about my health than what happened to Dominik. Charges seemed even more complicated and messy—a long, awful drawn-out process—and I wasn't sure I could handle the stress.

"Can't we call his mom and have her yell at him?"

That was my thinking. Although I thought making a slight joke was funny, Ted looked at me knowing better. The severity of the incident required a much different consequence and I was too overwhelmed to think about the long-term consequences. I squirmed in my seat as Ted explained the process and the importance of starting sooner rather than later. I decided starting the reporting process now with the possibility to drop it later would be best, rather than waiting to report the incident and nothing being able to be done because of timing.

I was nervous about the legal side but glad I was not alone. I can't imagine being a lone traveler when something like this happens. Heck, I can't imagine being in the States and having this happen without a medical team who knows what to do and staff who are more than willing to take care of business. This is not something I prepared for. How many employers in the States would fight for your legal rights as an individual? I was (and am) very grateful to have had this support system as a Peace Corps volunteer.

Ted gave me a hug before I left. His touch was both slightly uncomfortable yet comforting since I knew he was a safe person. I was still a little out of it. I would see him again soon enough.

I walked into the medical building to find the medical officers, Susan and Lisa, in the office at the end of the hall. For the third time that night, I relayed what happened, this time to Lisa. Another sad, yet supportive, response.

One person retrieved the rape kit while the other started gathering meds. The only food they could find was a cheese and bread sandwich left in the fridge by the off-duty nurse. I was instructed on all the meds and their usage. The emergency contraception typically referred to as Plan B or the Morning After Pill, was one pill right now and then one pill in 12 hours, or around 7 a.m.[4] To treat the possibility of gonorrhea and syphilis, one would require a shot in the hip and the other would require more meds. For PEP, I would be on another med twice a day for 30 days. I took a bite of food and then took a pill. Repeat.

I was nervous about the emergency contraception pills. All I could imagine was my whole uterus gushing out to prevent a small alien from growing finger-nails inside me. A roommate I had back in Indiana took Plan B once after she and her boyfriend had a condom break, and I remember her acting as if her abdomen was revolting which I guess is expected since common side effects include nausea and vomiting, breast tenderness, changes in menstrual period or headaches.[5] With all the meds the nurses were giving me, I had heard horror stories of sickness and nausea and I was not looking forward to ingesting any pills—especially PEP since the course of pills meant 28 days of feeling nauseated and irritated.

We went into the medical examination room so Susan could get a vial of blood to be tested for HIV. My veins are tricky and after two failed attempts in the right arm and one look at the left, my right hand was chosen to slowly drain out blood. They decided to wait on the hip injection since it was getting late and we needed to make our way to the medical facility to complete the sexual assault forensic exam.

Thankfully, there was a female nurse practitioner on shift to do the exam. Her night was coming to a close so we tried working as quickly as possible. We only had time to do the physical exam of vaginal swabs. It was an unpleasant feeling as the insides of my body were scraped, but it had to be done.

I didn't want to miss the conference nor have people ask what was going on. While everyone else would be hanging out, I would be at the follow-up appoint-ment completing paperwork.

Before I could leave, I had to see another nurse and get a shot in my hip. The hot sting of fluid running through my flesh was the worst shot I've ever received. Exhausted, I was glad to be finished for the night and allowed to go back to the hostel. Crackers and an apple from the convenience store was my dinner before one of the drivers dropped me of.

Exhausted, I walked up the three flights of stairs to find Bridgette still watching TV. Nate had not called back and Bridgette was bitterly disappointed. I kept telling her it was going to be OK. Dominik was the exception, not the rule. Nate was probably still making calls or something.

Bridgette offered to go with me to all the appointments and meetings but I didn't want her to. Maybe Bridgette wanted to be supportive but I had already felt so judged and cheated by her. The way she would gossip negatively around others, I felt like I couldn't trust her with the private information I had to tell the doctors, the police, medical officers and country director. She would probably bring up

4   Centers for Disease Control and Prevention, http://www.cdc.gov/reproductivehealth/unintendedpregnancy/contraception.htm

5   RX List, http://www.rxlist.com/plan-b-one-step-side-effects-drug-center.htm

Dominik and not believe me anyhow. Having her physically present would be more stressful than anything and I did not need that. I wished I could trust Bridgette. I wished people were more trustworthy.

As I pulled out med box by med box and explained how serious this was all getting, Bridgette became flustered. Her reaction was confusing and I couldn't understand her being flustered since I was the one having to go through the medical and legal process. Gwen came into the room to see how I was doing.

"It's getting really serious quickly."

"Why didn't you just tell the nurse the condom broke? You didn't have to go into details," Gwen stated.

The condom broke? That wasn't the truth. I didn't want the medical staff to think I was careless. Consensual sex with a simple broken condom would have been much more of a relief compared to the reality of what happened. Dominik had let the condom "slip" off inside me twice before I tried getting away.

I made some jokes about what would happen if the cleaning lady came in and saw a brown paper bag full of pills ("These volunteers are all druggies!"). I needed so many meds and so many different chemicals in my body to be healthy after a single night.

I didn't want this one night to define the rest of my life and I would do whatever was needed to live a normal life. This was the exception and not the rule and I would be OK.

I had to be OK.

While lying in bed before falling asleep, Bridgette asked me a question from the other side of the room.

"Sandi, did you get off at all with Dominik?"

Oh, God. Unlike what some people believe, sexual arousal does not equate to sexual consent. Apparently, sexual arousal or orgasm during sexually assault is more common than people think yet a taboo subject a topic isn't talked about.

Arousal is connected to physical biology and works from the same autonomic, reflex-driven system associated with heart rate, digestion and perspiration. Sexual organs are designed to respond to stimulation automatically. If there are two people and one person is forcing themselves on the other, even if the second person "gets off" that does not mean the intercourse felt good for them, they enjoyed it, asked for it or consented to the sexual interaction. If a person uses power and control over the other, what they committed was sexual assault.

I couldn't blame Bridgette for asking me if I "got off" with Dominik if one of the wrongful societal beliefs is that if an individual biologically gets aroused the person must have consented.

Right then, I did not want to answer any of her questions. I did not want to have to explain anything to her. I humored her with an answer, wanting nothing to do with her.

Taking Care of Business
Day 3: Tuesday, November 9, 2010
Kampala, Uganda

Another day of mid-service training. Another day of sitting in a chair staring at the speaker and my mind wandering off somewhere else. My right arm was sore from the normal mid-service immunization shots from the day before that all of the PCVs had to get. Unlike the other PCVs, I was starting to feel the effects of the other meds. I felt OK but mainly because I was in a daze, unable to feel.

I would have to leave early from training and slip away without anyone noticing. Luckily, the day ended early and, just as the van arrived to pick me up, we decided to do a group photo. While the driver was taking tea with a snack, I ran over for the group photos. As soon as the last photo was taken, I ran up the stairs toward the van.

"Sandi, where are you going?" someone yelled.

"Taking care of business! I'll see you later at the wine party!"

I didn't lie. I really did have to take care of business. No one really needed to know the details of what type of business. If nothing else, I could have been doing more research for the tailoring business we started at my school.

The van hit rush hour so the drive was slow on roads with giant potholes and fresh fruit stands on each side. I missed my village—with its one dirt road with a few side ones that were easily maneuverable. I could walk across town in 15 minutes. Kampala was messy and disorganized. My village roads were like giant sidewalks until the speeding nongovernmental organization (NGO) vehicle or lorry truck kicked red dust in your face as it passed. Kampala drivers were erratic and deaths from motorcycle accidents were common. I missed the simplicity of village life.

The night before at the medical facility was the simple part of the examination. I answered simple questions and then had a physical examination that required me to sit/lay there. Tonight would be the awkward night where I would have to answer intrusive questions. Details. Where, how, when and with what.

I sat down in the seat across from the nurse practitioner as she looked over the forms. Her thick European accent was hard to understand at times. The pages of forms contained words I had never seen before and drawings I had.

Depending on the state or country a victim is reporting from, the paperwork varies slightly. Common themes include patient history with the person's name, pertinent medical history, pertinent and post-assault related history, post-assault hygiene/activity. The forms ask if there are any injuries, were weapons used to hurt/injure/threaten, voluntary consumption of alcohol within 24 hours of the incident, had sexual abuse by suspect been ongoing, victim report pain, victim drugged by suspect, voluntarily taking controlled substance within 96 hours of incident, any other possible victims? Lots of questions.

I found a few sections interesting and oddly amusing:

Victim Demeanor Observed at Time of Interview (select all that apply) Include detailed description in narrative
- ❏ Afraid/Fearful
- ❏ Angry
- ❏ Calm/Controlled
- ❏ Confused
- ❏ Flat Affect
- ❏ Nervous/Agitated
- ❏ Shaking Trembling
- ❏ Tearful/Crying
- ❏ Withdrawn/Quiet/Flat Affect
- ❏ Other (describe)_____

I could identify with all the different emotions as she read off the list. Not necessarily three days later when we were filling out the paperwork, but throughout the last few days I had felt a little of everything.

I was afraid and fearful when I had lost control and Dominik's hand was around my throat. I was angry at myself for letting down my guard and ever going with him. Angry that he was so disrespectful, that he "let" the condom come off and that he violated my body. Calm and controlled as I walked out of the hotel. Confused on how this could be happening to me. Flat affect when I spoke with the others. Nervous and more agitated when he purposely had the condom come off inside me. Shaking as the water ran down my body and I tried to wash him off me. Tearful in the shower, as I lay in his bed trying to sleep. A part of me wanted to cry after every triggering thought related to that night. Withdrawn during brunch with everyone. Silent while surrounded by 40 of my fellow volunteers. I was not a fan of feeling. Anything.

POST-ASSAULT HYGIENE/ACTIVITY Not applicable if over 72 hours (check either no or yes)
- a. Urinated
- b. Defecated
- c. Genital or body wipes
  yes, describe:
- d. Douched
  If yes, with what:
- e. Removed/inserted tampon, diaphragm

f. Oral gargle/rinse
g. Bath/shower/wash
h. Brushed teeth
i. Ate or drank
j. Changed clothing

Practically everything had been done on the list. In the moment, all I wanted was to shower and to get his residue off of me. Had I been thinking properly or with the intention to press charges, I wouldn't have showered to keep evidence, but keeping evidence had not been my main focus right after being violated.

Maybe I could claim momentary insanity about my actions. But what about when I had told the other three? Thinking back, if any of them had been paying attention and suggested we seek help right away, I would have kept evidence. I was not thinking clearly on my own and needed them. They failed me in that.

The others didn't seem to think anything I said was that big of a deal or anything to be alarmed by. We stood on the sidewalk talking while I was wearing the clothes from the night before, we ate brunch and I told them more about the choking after I tried pushing him off because he refused to wear a condom. I could have used anyone right then to bring me to reality so we could have obtained more evidence immediately after the incident rather than three days later.

If those three had understood, knew the signs of sexual assault and had been informed on how to respond, they would have seen that I was in shock and pushed me to get medical help. Even with having friends who couldn't recognize what had happened and three days later, there was evidence of sex from the vaginal swabs.

And there were parts of the paperwork that weren't so entertaining.

ACTS DESCRIBED BY PATIENT:
- Any penetration of the genital or anal opening, however slight, constitutes the act.
- Type of sexual intercourse (oral, vaginal, anal).
- If more than one assailant, identify by number."

This included all the details that were hard to repeat. The type of things that made me embarrassed and uncomfortable once and then again when I had to check it over. But necessary information since these details make a case against the offender.

I had to describe the type of assault. Rape was defined as penile/vaginal penetration against the will, by force, threat or intimidation. Technically, he used manual strangulation as well. I hadn't sustained any severe physical injuries because my instinct was to freeze in fear. To some degree, the severity felt minimized when I didn't have physical proof to show. I couldn't pull up my sleeve and show knife marks. I didn't want any bruises or black eyes. I thought I was lucky to not have any physical evidence but the form had me thinking that, for reporting to police, it would have been better to have marks.

As soon as I told him to stop and he forced himself on me, he was committing rape. When he put his hand around my throat and used contemplated force, it became aggravated sexual assault. Why then was there still a part of me that felt like the incident was "too small of a deal" to report?

Type of Coercion/Force/Fear Involved:
- ❑ Disregarding the victims stated or otherwise communicated lack of consent
- ❑ Verbal pressure/coercion
- ❑ Position of authority (teacher, supervisor, boss, parent)
- ❑ Threat of physical force or violence
- ❑ Victim was incapacitated
- ❑ Presence of weapon
- ❑ Stalking
- ❑ Physical restraint
- ❑ Physical force
- ❑ Threat of death
- ❑ Abduction
- ❑ Other_____"

I had told Dominik "no" multiple times and even went into detail about why and he completely disregarded what I said. He had not been successful at the beginning of our encounter to coerce me into having sex without a condom. He was not in a position of authority, but he was in a position of greater physical strength. He never threatened me; he just took the intensity to the next level of control. There was no presence of weapons that I knew of. Stalking, no. Physical restraint, against the mattress and the shower wall. The more I thought about the interaction, the more he became a jerk in my mind. He was a selfish, manipulative bastard who sees women as little more than sexual conquests, mere objects for his personal pleasure.

In violence, this type of strangling is mostly done by men against women rather than against other men because of the inequality in physical strength between the two people. Depending on the strangling, it can compress the airway, interfere with the blood flow in the neck or work as a combination of the two. Manual strangulation can damage the larynx and fracture the hyoid or spine. When there is airway compression, it leads to fear of not being able to breathe and air hunger, which could lead to violent struggling. More technical variants are referred to as chokeholds, and are extensively practiced and used in martial arts, combat sports, self-defense systems and military hand-to-hand combat application. Some strangulation holds can be done from behind or from in front, pinning someone against a wall, or completely lifting them off the ground, which requires physical strength. An experienced person knows how not to leave bruises or marks. Strangulation can be used to violently hurt someone but can also be used as a fear mechanism to debilitate someone.

There doesn't need to be a weapon for an assault to be serious. Dominik's physique of an extreme body builder and his tactics were enough. Dominik compressed my airway and the blood flow in my neck. Although I was fearful, I did not go into violent struggling because I did not want him to push harder. When he put me in a chokehold in the shower, my back arched against his chest and I had to stand on my toes. This guy was definitely a fucked-up asshole. I was starting to understand why Ted thought filing a police report was a wise decision.

The rest of the report went quickly. At the end, like the victim assistance checklist said to, the nurse made sure my personal safety concerns were addressed. The interview lasted for about an hour and the nurse was nice and took filling out the paperwork very seriously. We parted ways, she wished me luck and I thanked her.

Ten minutes was all I had to wait for the driver. The sky was already dark but the evening was still young. I was back at the hostel before the end of dinner. I sat down with the group of ladies from Laura's birthday night with a plate of the leftover Ugandan food. Before I could eat, I received a call from an unknown number.

"Hello."

"Hello, may I please speak to Sandi."

"This is she. Who am I speaking to?"

"My name is Bruce Bradford and I am Dominik's supervisor. I've learned that there is a possible situation. Can you tell me what the situation is?"

"Well, we are trying to get a hold of him for some information. I can't really say anything but you can talk to my country director."

"Your country director?" I could hear a slight hesitation as he said this.

"Yes, I am a United States Peace Corps volunteer. I will give you his number. His name is Ted."

"OK, that will have to do."

"His number is in my phone so I'll have to end this call and text it to you right away. OK? Thanks for calling. Bye."

Apparently Nate had worked his magic in contacting someone who would know where Dominik was staying. I was surprised his boss was the one who called me, yet content that I could put him in contact with my boss if they wanted to go that route. Maybe this would all be sorted out quicker than expected. We now had a way to contact Dominik. Maybe the legal process wouldn't be as complicated as I thought.

I tried calling Ted to warn him about the call he would soon receive but there was no answer.

Dominik's boss called again four minutes later since the text with Ted's number did not go through. The networks in Uganda are fickle. I re-sent the number and called to make sure he got the number.

When I sat back down at the table, I whispered to Bridgette about the call I had just received and her brown eyes grew large. Others at the table asked what was going on.

"Just taking care of business!"

No one needed to know what type of business.

Lunging for Throats
Day 4: Wednesday, November 10, 2010
Kampala, Uganda

Another early day. I packed quickly since I knew the nurses were sending out a driver for the people who needed medical attention in town.

The van arrived and volunteers wanting the free ride back to Kampala poured in. We dropped off the majority of people at the hostel where we normally stayed and the few remaining rode on to the headquarters office. We arrived around 9:30 a.m. and I was told to first see Ted before we would head out to file the report and go to the forensic doctor.

What Ted had to say, I had no way to know. Dominik's boss had called Ted. Dominik's boss was a military man making Dominik a U.S. Navy sailor in Uganda short term. Ted called the embassy, Peace Corps headquarters in Washington, D.C., and our regional safety and security representative to see what protocol to follow. Never before had there been a case like this. As a U.S. servicemember, Dominik had diplomatic status and, although I was a U.S. Peace Corps volunteer, I still had to abide by Ugandan laws as an American citizen. No one knew exactly what to do.

To some extent, I thought this was humorous. A military man stereotyped as trained with guns and large ego rapes Peace Corps volunteer promoting peace and friendship. We both had loyalty to our countries but were living our service out in different ways. Maybe he was training Ugandan military on how to kill. I on the other hand, lived in a village and worked with a community scarred by years of war and murder.

Ted said the Navy Criminal Investigative Service (NCIS) would be sending a judge advocate general (JAG) to do an investigation. Because we wouldn't know how the Ugandan police would handle this information, we decided to leave out the military aspect while filing the report. Ted kept making calls and said he would let me know when the JAG arrived to conduct interviews and the investigation. For now, we would still file the report and do everything we could on our Ugandan side.

We had an amazing safety and security coordinator, Jack, in all his glory. He was a shorter Ugandan man (about my height) but had long arms and wore shiny pants. He was serious and passionate about keeping us safe. He kept a gun in his holster and walked with confidence.

Filing the report was smooth with Jack by my side. Our medical officer, Lisa, also came with us to the police station. I had never had to file a report of such severity, especially not in a foreign country. With the Ugandan norm of sexism and the perception that men deserve sex and a woman can't refuse or be unwilling, I was scared of how this might unfold.

As soon as we walked into the first floor of the station, Jack made small talk with a man in uniform next to the metal detectors. Apparently, this man was second in charge and Jack had worked with him closely at the embassy. Jack actually knew a lot of the people in the station, which helped us tremendously to get what we needed in a timely manner.

Jack was able to ask for a specific female to help file the report. We walked up four flights of stairs to a room with scattered papers and boxes with a couple of desks along the edges. We were told to wait until they could find a space private enough for us.

After 10 minutes, we were escorted into a room with a large desk and a couch. I was sure someone important belonged here and we were only allowed to use the room while he was away. Jack had left but Lisa stayed with me. I sat on the couch on the right side and the investigator was on the left. Lisa sat in a chair next to the couch.

The female detective introduced herself and we began with basic information like my name, date of birth, nationality, date of the incident and "this is my legal statement." I was American, Lisa was British and the investigator was Ugandan. I explained the basics of what had happened and where, and tried to keep it as simple and concise as possible while giving important details and nothing too graphic.

When the investigator read back what she had written, I shook my head and gave an odd look to Lisa. She had written things like "he lunged at me from the other side of the room and grabbed my throat with both hands," which was not true. Nigerian films are full of drama so I wondered if she had gotten that from one of them. I am sure she was enjoying writing this elaborate testimony but I honestly could not sign saying this was what happened to me.

There may have been disappointment when I asked if I could write my own testimony instead of her. I re-read my statement to Lisa and asked if there was anything else I needed to add for the case.

We left the room and headed back downstairs to turn the papers in. The room was old and smelled of urine. Once again, I could not imagine trying to file a police report on my own. I would have stood around for hours, and probably been given a male investigator who would have ridiculed me, as well as wanted juicy details.

Our next stop was the Ugandan forensic doctor for the official medical report that would be given to the Ugandan police. We went to a place that was in the part of town known for debauchery. When the sun goes down, vendors sell miscellaneous items including a small table full of different types of condoms.

This doctor was known as the best when dealing with sexual assaults and rape cases, but I was still nervous as we walked into the small clinic. At first, Lisa and I sat in chairs in the small hallway until a nurse asked us to go to the back. She asked what exactly we were there for. She started to prepare to draw blood since we were able to convince her that Peace Corps medical had already completed the physical examination. I was certainly glad to not have to go through another examination especially since it was now Wednesday and I was doubtful any physical evidence collected would be helpful at this point.

We were escorted to the doctor's small office where he sat directly behind a small desk. We closed the door and Lisa explained what the Peace Corps had already done and that we needed an official statement from a forensic doctor.

He seemed like a well-aged man and talked as if he had been working with sexually assaulted men and women for many, many years. His hair was starting to turn grey and his glasses made him look dignified. I was still surprised at the questions he had to ask and the details I had to provide. Sharing the events of the night felt like we were writing a drama as we went through the list of what Dominik did. I was having a hard time accepting that these events had happened to me, to my body. I was minimizing the actual events because I did not want to admit that I had been "weak," or at least not strong enough to defend myself, and violence had successfully been used against me.

After we finished the paperwork, we asked him a few questions about the legal system in Uganda and what normally happens after filing a report. He said the clinic will see six to 10 cases a week, whereas the police station said they only get a few a month. This meant young women and children were getting examined and filling out the paperwork, but never filing a report with the police.

Not believing the police would take sexual assault seriously, having to deal with the legal system and corrupt courts, fear of repercussions from friends or family if they knew, the perceptions of sexuality and women—take your pick: There are many reasons why someone wouldn't want to deal with filing an official report. Silence is one reason that offenders don't face any legitimate fear of consequences.

The more I had to repeat the story of what happened to me, the more I realized that what Dominik did not only deserved a slap on the hand from his mother but major legal consequences.

He is Such an Asshole
Day 5: Thursday, November 11, 2010
Kampala, Uganda

I knocked on Ted's door and, like usual, he seemed deep in thought. He explained what would happen since Dominik was in the military. Part of me was relieved that we wouldn't have to deal with the local court system and the other part was not looking forward to the long process that could be in front of us.

The NCIS was sending people to conduct the investigation later that day from Djibouti. We weren't sure how legal proceedings would work logistically since he was based in Virginia but was stationed in Uganda on a short contract and heading next to Germany. We learned that within days, he would be removed from Uganda and taken to Germany.

Complicated and complex. That's how I would describe the legal side. I did not understand some phrases that were tossed around but I made sure to ask. I learned that our American Peace Corps safety and security officer (PCCSO), stationed in Kenya, would also be flying to Uganda to oversee that interactions were taken care of correctly.

All of these important people were involved because Dominik abused his strength to violate a woman. The fact that I am that woman, a Peace Corps volunteer who chose to file a report, meant that there would be consequences for his actions.

As for medical, the medical officers asked how I was feeling since I started taking all the meds the week previous. The first few days weren't that bad. Between feeling exhausted and having to complete this interview or that examination, I did not really have the time or energy to take stock of how I was doing. I numbly floated through the week.

I started noticing that the PEP meds were wearing at me. Because I was so exhausted, I couldn't function at the level I normally did. I didn't have my usual patience or cheerfulness.

"Have you told your parents?" Susan asked.

"No, my mother's health is awful and I can't imagine how her health would be if I told her. She couldn't get out of bed for three days after I left for the Peace Corps because of the mental and physical stress of seeing her daughter leave for two years. I don't want her health to get worse because of me."

Normally, I was very open with my mom about what was happening. I told her about the riots where tires were burned in the middle of streets and gunshots could be heard at the top of the hill where I lived. There was the time I was walking home from dinner and a former child soldier turned security guard got drunk while on shift and started shooting at people while I was across the street. The time where a man barged into my thatch-roof hut, probably out of curiosity of what the inside looked like, while I was sleeping but thankfully left as soon as I started yelling at him.

I'd stayed safe and healthy through all of that though. This was too much for my mom. Not only had something bad actually happened, but I was raped. In a family where people are overly conservative, this was overly bad. I wanted to keep this as confidential as possible and I especially did not want my mom to worry and possibly get sicker.

I had been given the option to fly to Washington, D.C., for counseling, but the timing was inconvenient. So much was happening at site that I had been looking forward to for such a long time that I couldn't leave. People were counting on me for multiple large events and tasks and I felt obligated to stay. I didn't want to leave my Ugandan family right before the holidays. I wanted to stay until after the school semester had finished and holiday gatherings were enjoyed. I would possibly deal with D.C. after the New Year, while students were still on holiday and my social life had settled down.

We had already set up an appointment this morning with Lyla, the counselor from Europe. A friend had seen her a few times and had mentioned how they enjoyed working with Lyla. Never before in my life had I seen a counselor and I wondered what speaking to one would be like.

The appointment was in the same medical building that the forensic examination was completed. I waited in the lobby with other Westerners and Ugandans. Lyla came into the lobby and escorted me to a small library office space. It felt like an interrogation room with a single table and a chair on either side. I walked to the far end and sat under the window that looked out into the courtyard area.

Re-telling what happened never gets easier. I wish I could say that I did not tear up but that would be lying.

Lyla kept saying, "Ah, he is such an asshole," almost making me laugh. I am not one to usually curse but I liked hearing her call him that. Her calling him an asshole was empowering and validating since, yes, this guy was an asshole and what he did was wrong.

When I tried telling the others what happened, Crystal said the choking was kinky and was jealous I went instead of her. The way they had reacted made me feel guilty for not enjoying what they had set up for me, for not finding the interaction exhilarating and pleasurable. The way Lyla was reacting, blame was placed on him where blame was deserved.

"I am glad I was the one that went through this rather than the other women. Because of my previous work experience, I think I can handle this, where this would have torn them apart," I told her.

Since I had worked with young women at a home for pregnant and new mothers, had spent time in brothels in India with an organization helping women get out of the sex industry and had heard extremely horrific atrocities that occurred to women worldwide, what happened to me did not seem as damning.

Maybe that was part of the reason why I did not report the incident right away—the fact that my one night of aggressive, forced sex seemed like nothing compared to 15-year-olds trafficked from Nepal to India to be gang-raped, or friends back in the States who had been sexually abused by their fathers repeatedly from childhood through high school.

I could not understand how I had gotten to this point—from the supportive and helping side to being vulnerable and taken advantage of. I knew full well what happened to other women, yet all of a sudden, I had crossed the invisible separation and become one of them.

The rest of the counseling session went well enough. Not too many tears and I was starting to realize that maybe I shouldn't place all the shame and judgment on myself. We planned to meet again the following week after my other meetings with the NCIS.

After being in-country for 14 months, my clothes were feeling the wear and tear. Hand washing in a foreign country is not exactly the gentle cycle. Other than my underwear that stayed indoors, all other clothing dried out in the hot sun's warmth. I grew tired of the same 10 shirts and decided it was time to "update" my clothes by visiting Awino market in the center of town. Awino was the largest outdoor market in East Africa and sold everything from shoes and shirts to kitchen pots and pans. Plus, with the next day's interview with NCIS, I really needed to find something that did not make me look like a worn village woman.

Chuck—the volunteer who had contracted malaria—and I decided to go together after our morning meetings. He was recovering from being mugged and had cuts and scrapes along his right side of the face; he wasn't supposed to be alone in case there were complications with his pain meds. Me, I did not really feel like being alone in a market where women get harassed by the shopkeepers. The PEP meds were starting to kick in with the irritability and I could tell my temper was getting shorter and shorter.

We decided to walk the 30 minutes down to the market rather than get a ride in a matatu, which is a small 15-passenger van that holds roughly 20 people and stops along the road to pick up and drop off passengers. Chuck and I talked about Peace Corps life, stopped in the MTN store to have my phone looked at and looked at some hats, all while people kept looking at us wide-eyed, looking at Chuck's face and saying, "Boda (motorcycle) accident! Sorry! Sorry!"

At first, people's comments toward Chuck were quite annoying and we did not know how to respond. If someone has a physical deformity or something unusual in the U.S., courtesy dictates that you are not supposed to stare and you especially do not bring the abnormality up in conversation, much less physically point at it. Here, people follow you with their eyes until you are out of sight or make comments right in front of you.

We made up different excuses, some factual, some not so. People were shocked it was not a boda accident since those were so common. People who were the same color are automatically considered friends or family; it doesn't matter if one was born in Sweden and the other in Australia. If you were both white, you were friends or related. We turned this concept on the Ugandans and joked, "Ah, your friends did this!" with a punching motion. People we passed became even more apologetic. At one point, I said that he was my husband and that I punched him but then I felt bad because of the masculinity issues in the country and I would never really beat someone.

I realized that both Chuck and I were still in town for medical reasons, yet everyone was giving Chuck attention and saying sorry. I was invisible. I didn't have any outward physical evidence that anything was wrong. Only I knew the pain, sorrow and grieving in my heart.

To these people, I was another white person roaming the aisles of Awino. Sexual assault was such a private experience that hiding what happened was easy. Keeping the pain secret and not getting help was not healthy but I couldn't blame those who chose to do that. Maybe if I had large bruises on my neck and broken blood vessels in my eyes people would have noticed and said sorry. Instead, I had silent wounds that festered in an emotional and psychological cavern.

On top of that, I couldn't find a single thing to buy. Awino market was disorganized and there was hustle and bustle in every direction. Every three feet, there was some new shopkeeper trying to get you to look at hats, skirts, shoes, chickens. They yelled at you, grabbed your arm and made comments. The whole experience is overwhelming on a normal day.

Occasionally, I drifted away from Chuck for a few minutes at a time to see if other stalls had items that would catch my eye. I was looking at a pile of shirts, then looked up to see someone who I thought was Dominik, but was actually a fair-skinned African. Dominik was African American. My heart started pounding extremely fast, fearing that something bad was happening. Adrenaline flooded me. My breathing went from normal to quick short breaths, making me light-headed. I attempted to gather my composure, took deep breaths and walked back to where Chuck was looking at belts. No one noticed my small panic attack.

By the end of the day, I was able to find a few shirts. To exit, we had to pass the area with business attire, with suits and jackets of all shapes and sizes.

I wondered what I would wear the day I testified against Dominik: a power suit that showed a -business attitude or a flowy skirt that showed a softer side of femininity that was taken advantage of. Either way, there were going to be consequences for this internal pain.

Life as an Episode of NCIS
Day 6: Friday, November 12, 2010
Kampala, Uganda

I felt pretty comfortable talking to strangers who were trying to figure out who I was and where I fit in. Never before had I had an interview quite as important as the one with NCIS. The Naval Criminal Investigative Service (NCIS) sent over their judge advocate general (JAG) representatives to take an official statement against Dominik. My words could bring with them the weight of consequences and punishment.

I made sure to wear something conservative that still had some life to it—a gray skirt that fell past my knees and a loose maroon top that cinched at the bottom. My hair was down and the sun-bleached blonde streaks in the front were almost white.

People make judgments within one-10th of a second of meeting someone new: what they are like, their economic status, whether you could be friends or if the person would be a good boss.[6]

I had to walk into a room with people I had never met and share deeply personal and painful information with complete strangers.

The Peace Corps had a driver come and pick up a group of us from the hostel. We drove to the office and I checked in with the medical officers and the country director. The NCIS representatives weren't there yet, so I sat in the volunteer lounge at one of the computers.

I searched "military sexual assault consequences" and a few other phrases to get an idea of what would happen. The results were alarming. Apparently, military servicemembers had a bad reputation for sexually assaulting women around the globe, wherever they were stationed. There seemed to be a "what happens in Vegas stays in Vegas" mentality. American soldiers had been pillaging and raping host country national women, as well as fellow servicewomen, in the countries they served with little to no consequence for a long time.

There was an article from Asia where a host country national had been raped by a U.S. soldier. The article talked about how sexuality was viewed by men in the

---

6   Willis, J.; Todorov, A. (2006). "First impressions: Making up your mind after 100 ms exposure to a face". Psychological Science (17): 592–598. Retrieved 17 May 2014.

village and how the woman was powerless. The male villagers saw the military man choosing her as an honor. The soldier was able to pay some money to the greedy men in the village and nothing legal was ever done. Even if a soldier was sent somewhere to "keep peace" such as Okinawa, they could be committing atrocities of their own wherever they were deployed.[7]

I thought about the injustices women face all around the world, the harmful traditional practices being committed against women such as female infanticide, early marriage, dowry-related violence, female genital mutilation, crimes committed in the name of "honor" and maltreatment of widows.[8] While we definitely have gender inequality and violence against women in America, I am thankful for the individuals and communities who were brave and stood up against injustice and inequality. I knew I didn't want anyone else to have to face what I'd faced.

I knew I couldn't back out of pressing charges now. I had to testify, verbalize the details despite any feelings of embarrassment or violation. I couldn't let my fear of the unknown get in the way of a proper trial with possible consequences for my attacker. I had to use my voice despite how uncomfortable I felt inside.

Thankfully, Lisa who had gone with me to the police station and the forensic doctor, sat with me during the interview. She had heard me tell the story of what happened multiple times and would be able to remind me of missed details. I was still looking up information on the computer when she walked in and called me to come with her.

We walked straight through the building doors, left around the corner to the flight of stairs, right down the hall to a small conference room. I thought fleetingly to myself, Last time I was in this room was for a grants committee meeting. It is strange how useless facts pop into your head when you are on the cusp of doing something important.

The two men stood as we entered and shook our hands. Jake was the head investigator and a former lawyer. He was a little over six feet tall and looked like a family man. Aaron was the recorder and had wanted to get into the law enforcement field after getting out of the Marines. He was slightly shorter and more muscular. They seemed alright. They had calm voices and were relaxed—not as if they didn't care but rather to put me at ease and not feel like I was being harshly interrogated.

The hardest part of retelling the story this time was that they asked for specific details. I was acutely uncomfortable as I told them hand placements, sexual details having to do with genitalia, comments he had made to make me feel small, weak and deformed.

I started the interview with a decent composure but when I started talking about what happened at the hotel, I started to breathe slower and tried to hold back tears. Their questions were matter of fact but I could not help but imagine

---

7   Whose Security Is It? Military Violence Against Women During Peacetime by Cathleen Caron http://www.wcl.american.edu/hrbrief/v6i3/militaryviolence.htm

8   UN General Assembly, In-depth study on all forms of violence against women : report of the Secretary-General, 6 July 2006, A/61/122/Add.1, available at: http://www.refworld.org/docid/484e58702.html [accessed 10 July 2014]

their judgment as they heard my story.

Aaron handwrote his notes while I answered questions. They needed time to type them and have me initial the paragraphs with my approval. Another volunteer and I left for lunch but I was back within 40 minutes.

While downstairs, I saw Greg, our Peace Corps safety and security officer (PCSSO), who covered the East African countries. He was probably six-foot-five and a big teddy bear that you wouldn't want to cross on a bad day. I had met Greg when he was conducting a security assessment for volunteer placement of the northwest region of Uganda. That was in September 2010, right before I facilitated a training on "Working in a Post-Conflict Area" to the newest group of volunteers.

He told me he was there to make sure everything was handled professionally and with quality. I told him how amazing everyone had been and how smoothly the logistics seemed to be running, the NCIS guys were actually not as scary as I thought they might be and I was glad we were pushing forward with the investigation, even though I had been very hesitant at first. We talked for about 15 minutes before the NCIS guys were ready for me to return.

I slowly read what Aaron had typed. As I looked at the words, all I could think was, Goodness, that sucks for her! I still wanted to dissociate myself from the incident. I read back how the others responded. If this had happened to one of them and they had told me about it, I could only hope that I would have reacted differently, and been supportive.

Correcting spelling and grammatical errors took a while, although I told Aaron I was just being picky. Jake said I was a lot faster at typing than Aaron and that made me laugh. Toward the end, I just wanted to be finished and I didn't want to keep looking at the words that now described my life, what I'd been through.

They printed the four sheets of paper and I had to re-read it again initialing the beginning and ending of each paragraph. The grammar wasn't perfect but good enough. I couldn't look at it anymore.

Since Jake had been a lawyer in the past, he knew what to look for in a statement and the right procedure for creating a correct and effective one. He handed me a small pamphlet with victim rights and his contact information. He explained a little about what would happen next and then I was free to go. Four hours after walking into the room, I had shared and signed a statement that would help determine Dominik's fate.

They would finish their investigation today with interviews from Gwen and Bridgette. Gwen had already offered to help in any way possible and knew she would probably have to give a statement. Bridgette was more hesitant.

The next day, they would conduct interviews with other military personnel and Sunday wrap up with Crystal and then Dominik. They stated clearly they were interviewing all of us, but with him, they were interrogating him—which was not a pretty interaction. I learned that Dominik was with the Naval Special Warfare Group TWO Logistical Support Unit Combat Services Support Detachment. Within days, Dominik would be out of the country and at a post in Germany.

NCIS said they would speed things up with the next interviews since they already had the basic information of the night and my statement would be the longest. I didn't realize that Gwen would be back within 20 minutes. Bridgette seemed to be back in less than 15.

"Ugh! I can't believe how embarrassing that was!" Bridgette whined when she entered the volunteer lounge.

"What was embarrassing about it?" Gwen asked.

"Having to repeat what was said that night! I had to tell them about the conversation in the car. It was so perverted! Gross."

Did you have to tell them about his fingers pulling a condom out of your vagina? His choking you or his lack of respect for another human being? No. Didn't think so.

If Anyone Should Be Pissed, It Should Be Me
Day 7: Saturday, November 13, 2010
Kampala, Uganda - 1 week

Bridgette had been staying with some of her embassy friends the last few nights. She met a woman named Natasha who the year before had volunteered for a few weeks at my first organization in-country and suggested we all do lunch. I agreed and Natasha was the only one at the restaurant when I walked in.

I enjoyed being able to talk to her about my previous partner organization, Friends of Orphans. Bridgette came in about 30 minutes later while Natasha and I were laughing about the dysfunction and corruption of the director and organization.

"Crystal is on a bus and will be here tonight. She's pissed she has to come back to town for an interview," she said.

"If anyone should be pissed, it should be me," I said aloud, bothered by her statement.

I was quite proud of myself for speaking up. Everything she said made me mad. Bridgette might have good intentions or no intentions at all, but she was making things worse.

I put aside my frustration and continued with lunch. Bridgette left first, then as Natasha was about to leave, PCSSO Greg walked by.

When she left, Greg sat on a bench on the outside seating while I sat on a chair at the table closest to the open restaurant front. We talked about the legal process, the military judicial process, how long the process lasts, description of a victim's advocate—preparing me for what was to come. Somehow, sitting there and talking to Greg was comforting since I knew that the Peace Corps was going to be the support and help that I needed to get through this.

"There should be enough evidence against him. Even though these can become 'he said, she said,' he admitted to choking me to Bridgette and Crystal the next day. What an idiot. Someone had to see me come in and leave the hotel," I told him.

"The cameras have you coming in a little after 3:15 a.m. and leaving at 10:34 a.m.," he stated.

I wondered how the camera captured my face the next morning. Was the video from right after I left his room when I was just glad to be out of there, or when I laughed to myself about how ridiculous and awful the night had been when I took the stairs? Or did the video only see a tangled mess of hair on the back of my head as I walked through the front doors into the overly bright

morning?

I needed to get back to the hotel, which was a 15-minute walk down and then up a hill to the right. I still could not believe how Bridgette was acting. Her comment about Crystal being pissed she had to come back to town really didn't sit well with me.

I felt as if they were blaming me for inconveniencing their lives. Right after the incident, I was in too much shock to realize the depth and complexity of their involvement. I was extremely forgiving and took the blame and responsibility for everything. I told myself everything would be OK but all of a sudden I was doubting that.

Saturdays are a going-out night in Kampala. Although I wasn't drinking, I was trying to be social and to hang out with others. I rarely went out drinking or dancing in the States because it can be expensive, I'm an awkward dancer and I'm not into the overt sexual undertones. Here, with the right people, I had learned to have fun dancing in a familiar group.

Crystal and another volunteer, Amber, wanted to go out on a Saturday night. The routine would be to start getting ready around 7 p.m., take at least two hours to shower, do makeup and tease/curl/straighten their hair. After 10 minutes of brushing my teeth and applying makeup, I was ready to go. Chuck and I decided to leave around 8 p.m. for dinner and then meet up with the others later.

After dinner, we went to Bubbles O'Leary. The others weren't answering their phones so we didn't know where they were. A rugby game played on the TV so the Irish pub was packed inside. Chuck and I checked out the inside bar and found it overcrowded and hot, so we walked outside to the balcony.

While walking over, a guy passed by and said, "Thank you for your service" to Chuck and kept walking toward a table with five men. Slightly confused, we kept walking. Chuck recently had a haircut and Ugandans generally only give a short military-looking cut. Maybe this man thought Chuck was in the military and was thanking him for it.

Chuck ordered his drink and I ordered my Fanta Orange. Since there weren't any tables at the moment, Chuck and I stood talking. The same stranger came up and said, "It's good to hear a fellow American accent! There are too many Brits and Australians here!"

He seemed entertaining enough so we kept talking. His name was Gavin and he was about six-foot-two and muscular. He and his two friends, one about the same build but with a darker complexion and the other about five-foot-six and smaller, were in town for a conference. He told us they were presenting a paper about the effects of atmospheric pressure on malaria symptoms.

He left and went to say goodbye to a few of the people at his table. Chuck and I sat at a round picnic table outside the bar on ground level. All of a sudden, Gavin and his two friends were sitting with us.

They explained where they were staying, which was a very nice hotel next to the U.S. embassy. They had been in town five days so far. When I asked them how long they would be in Uganda, they said they were on an "indefinite vacation." We clarified that we weren't military but rather Peace Corps volunteers and said a little about our placements in different parts of the country.

"What you guys do is rough! What are you drinking? What can we buy you to drink?" said Gavin.

They looked at my Fanta Orange with dismay.

"What did you put in there?"

"Ice?" Sometimes being the only one not drinking can be awkward—especially if you are not drinking because of certain meds.

All of a sudden, Crystal and Amber sat at the table, each next to one of Gavin's friends.

"This is Crystal, Amber, also Peace Corps volunteers," I introduced them.

As soon as they sat down, I was a little uneasy about how the night would play out. Amber had been known to go out to Kampala with very little cash but then find a guy to flirt with the whole night who would buy her drinks. I had gone out with her a couple of times and she worked her magic well. She didn't sleep with them, but never paid for a drink if she could help it.

The atmosphere changed as the women started talking to the guys. They offered to buy drinks, and the ladies accepted. Crystal asked Gavin about his tattoos, having him remove part of his shirt to get a better look. Crystal then shifted her shirt off her shoulder so she could show Gavin hers.

This was all starting to feel a little too close to the last time I had gone out with Crystal. Is showing another person your tattoos a gateway action into being sexually assaulted? Of course not, but some might find it risky or rebellious.

Crystal started talking to Gavin's friend as he came back with drinks. Gavin and I kept talking, and he was actually really funny. We talked about whether or not my friends were interested in his friends—which, of course, was no—but they knew how to down the drinks his friends were buying.

He talked about when was in California, he'd tell a woman he's getting a drink and that she is more than welcome to come with him and buy her own. To some that might come off as rude, but I thought it was an amusing way to see if the woman was interested in him for free drinks or for the company.

Gavin and I kept trading tidbits back and forth, laughing while we people-watched. I asked him more about his scientific work and what he did. He answered, but his answers seemed suspicious.

"Are you here on contract with the military?" I posed.

I had asked before but I was getting more suspicious. I was on edge knowing that Dominik's boss and a few other military men were in town to be interviewed by the NCIS.

What if this was a trap to get me to say something about what was going on? They kept asking why I was not drinking and what I was doing in town. What if they were here to try to repeat what happened the week before? I was not about to trust short-term males who were in town for suspicious reasons at the moment.

"Of course not!" He said shaking his head back and forth.

"OK, it's just that there was an incident last weekend with these military guys, where one said he was a picture taker and the other was in construction. I really do not like being lied to, so please be honest."

He assured me he was not military.

"There is a lot you will never know about me," he said.

The laughter we had recently shared became brittle. While looking at Gavin, I heard his short friend make a quiet comment to the other two women.

"We are all former military and are here as private military contractors..."

"You're here with military! He just said so," I said as I pointed over to the short guy. U.S. military presence was not public knowledge to Americans.

Gavin threw up his arms in disbelief that their cover had been blown.

"What are you really doing here?"

"Keeping this guy's ass out of trouble!"

Even if the U.S. was trying to conceal that it had military and private contractors in Uganda, I didn't appreciate how difficult it had made my life. I had been lied to the week before by someone in the military.

"Let's just forget he said that."

I tried sitting on the bench and going back to the conversation but I couldn't do it. I sat there for five minutes before I decided to excuse myself from the table. I went onto the balcony to see another friend who had just arrived. Gavin followed a few minutes later, but talking to him now felt uncomfortable.

"What's going on guys?" Amber slurred as she came up to us.

"We were just having an honest conversation about life. Isn't that right, Gavin?"

"Sure is."

I left Gavin and Amber to get another Fanta. Throughout the night, I could see them talking but I didn't care. I stayed away, talking to other people I knew. Gwen had shown up at some point and it was good to see her.

Some time had passed and the majority of our group had migrated to the Latino club next door. Crystal had her NCIS interview at 10 a.m. and I had offered to go with her, so we couldn't stay out too late.

Chuck and I walked to the Latino club to see Gavin and Amber talking toward the entrance. I walked up to Gwen and Crystal to see how they were doing.

"Guys, Gavin asked me to go home with him! What should I do? He's really hot and he's staying at a hotel with a pool!" Amber slurred.

I stood there listening to Amber and became utterly pissed with Gavin. I left the group to confront him.

"Gavin, what's your deal with Amber? Did you ask her to go home with you?" I am sure he was caught off guard as I walked up while he was texting on his phone.

"Whoa, whoa, whoa. I did not ask Amber to come home with me. If that's what she thinks, I did not say it."

Of course, Amber walked over so we could not finish our conversation. I sat down in a chair next to Crystal.

"Now you know how I feel. Amber is always stealing the guys I am into."

What? Amber was not stealing anyone from me. I was not upset with Amber because she was talking to Gavin. I had chosen to walk away from Gavin earlier in the night. I was upset with Gavin for different reasons.

Crystal got up and left. A few minutes later, Amber sat on the arm of my chair.

"Sandi, what should I do? I am poor and do not have money for drinks. I live in a village where I only bathe a couple of times a week because of water shortages. He has hot running water! I told him I had not shaved but he said he had a razor. I am always lonely and he's really hot!"

She was slurring her speech, but I got the point.

"Amber, I would really advise you not to go home with him tonight. The reason I am in town is because of an incident of a good night turned bad. You might have more money if you came into the capital only one or two weekends a month rather than every weekend and then you would be able to purchase your own drinks. You are right, Gavin is really hot and he's staying at a great hotel, but how about you wait until you are sober tomorrow and the time is not so late to be alone with him? How about you stay with us tonight and then maybe go with Gwen tomorrow to use his pool or something? Come home with us, dear."

I felt I had to say this even if she would get upset. Amber agreed with the logic but sat with me. And sulked. She had already given him her number so he would be able to call the next day if he wished.

Before Gavin left, he came up to the sitting area where we were talking.

He put his hand on my shoulder and said, "Sandi, you're a good friend." He told Amber she was beautiful and that he'd call her.

I couldn't be mad at Amber because Gavin called her beautiful. She is beautiful and a good person as well. It was worth waiting 12 hours until she was sober and capable of making rational decisions. A good guy would see that any day. Why women feel like going home with a guy is do or die is bewildering.

I half laughed. I knew he meant his comment. I wasn't about to let what happened to me be Amber's fate as well. I knew I couldn't be the friend who pushed her onto someone or passively did nothing. I just wished someone had done the same for me.

Everything Is Not OK
November 14-20, 2010
Kampala, Pader, Uganda

The next week was a blur. I tried to act like nothing major had happened. I was told again about the opportunity to leave Uganda for a break and to see a counselor back in the States but I had too much going on at my site. Counseling would have to wait until after the holiday season when I had more time.

Gwen was still in town for medical and I asked her what she thought about staying or leaving. She was supportive and told me that I should do what I was comfortable with. She left the hostel to stay with her boyfriend. I found a tiny card on top of my red backpack, which made me smile.

> Sandi,
> Not sure I will see you before you go to GLOW or to the U.S., but either way I hope you have a great time, regardless of your decision. This has been such a tough time for you but I love how you have been able to remain positive. If you need any support just let me know. If you are around tonight maybe we can hunt down Martin for breakfast! See you soon. XO
> Gwen

Out of the three women, I felt closest to Gwen now. After brunch, she could have kept it to herself that she had been possibly violated by someone but she shared it with me. She even made the effort to leave me a little note. It was the small acts of kindness that I really appreciated.

I told medical I would be away a few days so I could do a full-day visit to my village. My direct Peace Corps supervisor was doing a tour of the North and would visit my village on Tuesday, November 16. I could have stayed in the capital because of medical but I wanted to be involved with the conversations she would have with community members. I thought being present, listening and contributing to conversations was important as she spoke to the director of my host organization and the head teacher, who was my direct supervisor in the village.

On Monday morning, I packed my belongings and walked 30 minutes to the bus park. I was tired, hot and hoping the day would go smoothly. At the bus terminal, a man grabbed my wrist to pull me toward his bus company. Without stopping, I quickly swung around my hand and slapped his.

"Frisky!" he said as I walked away. Why did people keep touching me? Frustrated, I could feel blood rush to my face as I became hot with anger. Ten hours later, after another bumpy African bus ride, I unlocked my front door.

In the morning, I gathered my bag with notes and the business binder. The meetings seemed to go smoothly other than slight tension about the name of the handbag business.

Since July 2010, I had worked with the head teacher, the tailoring teacher and a few others trying to brainstorm a name that would reflect what we were doing with a taste of the Acholi culture. Our team at the school agreed on Maleng Designs and the name was perfect.

I wrote this article months beforehand for interested parties who wanted to know who would be creating and benefiting from the handbag sales:

We are the young women of Northern Uganda. Yes, most of us grew up in internally displaced people camps because of a 21+ year insurgency caused by the Lord's Resistance Army. Yes, some of us were abducted from our homes and forced to become child soldiers and sex slaves to rebel commanders. Yes, some of us became child mothers while captured and some of us became child mothers after being sexually assaulted in the camps. Yes, a lot of us are orphans and have lived through extreme violence and ugly poverty. And yes, at one point we were unsure if we would even live to see tomorrow...

But today is a new day. With peace in our land after living in fear, we have hope for tomorrow. We are moving back to rebuild our homes from the ground. We may have physical reminders of our pasts such as scars and fatherless children, yet they also remind us we have been liberated and are alive. We are striving for a happy and healthy tomorrow for ourselves and our children.

We may not be able to attend a traditional school because we have a little one to breastfeed, because war and poverty have taken everything away from our families, but we have been given a second chance at our educational institution—the only secondary school in Uganda that is designed to help and empower young women and girls like us.

"When I am studying in class, I forget the tragedies of the past. I forget that I am a child mother. When I am in class, I am a student who is pursuing success in life."

Our pasts of tragedies do not define us. We are more than a number, a percentage or statistics. We are young women with unique and beautiful faces and names who have hope for the future.

Maleng Designs, "maleng" meaning "beautiful" in our local language of Luo, was founded in the belief that we are capable of a beautiful life where we are

self-sustainable by creating beautiful designs.
We are defining the path before us and we claim a beautiful future.

I wanted outside donors and buyers not to see our students as only victims of their surroundings but rather as individuals able to overcome tragedies, pushing forward toward a successful future.

For more than 21 years, Joseph Kony and his militia terrorized families in northern Uganda. Internally displaced people were forced to live in camps, relying on the government for food and shelter. Normal life was destroyed. Even now, individuals are dealing with the psychological effects, transitioning back into their villages and have a sense of helplessness and disempowerment. Communities are slowly trying to recover.

Peace Corps/Uganda specifically selected eight volunteers with international experience, who had worked with diverse populations and were mature to test the North. My group was the groundbreaker, Team Acholi, the first to be placed in the North since the beginning of the war. We were excited to take on the challenge.

Being a Peace Corps volunteer in a post-conflict zone is not easy for many reasons: It's difficult to integrate, people are hyperaware and on edge psychologically and resources are still limited in remote villages.

One of the blessings, yet also a slight curse, was the number of outsiders who were working or visiting there. There is a strong international NGO presence doing relief work and attempting sustainable development. Since the war had moved into the Democratic Republic of Congo, the North was relatively safe for outsiders to visit.

The numbers of expats had reduced in the deep villages since 2007 but there was still a fair number who came and went. I had seen all sorts of people from other countries: art therapists, counselors, documentary filmmakers, grad student researchers, medical teams, music therapists, international NGO staff on field visits, photojournalists, short-term missionaries from two weeks to one year and independent volunteers. Once, I was called "immortal" by a short termer since I would be staying long after they were all gone.

While the majority of these people had great hearts and were trying to do amazing work, sometimes situations did not sit well with me. Outside donors would visit to take photos of young mothers with their children—each wanting horrific stories from the students to help drum up potential funding. "War tourism" and "voluntourism" had people coming and going very quickly.

While a willingness to learn more or to help was great, sometimes the interactions between outsiders and the students felt more like they were visitors and exhibits at a zoo, respectively. "To your left, we have a former wife of Joseph Kony." Snap, snap, snap went the cameras. "To your right, you can see any one of the adorable African children who were conceived from a rebel commander raping a 13-year-old or older girl." Sometimes, I felt as though my girls, my students, these young women, were seen only as victims, or numbers on a grant proposal.

Because of the war, combined with relief work not transitioning into sustainable development quickly enough, there was a sense of severe helplessness and dependency on outside sources. With the handbag business, the idea was to help the school utilize students' skills who had been sponsored through the tailoring program. By having a local target consumer population as well as an international customer base, they could take more control of their situations and move forward with their lives. Although the name Maleng Designs would be a reminder of the beauty these young women possess, the name or title was not as important as getting the business up and running in the first place.

Day 10: Tuesday, November 16, 2010
Pader, Uganda

At 8:30 p.m., I got a call from the director of the organization I was partnered with.

"Sandi, you are going to have to change the name. It must be Megober Designs, after the Megober Restaurant. The name cannot be Maleng Designs."

"OK, I hear what you are saying. Before I am able to change anything, I must first speak to the rest of the team and discuss this with them. Once I have consulted them, I will be able to get back with you."

"Ah! You are not listening! You must change the name! If you do not believe me, ah, I have a problem with that!"

Over and over she repeated herself loudly in a thick accent I struggled to understand. Worse, the phone kept cutting in and out. I didn't have the energy to try to explain or argue with her. She kept going for nine minutes, ridiculing me. Her yelling at me was too much of a reminder of Dominik belittling me in the shower. I'd had enough.

"I am sorry but I can't talk about this right now. Goodnight," I said and hung up.

I needed to do more than just get off the phone. I was starting to feel the side effects of my meds. They were leaving me nauseated and extremely tired, making it easy to get agitated and sapping me of my motivation to do anything.

The director of the organization could be difficult to work with on a normal day. Being on meds that caused me to feel nauseated and irritated, I couldn't deal with an overpowering dictator and be level-headed. If I waited until January to go to America for counseling, the stress of being a Peace Corps volunteer with a dictator director was going to eat away at my soul. I decided leaving sooner than later was vital.

With that decision, I would have to leave behind all my prior commitments in Uganda. I would surely disappoint students, teachers, the photographer from Europe and other volunteers, and I would have to tell my parents something was going on.

When Bridgette had told me Crystal was pissed she had to come to Kampala to make a statement, I felt as if they were blaming me for an interruption and inconvenience in their lives. If only the "inconvenience" of sexual assault lasted only for however long the physical act lasted. Instead it felt like my pain and trouble were seeping out of me and into others' lives.

I traveled the 10 hours by bus back to Kampala on Wednesday. Thursday morning, the medical officer and I started the process for a medical evacuation to D.C.

Day 13: Friday, November 19, 2010
Kampala, Uganda

Telling my mom something had happened was even harder than breaking plans and letting people down in Uganda. She had called the week after the incident, but I had told her everything was fine. We talked like any other week.

I loved my mother. I can't imagine there is anything worse than finding out someone you love has been hurt and there is nothing you can do. Maybe I was trying to protect her when I didn't say anything the first week. Maybe I couldn't articulate the words, verbalize them to someone who is such an intrinsic part of my life. Maybe I was already overwhelmed and confused, and I didn't want to burden her with my feelings. If she were to start asking questions, I would break down and I couldn't let her see me that way.

I loved my mom and wanted to make her proud by serving in the Peace Corps. Right then, I didn't want her to see me struggling.

I swore I was strong, independent and able to take care of myself. Right then, I felt so alone, distant from everyone and frustrated with how I had let myself down.

I missed my family.

Not until two weeks after it happened, when the Peace Corps bought the plane ticket to return to the States, did I tell my mom I had been assaulted.

"Sandi, were you raped?"

I couldn't say those words. I was trying to be the brave and strong woman she had last seen at the airport before leaving for the Peace Corps, about to take on the world.

"Mom, I was assaulted and I am not going to say anything more about what happened."

"I think you already answered it."

"No, Mom, I was assaulted and that's all I am going to say."

The fact that she was thousands of miles away and could not hug her daughter, or have me sit on her lap and cry made her extremely sad and I could hear her sniffle on the other side of the phone.

Day 14

On Saturday, a Peace Corps driver and I went back to Pader so I could pack. I stopped at the school and all the teachers were away on a game drive. I would have been invited, but I had been in Kampala. I saw Lillian, a student I had nominated to attend Camp GLOW, a girls' empowerment camp, in December.

"Lillian, something has happened and I must leave now. I won't be able to attend Camp GLOW with you and the other four students. I am very sorry. I really wanted to go with you." I held her hand as I spoke.

"Ah! I am not happy about this!" she said as she yanked her hand out of mine.

I could see the confusion and hurt on her face. To her, she probably saw me as abandoning her like all the other "white" people had in the past. Her reaction hurt. I didn't want to abandon her or disappoint her; I wanted to be there for her, but I simply could not. My heart sunk as I knew I couldn't explain further.

Day 15

Sunday, we drove back to Kampala. Gwen was still staying with her boyfriend in town. She, Chuck, myself and a few others decided to go out for one last hurrah the night before I would get on a plane back to America. The decision was made and we went to Bubbles for a drink.

I saw Gavin in the midst of the crowd standing on the balcony. He was with the other military men and I indifferently said hello as I passed. I really thought Gavin was a good guy when we first started talking the week earlier, and I wanted him to prove that not all men would take advantage of a woman, to give me a reason to trust him.

And he did.

We talked about Amber and what happened with her before she decided to come back to the hostel with us. Apparently, she had asked him where he was staying, gave him big eyes when he talked about the pool and his hot running water for a shower and more or less invited herself to stay with him. Amber was pushing herself onto Gavin, and what guy is going to turn down a pretty lady?

A wise woman once told me that Peace Corps volunteers are put out on a L.I.M.B.—in a situation where they may feel lonely, isolated, miserable and bored. Granted, this can definitely happen back in the States, but the intensity and stresses of living overseas in a different culture can make the feelings even stronger. We can usually manage these feelings but sometimes we let our guard down. Something familiar, that can make us feel valued, connected, blissful or makes us feel alive—like someone we're attracted to—can be dangerous if approached unwisely. Sometimes we act in a way that the "limb" breaks and we land with a thump.

While at Bubbles, a friend from South Africa came up and said something that I needed to hear right then.

"Sandi, you aren't the type of girl that would go home with a guy that you just met."

He continued to talk about my characteristics as a woman and how I seemed like one of the last wholesome ones out there. The previous week, Bridgette had seemed to be rubbing in my face the fact she wouldn't go home with Nate because she had higher standards or some bologna. This guy had no clue that I was battling feelings of being a whore and being judged as one by someone I had previously trusted.

I started to tear up and told the South African the reason why I was leaving in the morning. From the other side of the large balcony, Gavin saw me starting to cry. He found Gwen, directing her to me so we could leave together.

The South African gave us a ride back. When we were inside the hotel, Gwen found a male friend from our training group to stay in the room until I was OK. There were two beds but he came and sat down next to me. I was still trying not to cry, but couldn't help the tears from flowing as he gave me a hug and held me.

"Sandi, you're a good girl. You didn't ask for or deserve this. You are such a good girl. Sandi, you are such a good girl."

He had struck an emotional chord and it broke my idealism of everything being alright. My life was not alright. I was broken and dirty and a mess.

I was leaning my head against his chest as I cried and I couldn't control how much pain was in my heart. I am a good girl, dang it. What happened to me was awful, uncalled for and unlawful.

And that's when I began to weep, with long, uncontrollable breaths where it felt like I was gasping for air in the middle. The kind of gasping sobbing that feels like it will last forever because you don't know how long the ache and torture will last. For the first time, I allowed myself to truly grieve over what had happened. I hadn't realized how dearly I needed to release my emotions.

Not a Newbie

Day 28: Saturday, December 4, 2010
Washington, DC

Ever since I was a kid, I've had a willingness and desire to help others. In 2008, I wrote in one of my Peace Corps application essays that, "Everyone has a story, yet people rarely take the time to listen. Some of these stories are full of joy and excitement while others are full of tragedies and pain. I want to listen to these stories and I want to help give those who live in desolation hope for the future—to give the rejected and forgotten a reliable friend who is not judgmental, believes in who they are and what they can become."

I was not new to stories of sexual exploitation and injustice. I'd been drawn to work and people who had tragic, painful stories. I had worked with victims of crime mainly in Indiana, India and then in Uganda.

In Indiana, I was a direct services advocate in a group home for pregnant and new mothers ages 13 to 23. Renee[9] was my youngest at 13 and had become pregnant after being drugged and raped by her boyfriend's best friend. Renee's mother had kicked out her father after he wouldn't clean up his cocaine habit and worked long hours to make ends meet. Her sister was 10 years older and would take Renee with her on drunken nights. Granted, at 11, Renee had been put on house arrest after driving a vehicle into a house while intoxicated, but she was trying to straighten out her young life when she was assaulted.

Renee's boyfriend's jealous friend, 19 at the time, wanted her to come over. Renee's only requirement was that his mother be home for accountability. After she walked the 45 minutes to his house, she found that he had lied and his mother was nowhere in sight. He offered her a glass of water and a seat on the couch to rest before she started the trek home in the summer heat. She was hesitant about staying but needed a drink and accepted the water. Within a few minutes, her body went numb and she could not move. This was most likely from him mixing ketamine[10], also known as a date rape drug, into her drink. He climbed on top of her and started saying how she wanted him and how he deserved her and not his friend.

---

9   Some names have been changed to conceal the identity of those individuals
10   http://www.medicinenet.com/date_rape_drugs/page2.htm

She tried to push him away but her limbs refused to move. Once she was able to stumble out of the house and report it to the police, they were slow to believe her. A girl with her legal history at such a young age was not taken seriously. Thankfully, the police eventually took the report and brought charges against him. Simply because of her age, he was found guilty of statutory rape. Her baby boy was adopted by a family friend who was unable to have children. Renee was able to get back home after a couple of weeks of recovery.

In 2009, I spent five months in Kolkata, India, learning about and seeing firsthand the effects of severe poverty and perversion. I went with an organization where half of our time was spent volunteering at two of Mother Teresa's Missionaries of Charity homes: Kalighat, for the terminally ill, and Prem Dan, for long-term care. The other half of our time was spent visiting young women in brothels and working alongside former sex workers who were employed with dignity by the organization to sew handbags and quilts. The products were sold online to provide fair wages and benefits for the women.

When I first arrived, I made friends with this tiny older woman named Anipa who was crouched over and silent. After laundry was finished, I would properly pamper her with massages and sit with her. She once said something to a lady who then translated for me, "She says you are a beautiful woman." Six of us went to Bangalore for an extended weekend and when we returned, I watched her mysteriously wither away. I spoon-fed her, then sat beside her gasping body and sung softly to her. After a month, her bed was empty. No more crying, no more pain. Although she was physically gone, I still teared up a year later thinking of holding her hand, seeing her in agony, not being able to speak the same language yet still caring deeply about her well-being and hoping that she felt loved during her last days on earth.

A week later, a woman named Nasrin was carried in on a blanket looking like she was just skin and bones. When I greeted her in Bangla, she surprisingly responded in English. Most of the women I interacted with in this house knew little or no English. The highlights of my morning were talking to her about Indian culture and her Bangla lessons. She had been abandoned by her family after paralysis took over her hips and lower body.

She had once been in love, she told me. She wanted to be loved, to have a family, to work, to be in control of her life, but her body had let her down. Her parents had abandoned her, and the man she had loved sexually assaulted her. During a low point, when a male friend visited her for Easter, I could tell her mind had been filled with thoughts of despair, feeling useless and needy.

"I have to ask someone to get me water or food, to lift me onto my bed, to help me go to the bathroom. I can't do anything for myself. I pray that God will take me away. I do not like my life; all I want is death. Pray that I will die," she told me one day.

It was a hard and honest conversation.

We had missed each other multiple times between her being in the hospital for treatment and then my holiday in Nepal. The day before flying back to the States, another volunteer, Aimee, told me that Nasrin was back and thought I had died. I couldn't let that be her last thought of me so I took an early-morning train to see her. When I got there, she had two walking canes next to her and was gaining back her health. I was only able to stay 30 minutes or so, but it was worth it. One of the hard parts of being in an area for a limited time is dealing with the unknowns that come after you leave. I was grateful I'd been able to see the life come back into Nasrin's eyes and her hope for the future before I left.

Most days I spent in India did not hold as much promise as that one. Certainly not the day I saw a 15-year-old Nepali young woman, caked with makeup and pulling down her skirt. She had been trafficked in with a promise from a family friend that a "job" was awaiting her. She was forced to sell herself. It was her second day of work as a sex worker in Sonagachi, where 12,000 other young children and women survive by selling their bodies.

We would visit these young women alongside an American translator stationed in Kolkata. One lady we visited had a daughter with severe cerebral palsy. She lived in a room smaller than most closets that she shared with her two sons and daughter. If ever there were a blurring of the line between work life and home life, this was it. The same bed where they slept was the same bed she worked in. Her sons were able to leave while she pleased men but her daughter was not. The daughter would lie underneath the bed as a man was serviced above her.

Another young woman, Sabita, had just gotten back from a "business trip" out of town. We talked about her beautiful long hair and using eggs as conditioner while she played with my glasses and took pictures with her wearing them. Through the translator, she told us how she wanted to learn English. Then her 4-year-old son walked in and gave his momma a big kiss on the cheek. When he walked away, "Would you ever expect a 19-year-old woman like me to have a 4-year-old son?" Sabita asked us.

She told us that she had been married early by her parents and he had his name tattooed on her body as a sign of ownership. She was his property. Not long after their marriage, he sold her to a brothel owner. Sabita burned her skin with acid to rid herself of his name. The black ink was masked by a long patch of raised skin.

In India, I lived in a small village outside of town. There was physical distance between where I slept and the severe sexual exploitation of the red-light areas. For four months, we would spend the day visiting children and young women and then go back to our home.

In Uganda, I lived in the heart of where tragedies had taken place—more than 21 years of tragedy. Since I was in Uganda for two years, I was able to build the trust that time and quality interaction create, which allowed my students to be more open with me.

One of my students, Agnes, watched the rebels kill 27 people in her village. Her uncle and three other men were then chosen to be boiled and fed to the rest of the village. The Ugandan military came in before anyone was forced to eat their family members and friends. Agnes was abducted that day but was able to escape the rebels within a couple of months. She was now studying computers at a vocational training school.

The people in my area all had unique stories. One of my students was a young "wife" (read: sex slave), to the leader of the Lord's Resistance Army (LRA). After becoming pregnant, she had complications from a fistula[11], also losing the child, and was sent to Nairobi for care. Although Joseph Kony had told her to come back after treatment, she heard about a school that helped reintegrate formerly abducted children and educate those who couldn't attend traditional schools due to gaps in schooling, severe poverty or because they were young mothers and needed to breastfeed their children. When I met her, she was our head girl and a strong student leader within our campus.

I wasn't new to working with women who had been victims of violence and who had suffered injustice. My heroes were the men and women before me who had dedicated their lives to serving the poor, the destitute and dying, the unwanted and forgotten—those who show unwavering love and support in the smallest ways, leaving immeasurable impacts. If only I could emulate the spirits of selfless trailblazing individuals such as Mary Slessor and Mother Teresa.

When someone quietly says, "All I want is death," being empathetic and as realistic as possible is essential to bringing her back to desiring life. If you blame her for things that were out of her control, she will emotionally shut down and sink lower. Judgmental looks and statements only create a wall of defensive behavior. In contrast, truly listening and being rational and accepting does a world of wonder.

I wasn't new to the harsh realities of this world. Young women had shared their stories and I had listened to their tragedies empathetically. I had walked with these individuals through the streets where injustices occurred. I had looked into their sunken eyes where hopelessness and pain lived.

But I had also seen their smiles and their joy. I had sat amongst a small group of my students singing beautiful songs of hope and love. In Indiana, knowing that my conversations with a 13-year-old girl helped her realize she didn't want to let her rape and pregnancy control her future was humbling and reaffirming.

My own feelings about listening to the words pour out of young women's lips about incidents in their lives were complex and difficult to understand fully. The pain they suffered broke my heart yet gave me joy when I saw what they had overcome. Whether they were seen as strong or not, women and girls who were able to come out striving gave me hope for others.

I think that might have been one of the reasons why I liked being partnered with my particular organization in Uganda. Young women who would otherwise be married off at 15 because of poverty, violated and sexually assaulted by village men, young mothers who would be forced to stay home and farm, female children who had been abducted and then shunned upon their return, the list goes on, but all these young women were able to pursue their education and better their lives.

---

11 An obstetric fistula is a hole between the vagina and rectum or bladder that is caused by prolonged obstructed labor, leaving a woman incontinent of urine or feces or both. - See more at: http://www.fistulafoundation.org/what-is-fistula/#sthash.VgYlACXW.dpuf

They had hope of a better livelihood to provide for their families.

While an international NGO was facilitating a group assessment of one of our programs, a child mother said, "When I am in the classroom, I am able to focus on studying and my future. I forget that I am a child mother and the past that comes with that. When I am learning, I am a student preparing for a better life ahead."

This was why I did the work I did. Seeing people go through the process of self-realization and empowerment created an amazing feeling of being able to take on whatever the world brought my way. If something bad happens that we can't control it shouldn't stop us from living our lives. We overcome and we become wiser and smarter because of it. We become resilient. I looked up to the young women I worked with because I saw their strength in the midst of and after much adversity.

When I accepted an invitation to serve through the Peace Corps, I willingly chose to take on an experience. I wanted a deeper understanding of life in Africa. I wanted to take on whatever unknown discomforts may come, not realizing that meant sleeping under a leaking thatch roof and using a smelly, fly-infested latrine. Building relationships with my neighbors and coworkers gave me a better understanding of African village life. I loved my community, the teachers I worked with and the students in my classes as we dealt with issues. Choosing to pursue the Peace Corps was the perfect fit for my life.

A year after getting to Uganda, when I left my friends in the car and walked away with Dominik, I unknowingly chose to put myself in a vulnerable situation. I was not new to injustice in the world around me but I never expected to be able to relate in such a personal way to the women I worked with. I had no idea how it felt until I went through it myself.

I felt betrayed, misunderstood, alone and overwhelmed in the morning. It took less than 12 hours to change my life forever.

The Journey Ahead
Day 17-65: November 23, 2010 through January 10, 2011
Washington, DC
2-9 weeks

I knew the journey back to the U.S. wouldn't be an easy one. I had never planned to travel back during my two years of the Peace Corps, let alone under these circumstances.

I arrived in D.C. a few days before Thanksgiving. In the morning, I went to the office for medical evacuation orientation and to meet my psychologist.

I was nervous about meeting him. I wasn't sure about a male psychologist after being sexually traumatized by a man. After our first meeting, I knew things would work out. He was an older, wiser gentleman, reminding me more of a cheerful grandfather than a brutal rapist. We met three times a week for the remainder of my stay in D.C.

There were three chairs in the room. The first was a large chair for the psychologist who would be sitting there all day counseling others. Next, the patient chair was set to the side of the desk—reserved for the one needing counseling. The last chair was set directly across the desk by the door. During our sessions, I sat in the patient chair.

Because of my work with young women and children, I had normally sat in the first chair. Sitting in the second chair was uncomfortable. I squirmed and answered questions that I would usually ask someone else.

At the end of the first day, I was given homework to look into Rape Assault Incest National Network (RAINN) and the DC Rape Crisis Center about group counseling. The only group counseling I found was a 12-week commitment and I wasn't going to be in town long enough to complete it. There were also personal defense classes, but I had just missed them.

I looked into Adult Sexual Assault Survivors. On the website, I found a measurement to check the emotional impact of the assault. In my journal, I scored myself from one, you don't identify with the emotion at all, to 10, you completely do.

Emotional Effects	Me?	Emotional Effects	Me?
Guilt	7	Distrust	6
Fear	3	Loss of Control	4
Avoidance	3	Numbness	6
Anger	7	Re-experienceing	6

November 25, 2010

Although I know what happened with violence was not my fault, I put myself in a vulnerable position which consequently was abused. This incident was the exception and not the rule so I cannot live in a world of fear. For sure I will avoid similar situations, yet I cannot let this one incident control where I go or how I live. I have never been one to accept blind leadership/authority. Words and actions that have no reason or justification that people try to push on me is not acceptable. I do become angry when others push their control. I want to trust others, but people are human and lie. I am much more aware and skeptical now. I let my guard down, I gave away control. I am numb to the seriousness. I want this night to be forgotten but can't. Numb sadness is what I feel."

I found helpful information on www.rainn.org. I wrote down what I thought was personally applicable (there is a lot more on the site dealing with sexual assault).

One out of six American women has been raped and even more have been sexually assaulted.[12] The FBI ranks rape as the second most violent crime after only murder and yet over 60 percent of rapes and sexual assaults are left unreported.[13]

I thought maybe what I went through wasn't that serious. Compared to other young women that I had worked with in the U.S., India and Uganda, this seemed like hardly anything at all. Shows on TV such as "Law & Order: Special Victims Unit" and "CSI: Crime Scene Investigation" only covered cases involving guns, knives, bruises and decapitation. My incident didn't fit any of that.

In reality, sexual assault is a serious crime no matter what the circumstances. Most rapes and sexual assaults do not result in physical injuries. Eighty-four percent of victims report the use of only physical force. Lack of injuries should not deter from reporting and doesn't make the sexual assault any less real.

When I left Dominik's hotel, all I could think about was how happy I was to be out of there, and how badly I wanted a shower and to sleep. Reporting what happened didn't cross my mind.

I felt like I had failed myself by putting myself in danger. Maybe I deserved this since I went against my better judgment. I trusted others rather than trusting myself. Afterward, I wasn't able to process the seriousness of what happened. Not until I sought medical attention a couple of days later and the nurse asked me directly if I was raped did I start to feel the gravity of what happened to me and adjust to using the heavy word "rape." I hadn't defined it as "rape" but instead a horrible night that I wanted to forget. According to the National Institute of

---

12   National Institute of Justice and Centers for Disease Control and Prevention. Prevalence, Incidence and Consequences of Violence Against Women Survey. 1998.

13   Justice Department, National Crime Victimization Survey: 2008-2012

Justice, about two-thirds of rapes are committed by someone the victim knows like an intimate partner, relative, friend or acquaintance.[14] The majority of rapes are not committed by someone jumping out of bushes or in a dark alley. Rarely do they resemble the dramatic episodes of "Law & Order: SVU."

I felt a tremendous amount of guilt, disappointment and loss of confidence in myself because I was taken advantage of and raped by someone whose name I had learned, face I had seen and personality I should have judged better. Had I been assaulted by a stranger in an alley, perhaps I would have felt less helpless. I had the means to protect myself and didn't. I wasn't helpless, I was just careless.

Some people don't report a rape or sexual assault because they think it's a personal matter, fear reprisal or believe police are biased. Even I had second thoughts about reporting, not wanting to ruin his life or destroy his family. Truth is, he's the one who chose to sexually assault me. He's the one bringing shame and dishonor to his family.

Fifteen out of 16 rapists never see the inside of a prison cell for their crimes.[15] By choosing to press charges, I chose to go through the legal system. I had faith it would hold him accountable for his actions. I could have stayed silent and nursed my own emotional wounds, but that would leave it to any future woman he might assault to take action.

Just because someone willingly and consensually begins a sexual encounter does not make sexual assault the victim's fault. As soon as one person says no, is an unwilling participant or even passed out from drinking and the other person continues without consent, it's considered sexual assault. The perpetrator had control of his or her actions and abused his or her strength and power over the other. He or she violated basic codes of morality and decency and committed a crime punishable by law.

Many victims claim that reporting is the last thing they want to do immediately after being attacked. The victim should do whatever they feel will make them safe and out of harm's way. The first 72 hours are crucial. Physical evidence will help in a prosecution case against the assailant.

The basics of Cognitive Behavior Theory help someone stop being victimized by one's own thinking. Essentially, I cannot control another person. I may not like the way someone else thinks or feels. I may wish the situation to be different. Other people's behavior is consistent with their personally biased thinking, which is a collaboration of all their past experiences. They have their issues and I have my issues: Both are a result of personal experiences.

We can focus on the problem rather than problem solving. Our own anger shifts to simple annoyance or irritation. This can be done by changing a (possibly) irrational demand to a simple preference:

Demand: Dominik should treat women with respect.

Preference: I would prefer that Dominik treat women with respect.

14   National Institute of Justice: Victims and Perpetrators, http://www.nij.gov/topics/crime/rape-sexual-violence/Pages/victims-perpetrators.aspx
15   Department of Justice, Felony Defendants in Large Urban Counties: 2009

I choose not to get upset about the incident, but I do get sad and am disappointed in people.

I choose not to get upset about the three other women's behavior that night because the incident is in the past and the threat is over. I would prefer if they didn't set up their friends with strangers. I would prefer if they didn't make rude comments. I would prefer them to evaluate their lifestyles and to be safer.

I found my experience designing training material on building trust in a post-conflict area insightful. In September 2010, I had attended the first "Working in a Post-Conflict Area" workshop hosted in Uganda. Twenty Peace Corps staff from different countries considered experts in the field and five volunteers from Uganda and Rwanda were invited. I met a couple of the headquarters staff while at the workshop and, a couple of weeks after arriving in D.C., sent them an email offering to volunteer in the office in any way possible.

I was welcomed with open arms and tasked with creating training material on building trust. During the workshop, one of the hardest challenges for volunteers in post-conflict areas is integration into their host communities and organizations. I was to organize information that would give volunteers information on the effects of conflict on societal and individual levels of trust, with the goal of improving their skills in carrying out cross-cultural relationships, community integration and volunteer personal and work satisfaction.

When I first moved to my site in northern Uganda, I didn't understand a lot of what was going on. Volunteers in other parts of the country didn't seem to be having as many difficulties and I didn't understand why someone who was so willing to integrate and so proactive hit a wall constantly. After investigating deeper about post-traumatic stress disorder (PTSD) while in D.C., my community started to make more sense to me.

I also started to make more sense of myself. I had started to react differently. I would get extremely upset or cry or become too exhausted for a normal routine. During my readings, I identified behaviors that I began to exhibit after being sexually assaulted.

Instead of trusting my own good judgment, I had trusted Bridgette, Gwen, Crystal and Dominik, which led me to second-guess myself constantly and be suspicious of the motives of every person I met. My self-esteem was shot and I doubted any empathy anyone had to offer, especially since the people I trusted that night gave me little to none.

Activities I would normally be interested in were stressful. If I had to travel on public transportation and the conductor touched my arm, I reacted by instantly pulling away or slapping their hand. My head wouldn't calm at night and I was left chasing after thoughts, trying to reason with myself about what happened to me.

The Peace Corps medical office was concerned that I was causing myself more damage by studying PTSD when I likely had it, but I felt like it gave me a reason to wake up in the morning. I had a purpose to wake up each day. I got dressed to go to the office on my own schedule and had the Africa Region staff as an adopted family. They let me borrow warm clothing, invited me to the Rwandan coffee shop down the road and we even put up Christmas lights together. Had I stayed in the hotel room watching TV or surfing the internet, I never would have been able to stop thinking about that night.

Even though the circumstances of being in D.C. were unfortunate, I was thankful for the opportunity to get to know the amazing people who worked behind the scenes on behalf of volunteers worldwide. Not only did the Africa Region staff make me feel welcomed, but I was able to meet the safety and security individuals who I'd be working with on the legal side of this journey.

You Should Have Told Me
Written in December 2010
Washington, DC

The night of November 5 kept replaying in my head. I couldn't sleep because of it, analyzing that night over and over again...

"Go to the bathroom," Dominik says without hesitation.

"My friends dared me to do this," I say under my breath as I walk past Todd to the bathroom.

I shake my head and roll my eyes at myself in the bathroom mirror. This could possibly be a decent time. I wash my hands. Toilets are not romantic. Dirty. Not a turn-on whatsoever, but here we are, and there Todd is.

The bathroom has a large corner bathtub with jets to the left of the door, a stand-up shower with glass doors to the back left, two sinks straight ahead with a wide mirror above, and a toilet on the right wall. Dominik walks into the bathroom and closes the door.

Dominik had been fun to talk to while watching Bridgette and his friend chat.

I do not feel comfortable with Todd on the other side of the door. Maybe if I was drunk and my judgment was impaired, if I was wasted like one of my friends, I wouldn't care.

Dominik walks across the bathroom with a sly smile, stalking me with his eyes. His head is cocked to the slight right as he leans in to kiss my lips and begins to undress me.

"Suck my dick."

"No thanks," I reply firmly.

We kiss for a moment but Dominik seems to want to skip everything and go straight into sex. He starts to come closer to me before I ask where his condom is.

"But it feels so much better without a condom!"

"I teach child mothers and women who have been violated by the risks of exactly that. There is no way I am going to be hypocritical to what I teach them."

He is losing points quickly. He rolls his eyes and then pulls a condom out of his jeans pocket. Both of us are slightly annoyed. I try to enjoy my friends "favor" that is supposed to "fix" me. I try to relax but my attempt is pointless.

I am anxious and hyperalert, especially with Todd on the other side of the bathroom door.

"Stop thinking and worrying," he says, clearly irritated. He can tell this tactic is not working. This is turning into a night of unfulfilling sex. Dominik goes to the bathroom door, opens it and asks Todd if he would leave the room.

"Seriously? It's my wife's birthday and I am talking to her on Skype."

Yep, that's the type of roommate you have. Sorry for your luck, Todd.

"OK, he left. Come on. What are you doing?"

"I am folding my clothes."

I like things to be orderly, especially when I am in someone else's space. In a systematic pile, first my green double-fabric Chacos shoes so my clothes won't touch the floor, then jeans on top of them, underwear hidden by my black tank top. Recycled paper purple beaded necklace and bracelet on top. I may be messy and uncomfortable, but my clothes are neat.

I ask Dominik to turn off the bedroom lights but he wants them on. I think, Men are visual. Maybe with moving to the bed and without Todd in the room, I will be able to relax.

While walking toward the bed, I try to take a little control in the situation and kiss him. I want there to be some sort of connection.

I turn toward the bed and he slaps my right butt cheek hard, leaving it stinging. He starts to have sex with me and keeps saying how he wants to be in me without the condom. I just keep repeating that I don't want him to.

He tells me to look down.

"Where is the condom?!" I exclaim.

"It feels so much better without," he says slowly.

I tell him to stop and he rolls his eyes again. He pulls out and has to use his fingers to find the condom inside me. I am too tired for this. He sloppily puts it back on and begins again. A couple of minutes pass and I can see that the condom is gone a second time. Not only is this bad sex, it is disrespectful sex.

I tell him to stop while pushing at his hips with my hands but he doesn't stop thrusting. He gives a look of intense pleasure. He says something about how great the motion of stimulating the tip feels. I get exceptionally frustrated as I see the delight in his face. I push harder at his hips with my hands, trying to end this.

"You've already had me in you without a condom, so what does it matter?" he says in his sweet Midwestern voice.

I am done. He has no right to be treating me this way and he is pissing me off.

I sit up before trying to get off the bed. Dominik is on top not letting me go. In the next moment, his right hand closes around my throat and keeps a firm grip, pinning my head to the mattress. Fight, flee, freeze—I freeze.

I don't know what's happening.

This is not two mutually consenting adults. He is fucking me. He didn't care who he fucked, I could be anyone. Frozen, I look at nothingness with glazed-over eyes as he thrusts over and over again.

I'm no longer present in the body lying on the mattress where a man uses his strength to get off. As I lay there, he continues to fuck my body, without emotion or an opinion.

He pauses for a few seconds and spits into his hand for lubricant.

Time stops. I don't know how long I've been there but I'm finally able to twist to the left and break free from being under him.

"I'm taking a shower," I say as I walk to the bathroom and close the door behind me.

I step into the shower and turn on the water. Hot. I am too muddled to figure out how to turn the temperature down. I let the water run down my body hoping it would scour every trace of him from my skin.

I hear the bathroom door open.

Locking the bathroom door had not even crossed my mind. Dominik steps into the shower with me. He quickly pulls away from the water when he feels the scorching temperature and turns the knobs so it's cooler. He rinses quickly, and stands in the back corner.

"Did you get off at all?" he asks. I shake my head. "I knew I shouldn't have gotten involved with a girl who had not been with a guy in two years. I had sex last week and she got off. What's your deal? How old are you anyway? You're acting as if you're 17. You're one of those girls that believe you have to be in love to have sex. I can tell by the way you act," he tells me in a rambling jumble of words.

I listen to him belittle me and feel the water run down my body.

Maybe at the club with the other women his goal was to "please" the lady, but after I saw his aggression it's clear that his ultimate goal is just about himself. This is a game to him and it's not going the way he imagined it would.

He drones on and on and I grow weary of his slightly high-pitched voice as he tries to tell me who I am and how I feel. I turn to face away from him, letting the water run down my back.

That's when my throat meets the inside of his elbow.

I can't breathe. Any pressure on my trachea makes me fearful he would crush my throat. Water is rushing down my face and his forearm is pulling my throat to his chest. I grab his arm and pull myself up on my toes, trying to get air and ease the pressure. Even then, the water is pouring over my nose and enters my mouth. I try to spit the water out and quickly gasp for air.

When he is done with that position, he pushes the right side of my face against the shower wall with his hand firmly placed around the back of my neck. I just want this night to be over. Dominik hasn't come yet this time, and I know he won't leave me alone until he does.

He keeps going. Either his hand is around my throat pushing my face into the wall or he has me in a chokehold. I don't move and am afraid of what could happen if I do.

At last, he climaxes, rinses and dries off. I grab the shower gel from the shelf to my left and pour the liquid into my hands. I do the best I can without a washcloth to thoroughly cleanse myself. My blonde hair is a tangled mess and mascara is running down my cheeks.

I feel naked inside and out. I want to be invisible and to disappear.

"I need something to wear," I manage.

He makes comments that I ignore but then one catches me by surprise.

"You didn't like the choking?" he casually asks while drying off.

I shake my head.

"You should have told me," said as if I was the idiot for not speaking up.

He could have asked if I was into that. Did he expect me to speak up before or after he surprised me with his hand around my throat making talking impossible and breathing difficult?

"Twenty minutes in the bathroom to begin with, 20 minutes on the bed, 20 minutes in the shower, how is it that you did not get off? Make sure to take your birth control," he says in one breath as I step out of the shower.

"Birth control?" I pause, "I am not on any." There was no need to be on any. Except for today.

"Oh. Well, my name is Dominik Jones. Find me on Facebook. I wanna keep that little kid. I've been having sex since I was 15 and I've never gotten a girl pregnant. I don't even think I can have kids."

I just stare at him.

He forced himself on me without a condom, got violent when I told him to stop, kept going until he came inside me and then flippantly told me to find him on Facebook if he impregnated me?

Fuck you, Dominik Jones.

He hands me black gym shorts and a T-shirt to wear. I want something to cover my nakedness. He wraps a towel around his waist and leaves the bathroom. I follow. I want to leave but can't. It is at least 5 in the morning, not a wise time to be walking the streets of Kampala alone.

I am tired down to my bones from everything so I take the side closer to the window, turning to my right side, facing away from him. He wraps his dreadful muscular arm around my upper body and I start to cry softly. I do not move my body closer to his. I do not say a word.

All I have to do is stay calm for a few more hours and then I'll be able to leave. My body is heavy with the need to sleep.

I don't know when Dominik started. Todd was back in his bed and I didn't want to make any noise. What if the roommate abuses women as well?

Dominik pulls at the shorts I'm wearing and I whisper out a firm, "No." He leaves me alone for a moment. But he's a persistent one. In a daze, what seems like a few minutes later, he pulls at the shorts again and I say stop again.

But then I remembered what had already happened when I did not play by his rules.

Sensing he was becoming agitated by my refusal and rather than him getting aggravated and start strangling me again, I give up. He wants his way.

The grey T-shirt never came off but the shorts did.

He fucks me again.

He doesn't have a condom and I know he won't put one on even if I insist. He penetrates me from behind, pulling my body closer to his, and then turns me over.

I don't put up a fight. The first time I made any effort to get away there was a hand around my throat. When he wasn't happy with the way that ended, he followed me until I turned around and he could put his elbow around my throat. My will meant nothing to him. I just want him to finish and for the night to be over.

He comes and I feel sick and ruined as I turn on my side, too fatigued to get up, hoping the sun would come up so I can leave. The hotel room has thick curtains made to keep the equator morning sun at bay and they show no sign of light through the cracks.

Around 10 in the morning, Todd, Dominik and I wake up.

"Oh man, we missed breakfast," remarks Todd.

"I have to go pack my stuff at my hotel and check out," I say, in an attempt to leave.

"Oh come on, the other girls can get your shit together for you," Dominick insists.

"No. Really, they are waiting for me."

"They won't mind if you are late. You can stay."

I go to the bathroom to change into my clothes and get ready to leave, no matter what he says.

Once again, I don't think about locking the bathroom door. Dominik walks in shortly after and tells me he wants a quickie.

No.

I want to get far away from here.

I wanted to shower.

I want to scald my skin until it is red with heat.

I desperately need to sleep.

Sleep for hours and hours and hours.

I keep putting on my clothes until he grabs my side. I hate the feeling of his skin touching mine.

Suffer through and then you'll be on your way, I think to myself. He has broken me. I feel trapped, suffocated by the bathroom air. But I am so close to leaving.

Once again, no condom.

Please, just let me leave!

I hold on to the sink in front of me. I look at the vacant face with dark circles around her eyes in the mirror try to make sense of who I see. That is my body in the mirror. That woman in the mirror is disgusting. She is a shell. I can't stand looking at the body bouncing as he thrusts again and again. I turn my face toward the shower and close my eyes.

Nothing makes sense.

That woman in the mirror is broken.

This is wrong. He shouldn't be doing this to her.

He shouldn't be doing this to me.

At least he is quick. I put my clothes back on as quickly as I can and finally walk out of the hotel room.

There's a clear difference between an unfulfilling or bad one-night stand and a night that was exploitative and wrong. Dominik Jones broke the law and raped me.

The reality is, this is how the night happened and I can't go back to change any of it. Of all the people I talk to about this night, I am the most scrutinizing and biased judge of them all. I will spend more time thinking about this than anyone else.

Usually, after a negative situation, I'd analyze what I did and how I can do things differently. Saying, "Next time a man chooses to sexually assault me, I'll do this and that differently," seems wrong in this situation. I will do all that I am capable of to prevent "next time" ever occurring.

Acquitted, Not Guilty
Day 114: Monday, February 28, 2011
Pader, Northern Uganda
16 weeks

Although I physically came back to Uganda mid-January, my mind was elsewhere. I was getting anxious about the legal proceedings and starting to get emails from different military personnel asking for information as they prepared the case. Paranoid, I answered the requests for information.

On February 24, 2011, I received an email forwarded from Ed, the associate director for safety and security at Peace Corps headquarters. Ed was a military veteran, a former cop and used to be a sketch artist who worked with sexual assault victims. He took special note of my case and we talked about the situation while I was in D.C.

David, the lead security specialist who guided and advised overseas security staff and volunteers like me, said, "Here is some information I found on the process. Just in case." Included was a link, which I clicked.[16]

Courts-Martial Attorneys Military Defense Lawyers
To be accused of a crime is a terrifying ordeal. To be accused of a crime in the military, however, can be even more traumatic for people because it is such a unique criminal system. While most people have a general understanding of the civilian criminal justice system, the unique nature of the military's approach can be very confusing. A criminal trial in the military is known as a Court-Martial. While many of the criminal allegations addressed in a Court-Martial have similar charges in the civilian system, the Court-Martial process is extremely unique and differs in many significant aspects from a civilian criminal trial. For that reason, any attorney representing a military member at a Court-Martial should have specific, military experience. At JAG Defense, our Attorneys have litigated hundreds of Courts-Martial: as prosecutors, defense counsel, and even as a military judge. We have done so with outstanding success, and we encourage you to review our Representative Cases.
- Murder/Assault
- Military Sex Offenses
- Child Pornography/Internet Crimes
- BAH Fraud
- Desertion/AWOL

---

16 JAG Defense http://www.jagdefense.com/courts-martial.php

Your future—to include your reputation, livelihood and freedom—will depend upon how effectively your lawyer can represent you. If you have been notified that you are pending a Court-Martial, please contact JAG Defense for a free consultation about how one of our experienced attorneys can help you with your case.

Some 3,500 words later, I had an idea of the military process and what's to come. The unknown is scary. Still curious to see what sort of consequences rape charges receive, I looked at their military success page.

Navy E-4 engaged in a 9-month sexual relationship with a 14-year old girl. This relationship included the girl taking numerous nude pictures of herself and sending them to our client, which constituted the possession of child pornography. Our client was charged with carnal knowledge, possession of child pornography and sodomy with/on a child under the age of 16, and was facing the possibility of 50 years confinement and Dishonorable Discharge. Using evidence we developed through cross-examination of the witnesses at our client's Article 32[17] hearing, we were able to convince the chain of command to handle our client's case administratively, rather than at a General Court-Martial. Result: Our client did not serve a single day in jail, will not have a criminal record, will not receive a punitive discharge from the Navy and will not have to register as a sex offender.

How is it that a man who had a nine-month sexual relationship with a 14-year old girl was not even registered as a sex offender?

Air Force E-7 was charged in 2004 with raping an Army E-3 while both were TDY to Germany. Due to our representation at his General Court-Martial, he was found NOT GUILTY of the charge against him (additional details below). In 2007, the same client was charged with indecently assaulting and attempting to commit forcible sodomy with an Air Force E-4 while TDY to Turkey. At his second General Court-Martial, the military judge permitted the previous alleged victim to testify again regarding the alleged rape from 2004. In addition, the military judge also permitted a former Air Force E-3 to testify that our client had indecently assaulted her in 1990 while TDY to Oman. Despite the apparent pattern of sexual assaults in TDY environments, we were still able to convince the officer member panel that our client was NOT GUILTY OF ALL CHARGES against him.

Germany, Turkey, Oman. 1990-2007. Three military women in three different countries. How many women could he have raped or assaulted that were host country nationals in a 17-year time span? What if I didn't report the sexual assault by Dominik and then 17 years later he was still traumatizing women around the world?

Navy E-6 was court-martialed for severely beating his first wife in 2006 and his second wife in 2007. Based upon the charges, our client was facing up to 30 years of confinement and a Dishonorable Discharge. In addition to securing a favorable pre-trial agreement, we were also able to convince our client's command to release him from confinement early. RESULT: Our client served only 29 days in jail and received an HONORABLE separation from the U.S. Navy.

---

17   Article 32 (Uniform Code of Military Justice) Investigation is similar in nature to a civilian grand jury hearing.

Apparently, if you are going to severely beat multiple partners, join the military. Domestic violence isn't something they find truly reprehensible.

Air Force E-4 was charged with possession of child pornography and indecent acts with his 4-year-old stepson. After securing a favorable pre-trial agreement on the child pornography charge, our client pleaded not guilty to the indecent acts. At his court-martial, we challenged the competency of the child as a witness and objected to his testimony. After repeated attempts by the government to establish the child's ability to testify as a witness, the military judge sustained our objection and ruled that the child was not competent to testify. Result: Our client was found NOT GUILTY of the indecent acts charge.

The defense challenged the competency of a 4-year-old child who was being sexually abused by his stepfather? As if the psychological damage was not enough. The kid was 4.

Air Force E-3 was charged with raping and engaging in indecent acts with a 15-year-old girl. At his General Court-Martial, our aggressive cross-examination of the alleged victim established countless inconsistencies in her version of what occurred. Further, we presented evidence of our client's innocent state of mind following the night that the misconduct allegedly occurred. Result: Without even having to testify, our client was ACQUITTED of all charges against him.

If the defense attorney is male and the individual who sexually assaulted her was male, aggressive cross-examination of the victim is going to be a nightmare. Young females who are 15 are very vulnerable to being taken advantage of by someone who is more powerful, or if they feel pressure to impress an older male who they may hold in high esteem. She could be afraid of rejection and was coerced into doing something she didn't want to do. He could have manipulated her into thinking what he was doing was OK. She could have been in shock and denial that someone she trusted betrayed her and took advantage of her.

Having the defense aggressively cross-examine her could have put her back into a state of feeling helpless and actually re-traumatizing her on the stand. She could have felt flustered and doubted herself, unable to think straight as the defense lawyer asks her invasive questions, switching her words, confusing her.

I had just turned 26, 11 years older than this 15-year-old. Reading about her made me extremely anxious. What if I am unable to perform under aggressive cross-examination? I am firm in what happened and I know the truth, but what if I get on the stand and they are awful to me? What if I make mistakes and then Dominik is acquitted like this guy? I wasn't feeling so hot.

Air Force E-7 was charged with raping an Army E-3 while both were TDY to Germany. At his subsequent General Court-Martial, we dissected the alleged victim's actions both before and after the alleged rape, establishing her consent to all sexual activity that took place that evening. In addition, we presented expert testimony regarding the effects of alcohol on the alleged victim's ability to consent and make decisions throughout her interaction with our client. Result: Our client was ACQUITTED of the charge against him.

In American culture, the common thought is that tranquilizer pills or something that makes someone pass out or black out are the only drugs that are used to take advantage of another person. Alcohol is the sneakier, not as obvious, technique that more sexual predators tend to utilize. What may seem like a nice guy who is offering to buy a woman a drink could actually be his preparations for raping her.

How many times have we heard someone use alcohol as their excuse for their behavior? "I wouldn't have made out with him; darn drunk goggles." Angry drunks, the happy drunk, the overly sexual drunk. The woman who gets super-drunk, passes out and then the next morning her underwear are at the foot of the bed and she doesn't have any recollection of what happened. She can't defend whether or not it was consensual because she was too drunk to remember any of it. "If she can't defend herself, well then, it did not happen and there is no case," the defense could say.

We allow perpetrators to lay the blame on the victim instead of holding them accountable for their lack of self-control or respect for another person. Dissect every action and word of the victim and, somewhere along the line, there will be inconsistencies or enough proof to accuse them of being a "liar."

At the end of the day, each one of these successful defense cases teaches people that there are no consequences for those who have a good enough lawyer to prowl on the vulnerable who will never have a chance of keeping it together on the stand.

After reading all of these cases, who am I to think we have any chance of getting legal justice of a conviction against the man who sexually assaulted me?

I was scared to know that JAG defense lawyers prided themselves in getting their clients acquittals in serious cases like child molestation. I was scared of testifying and then having the defense question my every action and word. I was scared that I would be re-traumatized seeing Dominik in the room and then having to answer questions about his penis penetrating me. I was scared I would fall apart, all charges would be acquitted and he would go on to sexually assault women.

I thought for a few days before replying back to David.

February 27, 2011

Thanks David,

Did you read the Military Sexual Offenses representative cases? It's disturbing that the lawyers were able to get the different charges acquitted. I do not like it at all...

Sandi

And his response later in the day...

February 27, 2011

It is. I thought you should see this however. Just so you know. The military is under a lot of heat right now, both publicly and before Congress so I do not think they will blow this off. Even if this doesn't go well for us, we will continue to press the DOD and exhaust all avenues in pursuit of justice. Stay positive and keep the course. You are very courageous for doing this and I have no doubt that you very well may be saving the lives of other women through your actions. Please keep me posted and remember that we are here for you. You can call me whenever you need to talk, discuss the case or simply vent.

Whether the crime is committed by military personnel, a parent, a partner or an unfamiliar person, if nothing changes—if sexual predators see that no one is convicted, abusers' lives aren't being negatively affected and there aren't risks outweighing the "rewards," unless there are serious legal consequences that outweigh the perpetrator's gratification from abusing someone—this will continue. If all charges are going to be acquitted anyway, then the seriousness of the matter isn't portrayed as a "real" crime.

The case summaries were nerve-racking. They truly made me wonder whose freedom we are protecting: the perpetrator or the victim?

Long-Distance Relationships
Day 115: Tuesday, March 1, 2011
Pader, Northern Uganda
16 weeks

I had never been a fan of long-distance relationships, but suddenly, I felt like the military was pursuing one with me.

My sexual assault led to a long-distance relationship with the legal military personnel. There wasn't a mutual interest like on a dating website and they didn't have a profile I could properly scrutinize to gather information. I wasn't given the choice to click the yes-I'll-abide-by-the-rules button before joining.

I was unfamiliar with my new match of the military legal process and I never planned on checking their dance card for an evening of fun. I wasn't sure what this dance was or how it worked. Out of obligation, we began the discovery stage of our relationship, sending emails back and forth, trying to make sense of where we each stood, confused by never really meeting before.

Whether it was for a man or a court case, I never wanted to feel like not checking my email could be detrimental or if cellphone service went out for a few days that I might be in trouble. I wanted to explore East Africa, not make trips to the States. Living in a rural Ugandan village did not afford me the luxury of keeping in constant contact.

Thankfully, I was not in this alone. Anytime I received an email, I was able to consult David, the Peace Corps lead security specialist in D.C. He had worked for the Peace Corps for over 10 years and was once a volunteer himself. The majority of his work involved incidents with a Peace Corps volunteer victim of crime and a host or third-country national perpetrator. Dealing with my case was tricky: It was the first time in recent memory the Peace Corps had ever dealt with the perpetrator in the U.S. military.

Since Ed, the associate director for safety and security, was a veteran, he had contacts in the Department of Defense and a greater understanding of the military system than the rest of us.

I had come to learn that their legal system was a monster of its own with different terminology, rules and procedures.

David had emailed a Navy contact of his. Below is Major Brent Cotton's response, which attempts to explain the process.

December 15, 2010

Sir,

My name is Major Brent Cotton. I am the Staff Judge Advocate (Legal Advisor) to Special Operations Command Africa (SOCAFRICA) in Stuttgart, Germany. I am the one who arranged for NCIS to conduct the investigation in Uganda. I am currently in Senegal, but will do my best to give you an update.

First, I've cc'd the Kampala RSO, Chris Bakken and Miss Sandi Giver. In a VTC a few weeks ago with the Kampala DCM, Mr. Bakken, and Peace Corps rep (Ms. Droegkamp) we agreed that all correspondence from PC, Embassy, and SOCAFRICA would be coordinated through the RSO and myself to avoid involving persons who were not privy to the details of the case.

I cc'd Miss Giver, because she was on your original message, and in order for her to establish direct communication with me. I've been asked to be the victim liaison between Miss Giver and the Navy unit that is considering the charges. I can answer any of Miss Giver's questions and will coordinate her further involvement in any following proceedings.

Your information is correct, the investigation is completed, and has been handed over to the Prosecution Team that services the suspect's unit. They will evaluate the evidence and make a recommendation to the commander on how to proceed. It is all very hard to explain over email, but is a straight forward process. I am available next week to discuss the process more fully with Miss Giver.

If the commander decides to move forward with a court-martial, Miss Giver will be asked to testify in a proceeding called an Article 32 (Uniform Code of Military Justice) Investigation, which is like a grand jury hearing. The Article 32 investigating officer will determine if there is sufficient evidence to go to a court-martial. This process and any follow-on court-martial will require the continued cooperation and testimony of Miss Giver, and as stated before, I am here to help bridge the gap between her and the Navy unit back in the U.S.

The entire process can take anywhere from four to six months depending on a number of factors. I will provide direct updates to Miss Giver, and to Embassy Kampala. The RSO will forward those updates to the PC. If you prefer to adjust that notification process, we have to talk with the Embassy. I must have direct communications with Miss Giver, but for the other updates, I am willing to adjust as long as the Embassy approves. We merely want to avoid unintended or unnecessary involvement. I'm sure you can appreciate this approach.

I hope this helps answer some questions. I apologize in advance for any confusion. A BlackBerry is not the perfect tool for such communication. Please let me know if you have any questions, and Miss Giver is free to ask me any questions she may have. Again, I am available next week for phone or VTC conversations if desired.

Very Respectfully,
Major Brent Cotton

In civilian life in the U.S., a victim is usually assigned a victim advocate—a professional trained to support victims of crime, offering information, emotional support, resources and help filling out paperwork. They can attend legal proceedings with victims and help them to know their rights.19

Since I was not enlisted in the military, depending on who I was talking to, military contacts kept saying they wouldn't be able to provide a victim advocate or that they were looking into it. I was learning that my new long-distance relationship partner was fantastic at procrastinating. Although I didn't have a specific victim advocate, I felt taken care of by the Peace Corps and especially by David.

The military kept changing my point of contact. In early January, I received an email from the Cold Case Unit, stating they would keep me apprised of the case review. A few weeks later, I received another email, this time from Lt. Matthew Sonn, asking for more information as well as providing a little information about the process.

January 5, 2011

Sandi,

The NCIS investigation into your complaint dated 10NOV10 has been transferred to the NCIS office located in Virginia Beach, VA. I will have oversight of the file while it undergoes a judicial review at the Region Legal Service Office in Norfolk, VA. The investigative reports have been provided to USN prosecutors for review. I will keep you posted on the results. If you have any additional questions please let me know. Hope you are well.

Special Agent Bill Heath
NCIS Cold Case Unit

January 24, 2011

Sandi,

Thank you for your contact information. Hopefully we can take care of most of this discussion via e-mail for sake of ease and time zones. I have a few questions for you which will help in making my recommendation about the disposition of this case.

1) How much longer will you be in Uganda?
2) I have read your statements to NCIS. Do you have any changes to what you have previously stated happened (additional details, misstatements in the previous statement, etc.)? If so we can discuss further on the phone.
3) Do you know how long your friends you were with that night will be in Uganda?
4) Do you wish to participate in the prosecution of BU2 Dominik Jones? Your decision to participate or not is not controlling on the convening authority, but is something that is considered when deciding how to dispose of a case.

Please allow me a moment to briefly explain the military justice process from where we are and where the case may go in the future. Currently I have the case file to review and make a recommendation to the convening authority. The convening authority is the commanding officer who will decide whether to send this case to court or not. If it is decided that this case will go move forward, the first step will probably be an Article 32 hearing. This hearing is conducted in by a neutral Investigating Officer, who will make a recommendation, based on the evidence if there are reasonable grounds to move the case forward to a General Court-Martial. This hearing is our equivalent of a Grand Jury hearing. Once the convening authority receives the Article 32's recommendation he will decide whether to send this case to trial or not. If the case goes to trial it could be at a General Court-Martial (felony level) or a Special Court-Martial (misdemeanor level). I recognize that our process may be confusing from the outside looking in, so please feel free to ask any question you may have regarding our process.

Further I have attached our Victim/Witness Assistance Program form. Please review this form as it describes your rights under this program.

Please let me know if you have any questions of me or about our process.

Matthew Sonn
LT, JAGC, USN
Command Services Attorney
Region Legal Service Office Mid-Atlantic

I was hoping the victim/witness assistance form would be helpful, but there were gaps in the information on who to contact depending on what information was needed. Although I appreciated being provided the pamphlet, it was not particularly useful.

January 25, 2011

Lt. Sonn,

Hope your day is going well. Thanks for the quick response. Over email will probably be the easiest way to get this accomplished since the phones can be tricky.

Let's begin.

1) How much longer will you be in Uganda?

My close of service is mid-October, 2011. I plan to travel for a few months after that and am unsure of when I will be back in the States full time.

2) I have read your statements to NCIS. Do you have any changes to what you have previously stated happened (additional details, misstatements in the previous statement, etc.)? If so we can discuss further on the phone.

When I gave my official statement to the NCIS I had completely spaced that we had gone to Iguana before Bubbles since the incident with Dominik started at Bubbles and that is all I was focused on. I've attached what I wrote during my counseling. This was to help process the night. It's more grammatically correct and fuller than my first statement. The actual alleged rapes start on page 4. The previous pages are the background of the night, how we all met, bits of this and that. If you have questions, let me know.

3) Do you know how long your friends you were with that night will be in Uganda?

Bridgette B., Crystal W. and Gwen S. are all in my training group with the same [close of service] of October. They have the option to early terminate their service though, so no definite dates can be given. When it comes to testifying, it would be best if the court could use their written statements. (Speaking of, I was told it is possible to get a copy of the evidence/official statements. I would like a copy of all statements sent this way.)

4) Do you wish to participate in the prosecution of BU2 Dominik Jones? Your decision to participate or not is not controlling on the convening authority, but is something that is considered when deciding how to dispose of a case.

I do wish to actively participate in the prosecution of BU2 Dominik Jones. Dominik shows certain behavioral characteristics of a power assertive rapist, which were only brought forth once I refused and was in a vulnerable state. I do not wish what happened to me to be repeated to another woman. I desire the maximum penalty that is possible. I have already been told that if this does indeed go to General Court-Marshal, the Navy will take care of all expenses for me to fly back to the States to testify. The sooner this can be taken care of, the better. I would prefer this to happen before I leave Uganda for good therefore it can be something of the past when I move on with my life.

Thank you for the Victim's form. If you have any questions, please let me know. Thank you for your work.

Sandi

There was not much I could do. The incident happened to me but I was not really able to do anything when it came to the legal side. So we waited.

Hurry up and wait. Each email seemed to be from someone different—NCIS, Cold Case Unit, Germany, Norfolk... even when I did send an email to one person, my contact person seemed to change.

February 25, 2011

Ms. Giver,

I wanted to introduce myself to you. I am the Naval prosecutor who has been assigned to the case concerning BU2 Dominik Jones. I work in the same command as LT Matt Sonn, who I believe you have been in contact with previously.

As an update to where the case currently stands, the command will be preferring charges early next week. Preferral of charges is our equivalent to filing or bringing charges in a civilian court. The next step will be to proceed to an Article 32 hearing, which is somewhat akin to a grand jury hearing. At an Article 32, the government puts on sufficient evidence to show a neutral investigating officer (IO) (sitting somewhat like a judge) that there are reasonable grounds to proceed to a court-martial. The IO will make a non-binding recommendation to the command of whether charges should go forward, and at what forum. General courts-martial are our highest forum with the most punishment available. Convictions at a general court-martial are treated like federal felonies. The next lower forum is a special court-martial, which has less punitive discretion and is treated like a federal misdemeanor. The lowest court-martial forum is a summary court-martial, which has less punitive discretion and is generally not treated like a federal conviction.

At the Article 32, we would like to present your testimony. If we can arrange for your travel here, and you are willing and available, then that can be in person. Otherwise, we can attempt to take your testimony telephonically. Even if that is not available, we may be able to submit your previous sworn statement, given to SA Guthinger from NCIS.

As the victim in this case, I will consult you with any potential offers to plead guilty in exchange for limitations on sentence, or any advice to the command regarding what forum to proceed to. The convening authority will take your input into consideration before deciding on any offers to plead.

Please feel free to contact me at any point with any questions that you may have. I understand that telephone may be spotty, but my number is listed below and I can always respond via email. I have also attached several documents that more explicitly describe your rights in this process. If you have any questions regarding those forms, please let me know. My contact information, as well as that of my paralegal, LN2 Marcus Thomas, are included on the forms.

I hope that we can assist you in moving through this process, and I want to thank you for assisting us in this prosecution. I'll be in touch soon to discuss further logistics for the Article 32 hearing.

Best regards,
LT Aaron M. Riggio
Region Legal Service Office Mid-Atlantic
Trial Counsel

Good day Lt. Riggio,

Thank you for your work in prosecuting the Jones case. Sonn and I communicated a bit in January. My latest email was from Bill Heath saying SA Isadore

Singleton is now assigned to the case.

In my last communication with Bill Heath, I conveyed:

"I would like to provide input to the Commanding Officer making the decision on the case. I want full action as allowed within the law. I want Jones to be court-martialed and to stand trial for the charge of rape. Three counts if possible because there were three different occurrences throughout the single night. Jones shows signs of a power assertive rapist and is a danger to women Stateside and abroad, on and off-duty. I do not want other women to go through hell as I did by Jones's hand. I am willing to participate fully in the trial and will provide testimony as needed.

Also, what recommendations did your office make to the Commanding Officer regarding sentencing and/or the next steps with this case?

Please get back with me about the Commander's decision as well as my rights for appeal."

With the Article 32 and presentation of my testimony, I am more than willing to present in person. Telephone communication rarely works where I live in the village and I've been having a hard time receiving calls from the States for the last few months. Would you give a timeframe of when this may happen? I teach psychosocial classes in a post-conflict area and will need to find a substitute in my absence.

Thank you for your information and if there is anything you need me to do, just let me know.

Thanks,
Sandi

I Know What You Are Going Through
Day 121: Monday, March 7, 2011
Entebbe, Uganda
17 weeks

I already believed you didn't have to live through specific experiences to be an advocate for change in public policy, for community organizing or social action or to support the poor, the oppressed, the marginalized and the disenfranchised. It was why I had volunteered in the Peace Corps and India, and had inspired my work in Indiana.

Now that I was working through my own trauma from sexual assault, I started to understand my students at a more personal and deeper level. I definitely didn't live through the extent of torture and exploitation my students did, but my compassion toward them increased. Every time they spoke about a personal experience, I was taken back to my own experience and partially re-lived the pain, betrayal and loneliness, regressing emotionally to a difficult time. But I was also able to pull empathy from that experience and think of how I needed or wanted support and provided that to my students.

Trying to focus on my Peace Corps work in-country while dealing with emails and complexities of the case wasn't easy. I wanted to focus on the students I should have been teaching, but I kept having to leave site for counseling or a medical checkup. Once upon a time, I rarely went to Kampala for anything other than scheduled volunteer events or trainings. Now it seems like I was heading there every other week, making the 20-hour round trip each time.

Before the incident, I was very involved with our Gender and Development (GAD) committee. In December, I missed our empowerment GLOW camp, which is Girls Leading Our World, because I had to leave for counseling in the States. This weekend in March, a group of about 40 volunteers were meeting in Entebbe for GAD to start planning the next year's events.

After the incident, I kept a lower profile than before. I didn't talk to people, I didn't discuss what happened. This would be the first time I would interact in person with a large group of people that I'd known for the last seven to 20 months, with varying depths of personal relationships.

Thankfully, only a few people there knew that I'd even left for the States.

Three people from my training group were there: an amazing married couple and Abby.

Abby had gone back to the States on a medical evacuation for psychological reasons. Combined with malaria prophylactics, the stresses of overseas life can make someone dangerous to their own health or depressed. She had been medically cleared and was back in-country.

Abby started asking me how I was, but her tone and manner rubbed me the wrong way: I could hear pity in her voice. She asked about my trip to D.C., her tone implying she was an expert in all Peace Corps D.C. with an air of superiority.

"I know what you are going through."

Really? I tilted my head as I looked at her. She may have meant it in a supportive way but her superior approach came off harsh. In my current state of hypervigilance, I was probably being extra sensitive, but we definitely did not go to D.C. for the same reasons. I didn't appreciate that she just assumed we had, though we'd never talked about what happened.

"Abby, I was raped," I said flatly and matter of fact, not interested in continuing the conversation.

I walked away, unhappy with her comment.

I needed some time to relax and be alone. I borrowed a computer and sat on a bed as I checked my email, not knowing what to expect.

March 7, 2011

Ms. Giver,

In response to your email to SA Heath that you excerpted below, I can provide the following responses.

As I said before, charges are currently being preferred against BU2 Jones. That means that we are prosecuting him in a Navy court-martial, and we are charging him for several offenses that stem from that evening. Specifically, he is being charged for the four instances that we consider to be nonconsensual intercourse. The first is after you told him to stop and he refused. The second is when he followed you into the shower. The third is in the bed in the morning. And the fourth is in the bathroom in the morning. We have charged the first two assaults under alternate legal theories, meaning that there are actually two charges for each of those offenses—one of forcible rape and one of aggravated sexual assault. He could only be found guilty of one of those charges per assault, but we charge them separately to ensure that both theories can be considered by a jury.

Once again, I will contact you with any offer to plead in exchange for a sentence limitation, or for any other matter that affects the trial process. Your input will be delivered directly to the convening authority—the commander responsible for the case.

Regarding the Article 32 hearing, it is currently scheduled for March 22. However, I anticipate that BU2 Jones' defense counsel will likely ask for a continuance for the hearing. In that case, it may be moved out as much as three or four weeks. The Navy will pay for your airfare, lodging and per diem. I can ask about paying for someone to accompany you. It is not a practice that we typically do, but I will see if it is possible in your case. Certainly, regardless of cost, you can have someone accompany you if you desire. Article 32 hearings are generally open to the public, so anyone that accompanies you may sit through the proceedings provided that they are not a witness.

I am attempting to contact anyone else that may have been a witness that evening or the next day. Do you remain in contact with your friends that you were out with, or do you have email/phone contacts for them? I also understand that you provide training to Ugandan women on how to respond to a sexual assault. Did you receive any formal or informal training on that? If so, are there any materials that you can provide to me that show the training that you received or the training that you give?

In order to begin arranging travel, we will need some information from you. Specifically, please let us know what the nearest airport is for you, your full SSN, and a checking account and routing number.

Thank you again for your interest in proceeding in this case—your testimony is important and we appreciate your willingness to assist us in prosecuting this offense.

I felt like Bridgette never believed anything I had said about the events. I hadn't cried wolf in false pretense to the other three women and here was proof. I couldn't believe what I saw. The words jumped off the page, validating the significance of what had happened. Legal personnel had found a significant crime and my search for justice was becoming reality. I was not excited to remember that this particular crime was against me. Emails like this were needed, but brought me back to difficult feelings of sorrow.

I sat on the bed a long time after reading the email, letting it sink in and processing the information. Four counts? I had considered the first two events as one but having them count as two separate counts made sense. I was able to get away after Dominik first put his hand around my throat in the bed then he followed me into the shower. I did not give consent for either one.

I wanted to be able to focus on the here and now of the GAD meeting, hanging out with other volunteers, but I had this whole secret long-distance relationship to deal with. This had become serious. Even more serious than before. It's as if he had surprised me with saying, "Not only do you need to come and see me, I am going to throw in an extra-sweet bonus to entice you!" My head was in two places.

All the other volunteers in Entebbe were hanging out and deciding on dinner plans. I didn't want anyone to know what was going on, so when I left the room, I left the news locked in my email. I wanted to shout for joy, yet I had no one I could openly rejoice with. Here was more internal turmoil.

I almost wanted the other women from that night to be there just so I could shake them and say, "See! Something wrong happened and even though you didn't listen to my words or observe how I was, someone else is!"

Knowing the intensity of the situation increased my anxiety. There was so much I didn't know about testifying in court, so much to learn. In the training group a year after me, I knew there was a woman who had been a victim advocate for many years in the States before joining the Peace Corps. I didn't give her any details, but rather asked about the civilian court system, what typically was asked of a victim and how the procedure went.

We were sitting on a porch bench away from the rest of the group. Quietly talking to her brought down my anxiety level and gave me an idea of what to expect. I had a lot of questions to ask and she explained things in ways I could understand.

I wanted to keep talking but Abby decided to bounce over to the bench and literally sat right between us. Abby was touching my leg with hers and I didn't want anyone touching me. I wanted to scream and tell her to leave because we were having an important conversation. Not wanting to be rude, I sat there calmly disappointed, not saying a word.

By this point, the majority of volunteers had left for dinner or ate at the hostel. Holly, the new volunteer who was the first volunteer I saw within minutes of leaving Dominik's hotel, was having a small birthday dinner at a pizza place on Lake Victoria. A small group of about seven of us went. Unfortunately, Abby invited herself.

Dinner was going great with tasty cheeseburgers and funny conversations. Other than Abby and I, the rest of the group was from the August 2010 training class. They had just had an in-service training a month or so earlier and the conversation started to focus on issues that were raised during that, especially safety and security of volunteers.

I listened as the others passionately discussed ways the Peace Corps could improve safety and security issues ranging from riding motorcycles and taxi accidents to house burglaries and sexual assaults. Each group of new volunteers goes through a similar cycle. A year earlier, my group had once been passionate about figuring things out, wanting change. A year in, we accepted the way things were and tried to keep off the staff's radar.

I found their discussion interesting, yet I had already heard the majority of what they were saying a year ago when my group was the new group. I liked watching the process of people discussing and coming to conclusions. I didn't want to cheat them of their experience by giving them the "answer" or disrupting their flow. When I selectively chose to speak, I kept my input abstract and distant, just like everyone else.

"20/20" did an episode on the Peace Corps' responses to sexual assaults, airing in January 2011. Their volunteer group had been shown the whole program during their training. I had just returned to Uganda, missing the airing, and was only able to view a few short clips that ABC News had uploaded to its website. I was upset with the portrayal of the Peace Corps, since I knew individuals in D.C. who had been working diligently on behalf of volunteers. I felt that they had portrayed the Peace Corps as a cold monster. After watching the clips, I sent an email to the chief of operations support for Peace Corps Sexual Assault Risk-Reduction and Response Program, Claudia, who I had met when I was on medevac in D.C. She said she would forward my letter to Carrie Hessler-Radelet, then-deputy director at the Peace Corps.

Atrocities happen if you are in the States or overseas, alone or with a group, working independently or with an organization. The majority of women worldwide have had unwanted attention, sexual advances from men they do not know and have been grabbed in some fashion. Every organization has its flaws and humans are unpredictable.

Sexual assault is horrific whether it be in a street alley by a stranger, college campus dorm by a "friend" or your own bedroom by a relative or partner. The act of rape is not something forgotten, yet we cannot allow the atrocities of the past define who we are and destroy our futures.

No one asks or deserves to be raped or sexually assaulted. When interviewed and asked what events lead up to the incident, I truly doubt the Peace Corps purposefully makes the survivors feel guilty. Rather, the individual's disappointment in not being able to control the situation and being vulnerable may bring about feelings of guilt. Peace Corps must ask difficult questions of the individual to analyze and learn from the situation therefore being more aware and able to prevent them from repeating.

As a current Peace Corps volunteer, having had my own incident recently and going through hell to sort things out, I am thankful for the support and professionalism that Peace Corps has provided. I cannot imagine having to deal with this on my own.

Peace Corps is working vigilantly on behalf of volunteers to improve safety and security, especially when it comes to sexual assaults and rape. I could only hope that ABC News would take their influential powers to address the reality of silent rapes and assaults across America.

The conversation turned to the "20/20" coverage. Any time the words sexual assault were spoken, Abby would physically turn and stare at me, as if waiting for some sort of crazy reaction. She didn't try to be incognito either.

I tried to outwardly show myself as calm and collected. She mentioned something about an event that happened a year earlier; bringing it up in front of the group was extremely inappropriate and rude. Large breath. I might have said something at the table but I didn't want to bring unneeded attention.

As we were leaving, I walked beside Abby.

"Could you please stop looking at me every single time the words assault or sexual assault is said? I really don't appreciate it."

She gave several excuses but I wasn't having it. I was ready to go back to the hostel. I was done with conversations for the night.

The next day, we all prepared to go back to our sites. Danny and Eliza had both stayed with me in Pader when they were doing their technical immersion week. They were good people and I wanted to be able to catch up with Eliza. We shared a taxi back to Kampala and later that night joined up with a few other volunteers at a casino.

I'm not a fan of gambling but I am a fan of hanging out with women as the guys gamble. Holly sat at the end of the blackjack table and, once she was finished, I nervously asked her a question.

"Do you remember the day I ran into you on the sidewalk outside Golf Course Hotel? You were on your way to the post office."

"Oh yes. And then we saw the others in your group."

"Do you remember what was said? How was I acting?"

I wanted to know what she remembered. I wanted to know how I had presented myself and what she thought of that encounter.

As she spoke, I listened intensely. Eliza came back from using the bathroom at the tail end of what Holly had to say. Since I trust Eliza, I was OK with her staying and finding out.

When I told them about what had happened right before I had seen Holly and how it was now a giant legal mess with the military involved, they were shocked.

"Sandi, I had no clue. I should have picked up on it!"

Holly had once volunteered on her college campus with a group that had a rape hotline, helping female students go to the clinic if they wanted. I started talking about why I passively said the night had been OK and downplayed everything to the others while Holly was standing there.

"Of course you would! That's a natural response after going through something traumatic and then feeling judged. You were still trying to figure out what happened! I am so sorry I didn't realize."

We moved away from the playing table to some comfy chairs to eat our free casino food. I may have started to tear up as we talked, finally talking to two awesome women who were responding the way I needed. They listened, they believed, they didn't criticize, they were concerned for my well-being and apologized on behalf of others, validating my experience.

A few nights earlier, while a group of us were eating dinner in Entebbe, a couple of random guys turned around from their barstool seats and started talking to our large group. Since I was the closest to them and had been in-country longest, I felt slightly obligated to entertain their questions. Once they mentioned they were military, my answers to their questions became clipped.

"I do not know if you noticed the change in my answers, but right now I am not so fond of military men."

As I shared, they opened up about their own experiences of being sexually assaulted in the States and while traveling.

Together, we sat there, each tearing up as we shared about our different experiences. One of theirs was while backpacking Europe. She woke up to a man on top of her in her own hotel room. Since she was only traveling through, she felt helpless by herself and quickly left. She never saw the guy again.

"There's a reason I don't like Irish men."

I wasn't alone. At the end of the night, we hugged each other, as if to say that we were here to support each other, no matter the pain that we might be working through ourselves. I was very thankful for them.

Stand, Stand By Me
Day 122: Tuesday, March 8, 2011
Kampala, Uganda
17 weeks

"If someone is truly my friend, his or her deepest concern is for the well-being of my character, my soul." - John Ortberg

I would never forget the look in Alyssa's eyes on that crisp autumn day when she said, "You should have warned me—I wish I would have known."

I had been working with the mentally handicapped in residential group homes for about three years in Indiana at the time. Each house had eight residents and the number of staff changed based on the difficulty of support each resident required. Each house had a different feel depending on the employees and residents' collaboration.

They opened a new behavior-intensive group home in the spring and I had offered to help with the transition of new residents and staff. This house was, for lack of a better term, intense. Very few of the new staff had worked with mentally handicapped individuals previously, so training was extensive. Because of physically violent behavioral outbursts, there was a need for men who were taller and broader since strength is needed when doing a takedown to prevent harm, bites, head banging, punching and broken windows.

A couple of months in, I learned that the younger guys had a bet to see who could get with the new female staff first. Since I had been in a committed relationship for over a year, I wasn't a target and they would talk openly about their pursuits with me. I told them making bets on getting with women was not the most professional idea they've ever had. They saw it as a challenge.

Alyssa had been assigned to shadow me at work to learn the ropes of the group home. She was new to town, with a husband and young son, and was excited about landing a job in the bad economy. She was extremely happy and helpful and I was glad that she was joining our team.

In between talking about the medication schedule, cooking rotations, individual life skills workbooks for each client and what to do when one of the patients became violent, I shared with her about the bet the guys had about new female staff. Since Alyssa was married, I didn't think they would bother her.

That was before I knew better. Alyssa stood in front of me a few weeks later sharing how she and one of our male co-workers had gotten involved romantically and she was scared that her husband was about to find out. I felt sick inside about her marriage and well-being. She hardly smiled anymore.

"You should have warned me—I wish I would have known."

I thought I had done everything I could have. To the best of my knowledge, warning her about the bet among the male staff was the best I could have done. I befriended her and was someone she could rely on for any help. How was I to know she wouldn't be faithful to her husband or the men would have such disrespect for her and her marriage? As much as I hated hearing about what had happened, I didn't feel responsible.

Ever since though, if I have knowledge that could potentially keep someone out of danger, from a bad situation or from a broken heart, I have always made an effort to not stay quiet but rather say something in a caring way. Though it's hard to see tragedy affect another's well-being, it's even worse when you know you could have helped prevent it.

The few times I had shared what happened to me, I got confused looks when I talked about the three other female volunteers. I got a sour taste in my mouth thinking about them. I felt like a tornado passed through my life, putting me on one side hanging off a cliff and the three of them closer together happily playing hopscotch in the bright sun. Not one of them was helping me as I dangled off the cliff.

The week I was sexually assaulted and multiple times afterward, I asked our Peace Corps medical team if anyone had talked to the other three. I was concerned about their well-being and mental health. Although the incident happened to me, they were an intrinsic part of the before and after.

To be honest, Dominik did the physical act of choosing to sexually assault me, abusing his strength and power over me but the violence wasn't personal; we had no previous relationship. A much more personal struggle for me was working through feeling betrayed and judged by the other three women.

There was hardly any communication between myself and the others once I left Uganda for medevac in the States. I detached myself from Uganda and let myself enjoy hot showers and breakfast options. In December, while on medevac and during counseling, my psychologist and I talked about the incident, but also about the relationship dynamics of Bridgette, Gwen, Crystal and I.

While on medevac, I was assigned to create a training session on building trust in post-conflict areas, working with the Africa Region staff.

The safety and security personnel for the Africa Region was curious about what it was like to work in a post-conflict area. We talked for about 15 minutes and briefly discussed dangers, the spike of crime throughout all of Africa and prevention.

A couple of weeks before I had left, our country director had sent out an email about stricter travel to and from the capital. Bridgette and Gwen decided to write a petition since they didn't feel it was right for the Peace Corps to parent them.

Although I didn't necessarily agree with Bridgette and Gwen's petition, and was not overly concerned with restrictions to Kampala since it was very expensive and time-consuming to get there from my site, I was curious about the outcome of the petition and what others were saying.

I meant well when I sent an email to Bridgette, the first since arriving in D.C.

Sandi: December 1, 2010, 5:32 a.m.

Hey Bridgette!

How was your Thanksgiving? How is Uganda treating you? Today I spoke to the Africa Regional security advisor. We talked about multiple things about a post-conflict area but we also talked about the spike of crime and violence toward PCVs throughout the continent of Africa. I spoke to her about the proposed ban on Kampala travel as well and suggested the country director work more with VAC rather than having it be top heavy. I am sure you have talked to more volunteers since you and Gwen sent out the email. I was wondering what you guys would suggest instead? What ideas do you have about decreasing incidents against PCVs? 40% of incidents happen in Kampala, is there a way to decrease travel and stays in Kampala? I've already given my thoughts but was wondering if you have heard anything that stands out as good ideas. I am working on a project with the person in charge of programming and training, met her at the post-conflict workshop in September. I have an official photo badge with electronic reader which is sweet and a window cubicle, haha, on the 7th floor so a lot of important people to our region are there. So, if you want voices to be heard, I could see what I can do.

Bridgette: December 4, 2010, 1:56 p.m. Report

Sandi,

Gwen, I and many other volunteers are trying to make it so that staying in Kampala is still a possibility. It is fine if you would not like to go to Kampala, but most of us PCVs do. Please do not ruin our chances and please stay out of this. (you, "is there a way to decrease travel and stays in Kampala?")

I hope you are getting better in Washington and enjoying your stay.

Bridgette

Sandi: December 4, 2010, 4:53 p.m.

Wow, Bridgette, that was rather cold and undeserved.

Did you read how 40% of incidents happen in Kampala which was typed right before the "is there a way to decrease travel and stays in Kampala?" Do you understand that it is not only Uganda but many other countries that are decreasing travel to the capitals because of crime and violence against PCVs? Do you not understand that this is not an attack on volunteers but rather people in Washington really wanting volunteers to be safe and healthy? You have no idea how hard the people here and the team in Kampala are working on this and it is belittling to them to push back in undeserved ways. Other countries already have a ban on their capital cities and volunteers lose vacation days if they are found there without permission. Just because we live in Uganda doesn't mean we should get special treatment.

I should have sent the original email to Gwen. Sorry you feel like I'll ruin this for you. I am not staying out of it. There is no possible way I could ruin your "chance" of anything. This is coming from Washington and people who have been working with Africa for years. If you do start going off about this email to others at the gossip tables...let it be. You guys need something to talk about I guess.

I am having an awesome time while here. Thanks for being so concerned about my safety and security a month ago and for playing your part in choosing me to go home with Dominik. What are friends for?

Sandi

She didn't want the ban on Kampala because she would rather hang out with embassy friends than spend time in her village. Using Dominik's hotel pool, her kiss with Nate, the next day when we saw him at Garden City, her comment about how embarrassing it was to spend 15 minutes with the NCIS investigators recapping perverted conversations, saying Crystal was pissed about having to travel in—everything seemed so selfish. I was tired of her only thinking of herself without realizing the ripple effects on others.

Bridgette December 13, 2010, 4:05 p.m. Report

Hi Sandi,

I am really sorry you feel that way. Once again, I really do not think we should be friends and this time I will say no if you try to crawl back.

I know it was not my fault you were raped. I know that I was a very supportive friend. Sometimes you have to take responsibility for what happened to you. I know it's hard.

Please do not email me or Facebook. I am going to block you on both and even if the blocking did not work, I still would not read what you sent me. Honestly, the negativity is too much.

I seriously hope you find peace, you definitely need it.

All the best

Bridgette

I was taken aback by her line about taking responsibility for my actions. I did take responsibility for my actions. I just wished Bridgette would see how she didn't help the situation. She had no clue what I was dealing with. Dominik didn't rape her; he raped me. She didn't have to go through the rape kit or deal with the impending legal issues. She didn't have to cope with people who she once thought of as friends judging her.

Before these emails, during counseling, I had worked on a letter to the other women. The main purpose for me was to get out all my frustrations in a concise well-meaning fashion, but to also bring to light how their actions affected me. It detailed what happened before, during and after that night, their actions, how they impacted me and how I felt about what they did and said. If there was ever another situation where another woman was raped after hanging out with Bridgette, Gwen and Crystal and I had not said something, I wouldn't be able to forgive myself. I felt it was my responsibility to do my part in preventing another possible dangerous situation.

After a long debate on the Uganda side, the letter was sent. Since Bridgette had tried erasing me from her life, I felt like a respected third party should send an email to tell them my letter was coming. Medical wanted nothing to do with it and didn't even think it should be sent (although the counselor and psychologist thought it should). I thought it would be best received if presented by the in-country counselor for volunteers and if all three could read a paper copy, so they couldn't keep it, at the same time. Finally, after months of people tossing it around, our country director emailed them on Monday and I sent my letter on Tuesday, March 8. Gwen responded on behalf of the three.

Gwen Tue, March 8, 2011, 10:38 p.m.

Sandi,

I have tried calling you several times to discuss this letter. I do not want to get into debate with you about what happened that night, you have your interpretation and I have mine. What I do feel strongly about is that if you had any sort of issues regarding our involvement that night you should have spoken to me, Bridgette and Crystal directly.

I feel that your letter was very one-sided in its nature, and you over-exaggerated the role that we had in you making the decision to go home with Dominik that night. Regardless of your opinions of us, I do not feel that you had the right to share it with Ted, our mutual boss. I also have heard from several volunteers that you are telling people that we forced Dominik on you, among other things.

I hope you are finding peace in your own way regarding that night. Bridgette, Crystal and I have listened to what you have to say through the letter, and we have put it behind us. I can speak for my friends and I when I ask you to please leave us alone, don't talk to other volunteers about us and in general stay out of our lives.

Gwen

I debated on responding, and even started to, but then decided there was nothing I could say that they wouldn't twist my meaning or intention.

I would have said that the reason I didn't answer Gwen's calls was because I was getting my eyes checked for new glasses. Of course the letter was one-sided: It's my opinion and I used "I" statements to try to make that clear. I didn't overexaggerate their roles. After speaking to the counselor in Uganda, the psychologist in D.C., the sexual assault expert who was creating training material on bystander intervention, it was clear they played a role.

Ted was also my country director and concerned about my well-being. I don't know what he said to the other three women but he was already concerned about them before he sent his email.

When it comes to other volunteers, I sent this letter five months after the incident, feeling like I'd been suffering in silence. I'd spoken only to a few trusted friends about this atrocity and how the night unfolded. After a social event, another volunteer kept saying how amazing Bridgette was (she thinks everyone is amazing). I couldn't stand the fact I had felt such betrayal and awfulness from Bridgette. I said a few truthful things and certainly wasn't spreading any lies. I didn't know what they heard but what came out of my mouth surely wasn't as horrible as whatever this other person may have told them.

The last paragraph just made me sad.

Though I had been sincerely concerned about them, now I wanted nothing to do with them. After I read Gwen's letter, I chose to not be reminded every time I logged onto Facebook that they were off having holiday adventures, roaming Kenya and posting happy photos, while I was going through counseling in D.C., having to deal with court dates and flying logistics, taking meds to help me sleep due to anxiety and depression. I didn't want to be reminded of how this shouldn't have happened.

I don't expect people to know how to be sensitive upon hearing that their friend was raped. I do expect people to have the decency to be sensitive afterward. I can't say how many times I'd heard other volunteers had gotten upset with Crystal and Bridgette, talking about what happened—that I approached him and led him on or that flirting with someone gives them reason to force sex on you. It made me angry just thinking about it.

I couldn't manage being "friends" with people who reacted in this manner.

Serving to the Best of Our Ability
Day 124-146: Thursday, March 10 – Friday, April 1, 2011
Pader, Northern Uganda
17-20 weeks

As if dealing with the emotional side of being sexually assaulted was not enough, I still had to deal with all these emails asking for information. Sometimes, I wished I could have just walked away from the night and never seen Dominik again. The end. I knew I had to keep going to prevent this from happening to another woman.

I emailed the lieutenant with the requested contact information as well as information needed for travel logistics. In response to the question regarding my training of Ugandan women on how to respond to sexual assault I responded thus:

> I don't provide trainings directly related on how to respond immediately after a sexual assault. The classes deal with the issues that ensue with post-traumatic stress disorder whether they were abducted by rebels, forced sex slaves, sexually violated, and the like from living in a conflict zone. I can send you an electronic copy of the Peace Corps Life Skills Manual which I used at times, but I really don't think it's what you are looking for.

I was not sure what they wanted with the Life Skills manual. It felt like they were fishing. I also asked about how soon we would know about a change in trial date.

> March 10, 2011
>
> Ms. Giver,
>
> Thank you for the information. We will begin setting up travel arrangements, and if we need any additional information I will be in touch for that.
>
> The defense can request a continuance at any time. If they do request one in advance of you actually setting foot on the plane to travel, then we will rearrange your travel to coordinate with the new date. That said, the discretion of whether to grant a continuance or not rests solely with the convening authority, who is the same command that brought the charges. While request for delay is expected, I do not anticipate that it will be very far in the future.
>
> If you could send me a copy of the Peace Corps Life Skills Manual, that would be greatly appreciated.
>
> I will be in touch regarding any changes to the date of hearing or any

information regarding travel arrangements. Please email if you have any questions.

Very respectfully,
LT Aaron M. Riggio
Region Legal Service Office Mid-Atlantic Trial Counsel

We exchanged a couple of emails with the internet link to the Life Skills manual as well some other information about logistics. Because it took a day to travel to Kampala and then possibly a couple more hours to get to the airport, I reiterated the importance of timeliness on date information as well as gave the prosecutor contact information for Peace Corps staff who could get a hold of me if he was unable.

I knew it seemed like I was being difficult. The fact that I was not in the military complicated the process. I wanted to do things right, which made me check and recheck things. I sent an email to the prosecutor to thank him:

March 14, 2011

Hello again Aaron,

I want to thank you for your patience and willingness to explain the military process. This is all new, sometimes confusing, and very complicating to me. I've always been the supportive friend or housemother seeing the brokenness and trauma aftermath of a man abusing his power and strength over a woman. I am inexperienced with the legal system and I've never before been on this side—the one who was raped.

Never in a million years would I have expected to be raped by military personnel while serving my country through Peace Corps. Dominik and I both volunteered to work for a federal agency, serving the United States government in different forms. We both took the oath to support and defend our country. You would hope as representatives of the U.S. while overseas, we would both conduct ourselves in a way the U.S. would be proud.

For the most part, I believe men and women serving our country do so to the best of their ability. My father, David, was in the Air Force many years ago, my brother Frank was a Marine with an honorable discharge after breaking both of his legs while on a mission in Iraq. They were men of integrity who served their country and mankind well. Unfortunately, I have learned firsthand the hard way that not everyone holds the same regard and respect for others.

I never thought I was vulnerable to the amount of disrespect and lewd behavior Dominik showed to me as he raped me multiple times within a single night. I had been assertive and felt somewhat in control of the situation until I had had enough of his disrespect and tried getting away. When he put his hand around my throat the first time, intense fear for my life swelled within my being. Three more incidents throughout the night is depressing and heartbreaking.

The morning after Jones raped me, I was in too much shock to realize the severity of what he did to me. I was happy to be alive and out of his hotel room. To me, I was a lot luckier than the women I had worked with who had been sold into brothels, raped by a boyfriend's jealous friend, a forced sex slave to Joseph Kony of the LRA. My incident did not leave me with the physical wounds or impregnation that they had been left with.

But that doesn't mean that my being raped by Dominik deserves to be seen as anything less than serious. I've listened to women share their tragic stories, the violence and manipulation used by men. I never thought I would go through my own incident of being raped, sharing their pain. Yet, here I am.

I may not have understood the complexity and depth of Dominik abusing his power and strength over me at the time, but now I am very much aware. This is the most serious thing I have ever been involved with and it's scary.

It's scary that Dominik is military who goes overseas on contract. It's scary to think of how many other women may have been raped by him and how many women could still be raped by him if he walks free.

Having justice through the legal system is so important to me. If I were to not report, to not testify, to not do everything I can to prevent him from raping other women, I would be a disappointment to myself and to women worldwide.

Thank you, Lieutenant, for being involved with the prosecution of Dominik. I know this is probably just one more case to your pile, but to me, this is the ONE case that makes the difference of whether or not other women are raped by Dominik.

I know that before I said emails would be the best way to communicate. Starting tomorrow, I will be in my village and not able to check my email except for once a day. Because of timing and how crucial information is right now, would you please call instead? Or, at least call so I can know to check an email with important information.

Thanks again.

Sandi

I did not actually get a response in direct relation to the thank-you email but I felt better sending my thoughts to him. I did get an email saying that, as expected, the defense submitted a continuance request for the Article 32 hearing scheduled for the following week. The defense wanted to wait until May 24, roughly seven months after the incident.

Thankfully, David from Peace Corps safety and security in D.C. was on the ball on keeping track of what was going on. All of the emails back and forth were overwhelming. Given the logistical matters of getting an individual from a rural African village to a courtroom thousands of miles away, one week's notice of postponement was not happily received.

The defense got their way on the postponement, but not the date they wanted: The new Article 32 date was set for Thursday, April 21.

Dancing With the Defense
Day 156: Monday, April 11, 2011
Pader, Northern Uganda
22 weeks

In the eyes of the military, I was not a victim. I was only another witness who just happened to have a crime committed against her. I was told that in the military system, anyone involved with the case is required to speak to both the defense and the prosecuting attorneys. I didn't find out until much later that anything that I wrote or said to the prosecutor was passed on to the defense.

April 4, 2011

Ms. Giver,

My name is Lieutenant Lauren Mayo. I am a Navy defense attorney in Norfolk, Virginia. I, along with LT Dan Sullivan, represent Mr. Dominik Jones. LT Aaron Riggio provided us with your contact information. We would like to interview you concerning this case. Please let us know when and how you may be contacted so we can facilitate an interview. Thank you for your assistance, and I look forward to speaking with you.

Very respectfully,

LT Lauren Mayo
LT, JAGC, USN
Naval Legal Service Office Mid-Atlantic

April 7, 2011

Good morning Lieutenant,

Hope all is well in Norfolk. I live in Northern Uganda which I believe is 7 hours ahead of Norfolk. I am busy the rest of the week and as long as there is power in my village over the weekend, my phone should be charged and ready to answer on Monday. Usually, calls from 8-10 a.m. from the East Coast are manageable.

Sandi

Since the day was late in Uganda and early on the East Coast, they answered within a few hours.

April 8, 2011

Sandi

Thank you for your quick response. Would Tuesday at 5:15 p.m. your time work for you? I believe that is 10:15 a.m. Eastern. Also, are you planning on attending the hearing on April 21? If so, when would you be arriving? Thanks again.

I decided to email the prosecutor to see what he would say about this predicament. He had tried to call the night before "to set up a time this week to discuss the facts surrounding the assault in preparation for the Article 32 hearing" but I had missed the call.

April 8, 2011

Lieutenant Riggio,

Have you worked with the female and male defense attorneys who are representing Dominik? They have asked to call and interview me concerning the case but now I am thinking that is not legal since I won't have a lawyer present. OR, does the military have a very different way of doing things?

Sorry I missed your call last night. I had just gotten back to my house and my mother called. If you are able to call in the next few hours or after 10 p.m. my time, that would work for today. Otherwise another day should work as well.

Cheers,

Sandi

April 8, 2011 at 12:55 p.m.

Sandi,

I have worked with the LT's previously. They are allowed to speak to you, and since you are not suspected of any criminal wrongdoing, you do not have to have an attorney present when they talk to you (military and most jurisdictions that I know of).

I will try to call you after 10 tonight. We can talk then more about speaking with the defense. No worries about last night, we will be able to connect soon. Thanks for your patience.

LT Riggio

I was at dinner with a few other expat volunteers in Pader when I received the call from the prosecutor, Lt. Riggio. While walking home along the moonlit dirt paths, we discussed the events that led up to the rape. He said we would wait until I was in the States to talk about the actual event. We then went over the pros and cons of speaking to the defense.

If I did not speak to them, they could request a continuance using the excuse that I was unwilling to speak and they needed more time to prepare their case. If I did speak to them, we would get an idea of what they would ask possibly but they would also have the benefit of having a pre-conversation with me. Either way, I got anxious talking about serious subjects over the phone. Adding to that not being able to see facial expressions or get an idea of their manner, I decided to wait.

April 11, 2011

Morning Lauren,

Hope all is well Stateside. I haven't been given exact dates of when I will arrive on the East Coast, but the prosecutor is requesting I be in around a couple of days prior to the Article 32 to prep and whatnot. I would prefer to have our interview in person although I know with timing this might be difficult. I'll contact a few people and see what I can come up with.

Take care,
Sandi

To Infinity and Beyond!
Day 165: Wednesday, April 20, 2011
Kampala, Uganda
Norfolk, Virginia
23 weeks

Of course, there were complications to get me to the U.S. The military was not sure if they had the budget to fly me in for the Article 32. There was a possible government shutdown that would begin the weekend before I would need to be in the States.

In all my 26 years, I had never been that interested in politics or what the government was doing. Of course, the one time I needed the government to have its act together there was a shutdown looming because of the budget. Thankfully, Congress approved the budget with minutes to spare.

Peace Corps/Uganda staff wanted dates, times, details—but I had nothing to pass along. I stopped worrying and figured I'd get to America somehow. The Peace Corps said they would pay for the flight and all costs even if the military refused.

With two days before I needed to fly out, the military decided they would cover costs. I sat at a computer checking my email on the Friday before the hearing and had three different flight itineraries. I met with staff in Uganda to attempt to figure out what was going on. I handed them papers and sat back to watch them try to make sense of the stack.

At least the first flight number to Amsterdam was the same on all the tickets. A driver picked me up from the hostel just before 7 p.m. Sunday, and my flight left at 11:45 p.m. that night. After a seven-hour layover in the Amsterdam airport, over 16 hours total in the air and a seven-hour time difference, I reached my final destination of D.C. at 3 p.m. on Monday.

I had to admit, stepping foot back on American soil felt amazing. Daryl, another safety and security staff member, had brought his 1969 Mustang Convertible to pick me up. Mocha in hand and the car top down, driving on paved streets where there are speed limits and the smell of cherry blossoms brought me back to life a little bit.

Although I was given the option to stay in a hotel, my friend Kelly offered to let me stay with her instead. We ate chips and salsa, her roommate grilled burgers and I, with Uganda a full day of travel away from me, could breathe a little easier.

Tuesday, David and I met at the end of the Metro Orange Line to begin the 200-mile trip to Norfolk, Virginia. Both of us were wearing jeans and a grey, long-sleeved shirt, which we from then on referred to as "the uniform." We never discussed the case other than logistical details. Instead, we filled the time on the train and then his car talking about his kids and what was happening Stateside.

We checked into the hotel in Norfolk and I was glad to have some time alone before meeting with the prosecutor. While packing, I had to consider what clothes would be appropriate for the occasion. I'd been living in Africa a year-and-a-half without having to worry about wearing a suit. My professional clothes were in storage in Indiana. A brown wrap-around skirt that I had bought in Nepal and decent shirts were the most professional clothing I had at the moment.

Everything in the Norfolk area was military. There was Military Road, military banks, military this and military that. I was surrounded. While still in Uganda, I had received a logistics email about lodging.

April 14, 2011

Ms. Giver,

Now that we have your itinerary underway, I would like to discuss lodging. The government will authorize up to $56.00 per day for your lodging. If you would like to stay on base, please call (757) 402-7002. If staying on base, please arrange to stay at Maury Hall, building A54 because it is right beside our legal office building. However, if you choose to stay off base, please keep the lodging allowance in mind. Ms. Dixon, our travel coordinator, will explain how to file your travel claim upon completion of your trip. You will need to make all lodging reservations on your own because they usually require a credit card and need to speak with the credit card holder directly.

What if I were to run into Dominik in the middle of town or on base? What if he became extremely upset and violent again, but did more physical harm this time?

Thankfully, when I told David my concerns, he agreed that staying on base was not acceptable. He booked two rooms at a Holiday Inn 15 minutes away from the base.

As we drove to meet with the prosecution lawyer, I could feel my skin get tight. Part of me was excited about getting the Article 32 over but a larger part of me dreaded everything that was about to happen.

David used his military pass to get onto the base. We drove a few minutes, found the legal office and parked across the street. After entering the building, I placed my purse in a basket and handed them my passport before walking through the metal detector. We sat in a large room waiting to be escorted upstairs to physically meet people I had only emailed before.

When Dominik said "find me on Facebook," I tried. I couldn't find a single Dominik Jones profile picture that was him. I wasn't able to find him until a couple of months later when I received an official email with the correct spelling of his name

His profile pictures were available to the world. I could see photos of what looked like him and his family, his military buds, him with a headset as if flying a plane, next to a motorcycle, a summer day with a group of guys and young women on a boat, one woman who was in more than one picture.

I Googled the correct spelling of his name and found a short video of him. He must have been deployed in May 2007 since there was a holiday greeting to his mother from Defense Video & Imagery Distribution System—"Video: Petty Officer 3rd Class Dominik Jones." There was a pipl.com page where he talked about some cars (or something). I also found a military page saying he was the top boxer in his weight class. I knew there was a reason I wasn't strong enough against him. He was also on a handful of dating sites.

In some ways, before I was able to find Dominik on Facebook, I still thought of him as a bad dream that didn't really exist in my world. But once I saw his face again he became a person with a family and hobbies. It didn't take long for me to check his Facebook page daily to see if there were any changes. Right before the Article 32, he posted a picture of himself and a woman snuggled up close. I wonder if she knew what Dominik had done during his stint in Uganda.

Not only had I searched for Dominik online, I also searched the majority of names of people who had been emailing me. I saw a picture of Lt. Riggio sitting at his office desk. When David and I were escorted by his assistant, I was able to point him out.

Tuesday afternoon was spent in a room going through the details of the actual event. Riggio the prosecutor, his legal assistant and another woman were present. Although he would apologize for having to ask certain personal and intrusive questions, I knew I had to answer honestly so he could fully prepare his case.

At the end of the day, we went to the courtroom where the Article 32 would take place. The room was dark and hot. Soon, I would be sitting there testifying against my rapist.

Wednesday morning, we went back to base and met with Lt. Riggio to go through more questions. He set up a meeting with the defense in the afternoon. They asked another legal person to do a mock cross-examination after the meeting with the defense.

"What are Lt. Mayo and Lt. Sullivan like?" I asked.

"They are nice and level-headed. They aren't trying to be conniving."

When we went down to the ground floor to meet them, I held my hand out for a firm handshake. Lt. Mayo, who I also searched on the internet, had just recently been married. She was awarded the legal assistant of the year. Her hair was now brown compared to the blonde in her wedding pictures and photo in the legal section of the military newspaper.

Lt. Mayo didn't seem awful. Her eyes were open wide and she had the flat face of a serious person as she introduced herself. When the time came to walk into the board room to discuss the event, we had a slight conflict.

"David has to stay out in the waiting room. He can't come in."

"I'm sorry, but I don't have a lawyer present. If we are going to meet today, I want David in the room as well," I stated matter-of-factly. I wanted someone to keep them accountable and to also watch out if anything crossed a line.

"That's not allowed. He could be a possible witness and this could taint his testimony."

"He knows nothing of the case. His connection to me is only the logistics," I explained.

"If you aren't willing to speak to us, if you are refusing, we'll have to tell the commander that you weren't a willing participant."

"Sandi isn't refusing to cooperate. She has stipulations and doesn't want to be alone in the room," David clarified.

"The military doesn't own me therefore I technically do not have to speak to you."

"I am only familiar with the military system and any witness has to speak to us," Mayo responded.

"I am a civilian and if you want to speak to me, you will have to let David sit in as well. Otherwise, we aren't having this meeting," I stated, holding fast to my demand.

Lt. Mayo was not happy but David and I insisted. A couple of people I had talked to about meeting with the defense were extremely unsure if it was wise in the first place. I had decided that as long as things stayed calm and appropriate I would be OK. At the first sign of anything ruthless, I would leave.

I was escorted into the board room while David waited for her to check with the commander to see if it was OK for David to sit in. Lt. Sullivan and their legal adviser sat with me and we talked about what the meeting would be about. No one seemed comfortable.

David and Lt. Mayo walked back into the room after a while and took a seat. In the next hour, they asked a lot of basic questions.

"Where are you from?"

"What did you study in college?"

"Where are you working now?"

"What happened the night of November 5, 2010?"

I thought I held my own during their questions: I was sad at parts, stronger at others.

"You know he has a family and that this will affect them as well?" asked Lt. Mayo.

I wanted to say, "Dominik should have thought about his family before he chose to sexually assault me. As much as I hate to see others suffer, he is the one that is causing their suffering and I hope and pray that he is held accountable for his actions. Would you also like to ask how this has affected my life and my family?" But I sat quietly and shrugged, not wanting to come off as rude.

We were escorted back upstairs to the prosecutor's office around 6 p.m. to recap what questions they had asked. Since I was tired and needed to save my energy for testifying the next day, I passed on practicing with the mock cross-examination.

As I left, we passed the woman in the hall who had volunteered to question me. I asked her about Lt. Mayo's style in court.

"Some would say that she's bitchy." Fantastic.

When You Choose to Prosecute a Rapist...
Prepare to defend your very being.
Day 166: Thursday, April 21, 2011
Norfolk, Virginia
23 weeks

My whole body was exhausted. Lying there on the bed, I wanted to curl up and wither away. I felt heavy, like someone had strapped weights to my chest.

Testifying was brutal. Even sitting in the waiting room made me anxious. I wanted to hear what was being said and argued. No matter how you slice it, my character, my every word and action, were on trial even more than Dominik's.

I wasn't worried about what the Peace Corps staff would have to say: We had good relationships and I'd fully disclosed everything to them from the start. It was the trio I was worried about—Bridgette, Gwen, Crystal.

Afterward, I was told that Gwen had apparently said she wished she had done things differently after I told them what happened. Bridgette reported it could not have been that bad or else I wouldn't have let them go to Dominik's pool. Crystal, the legal assistant, said nothing.

They finished telephone interviews with the three women around 5:30 p.m. and took half an hour before they were ready for me.

6 p.m. Norfolk, Virginia, time. 1 a.m. my African village time.

I calmly walked to the stand with my purse and a water bottle and sat down. I said, "I do," after the swearing statement like some perverted wedding vow. The room was small with a few rows of seats for the audience. They wouldn't allow my psychologist to sit in since he could be a "potential witness." David wasn't going to be able to either, but they questioned him before me so he ended up in the room. The defense was throwing out anyone who was with me on the basis that they could be a potential witness. There wouldn't be anyone who would be able to give a summary of what was said. Had I brought my mentor or my mother, they probably would have done the same with them. This was not victim-friendly.

I let my eyes slide over the observers in the audience. David was able to join the audience and sat next to my "victim advocate." That was a joke. The day before, I had been assigned someone who was about to leave the military and that's all we talked about—how she was leaving the military. Today, my victim advocate was 24 and on grounds-keeping duty on base. I had more knowledge in the areas of sexual assault and trial procedures than she did. For months, I had been asking about a victim advocate and the military kept delaying and not giving a straight answer. Lt. Riggio had emailed David stating that he was looking for a victim advocate from external resources since I wasn't military and there was confusion about me being assigned a military victim advocate. At least with assigning a victim advocate at the last moment they wouldn't look completely heartless.

The audience also included a reporter from the local newspaper and his military escort, who had to walk the reporter around the building. The escort alternated between looking bored out of his mind and dozing off during the proceedings.

There were a couple of older women taking notes behind the defense table in the audience area. One of them I remembered from the day before. I finally glanced at Lt. Mayo and Lt. Sullivan and pushed my mind only to see a blob of his Navy Enlisted Dress White uniform sitting next to them without taking in any details. That was Dominik.

The prosecutor went first, starting with asking me to state my name and basic information. We went over the events of the night: who I was with, what time it was, where we went. The basic data.

7:30 p.m. Norfolk, Virginia, time. 2:30 a.m. in my African village. I already felt tired.

As the convening authority called for a break, the defense table rose to exit the room. I saw the white blob get up with the rest of the group and I looked down, pretending to fidget with something in my purse.

They returned 15 minutes later. I played with my water bottle and took a deep breath.

This Article 32 had few rules and loose guidelines compared to a general court-martial. Lt. Mayo fired questions away at me with disdain. I wasn't answering questions the way she wanted me to. She would look at the papers in front of her, ask a question and, after I answered, she would nod disbelievingly and sneer. One of the legal assistants had said earlier in the day that Lt. Mayo was bitchy. I didn't think that was the right word; she was just annoying.

Before we even started questions on the actual event, she asked me all these questions on my background. Again, "Where are you from? What clubs were you in during college? What type of people do you work with?"

She attacked everything I'd ever been a part of. Because I've lived in small towns all my life with little diversity, she tried to make me appear to be racist. Because I would go to church when my work schedule would allow, she tried to make it look as if maybe I felt guilty about having sex therefore I had to call it a rape so it wouldn't be my fault. Because I've worked with young women who have been sexually assaulted before, she tried twisting my answers to make me look as though I had an agenda against males.

"Who do you teach and what material do you cover in Uganda?"

"I teach formerly abducted sex slaves, child mothers, young women who have been sexually violated and the poorest of the poor due to 21-plus years of an insurgency. The classes deal with the psychosocial effects of war in a more basic and interactive educational way. We cover topics such as self-esteem, decision making, controlling our emotions, consequences, love vs. lust, relationships, qualities of a good friend, goal making," I told her.

"What is love?"

"Love is a deep feeling of respect and care for another."

"What is the difference with lust?"

"Lust is a strong selfish sexual desire for another."

"What is a wrongful lustful action?"

"Forcing intercourse by placing your hand around the other's throat would be considered a wrongful lustful action," I stated clearly.

An old friend used to call me Mother Teresa because I volunteered and worked with mentally handicapped, pregnant teens, sex workers in India and because I had strongly instilled values and morals. But as I sat at the trial, I just felt empty. The defense attorney was trying to make me look horrible.

Every time I said, "I don't know" to one of her questions, she didn't like it. She wanted answers she could twist. For a while, I gave my very Ugandan "mm" noise, which means neither yes or no but rather that I've acknowledged that she said something.

"Say yes or no," she snapped at me.

"Yes."

"Yes what?"

"Yes."

They made me draw a picture of the hotel room on a large flip-chart on an easel. I used to play a lot with a computer program where you design houses, so I was very exact. I drew the door coming into the room, sinks, toilet, hot tub, shower, TV, chair, one large bed for Todd and one small bed for Dominik. I even put pillows on the beds.

Standing there, I went into teacher mode. I drew lines to where each event took place and numbered them. Instead of looking at the defense lawyer as I answered her questions, I stared at the drawing.

Here, the questioning got really difficult. The location of hands, what sex position, where performed were big topics for her. If I were more knowledgeable about sex position names, perhaps I might have been more help. Each time she wanted an answer, I would have to think back to his skin on mine, how he used his spit as lubricant, how his hands pinned my throat to the mattress.

"On the bed, where were his hands?"

"One of them was placed on my throat."

"Where was his other hand?"

"I don't know."

"What sexual position where you in? Show us the position on the ground."

Instantly, I shook my head. I felt physically sick. I was not going to put myself back in that position with Dominik sitting 15 feet away from me.

"He was laying on top of me, forcing his penis inside my vagina."

"And where was his other hand during this?"

"I don't know."

"What do you mean you don't know?"

"I know that one of his hands was on my throat and that was the only hand I knew where it was located."

"When you were in the shower, what position were you in?"

"He was standing behind me, forcing his penis inside my vagina, one hand around the back of my neck pushing my face against the shower wall."

"Where was his other hand? Was it on your shoulder?"

"I don't know. What does it even matter?"

"A man's life is at stake during this trial. Where his hand was makes all the difference."

Where his hands were that night, violating my body, made all the difference to me.

9:15 p.m. Norfolk, Virginia, time. 4:15 a.m. in my African village. Her constant back and forth of hand placement and sex positions lasted for an hour-and-a-half.

"How many more times are you going to ask? I honestly was not paying attention to where his hands were unless they were around my throat. It is now 4 a.m. my time and I am tired."

The convening authority agreed that the questions were becoming excessive and that, after two hours of questioning, the defense needed to wrap things up.

"Which one of his hands was around your throat?" she continued.

"Exactly where on your throat was it?"

"Can you please demonstrate?"

Again, remembering his hand around my throat made me uneasy and my throat began to tighten.

"Can you please demonstrate his hand in the shower?"

"I'm sorry, but for the initial assault in the shower, I can't properly get my throat in the crook of my elbow for my arm doesn't stretch that way and isn't long enough," I responded curtly.

"How come at no point you chose to scream?"

"It's hard to scream when there's a hand around your throat."

"Is it because the choking was actually foreplay?"

"Choking someone against their will is not foreplay in my book. Dominik never asked for my consent to be choked."

Lt. Mayo kept going back and forth between the timeline and questions. Three hours in, I became frazzled about whether I pushed his hips the first time I noticed the condom had "slipped" off or if it was the second time. Was it the second? My mind was fuzzy and her repeated, slightly reworded questions were worming into my brain. I didn't want to say yes or no to a question I had already answered two hours earlier. She pushed and pushed after I said "I do not know" to a question. She was getting to me and she was happy about it.

"Do we need to take a break?" asked the convening authority.

"I just want this over with. We can keep going," I replied.

I sat there dazed and unhappy with myself. At the end, she went through every single email I had ever written to one of the other women involved or military person, my letter to the others that I wrote during counseling, the longer write up I had written after the NCIS interview, which I had given to some other guy after he asked if I wanted to change anything.

"Did you write that 'the conversations were hilarious' in the vehicle on the way to the second location?"

"Can you finish the sentence? There was more to that sentence. It's on the paper right in front of you."

"Did you say it or not?" She shuffled the papers around pretending to look for it.

"That is not the full sentence. The second part says something about how the conversations were vulgar and embarrassing as the driver was listening."

She then proceeded to take out of context a sentence right after Dominik flippantly said to find him on Facebook. I had said something about how if I got pregnant, I would lose my job, return back to the States and have a bastard child. She painted me as someone who calls their unborn, imaginary child a bastard. The last part of that written statement had been "because there is no way on earth I would let it learn manners from you." She wanted me to look like I was using the negative connotation when in reality the definition is a child who does not know their father.

I admitted to having had said it. In one email, I had asked a question about seeing the statements and had used "pretty please" at the end of the sentence. The way she said it with vinegar in her voice made me chuckle. I was done with her questions.

I take it back, Lt. Mayo was malicious.

9:40 p.m. Norfolk, Virginia, time. 4:40 a.m. in my African village. I was exhausted.

Almost four hours after first entering the room, the prosecution was able to cross examine me.

"Is there anything you would like to further explain or clarify?"

"No."

If the fact that something unlawful had happened wasn't apparent by then, I didn't know what else to say.

The questions finally stopped. The prosecution's legal assistant took out the cassette tape that had been recording the whole thing. We had a short debrief with the lawyer and agreed to meet the next day for a follow-up of the last day.

I was glad the Article 32 was finished, but I still felt heavy. I answered everything to the best of my ability but I felt like I had failed since I was not able to answer each question the way I wanted to.

David, the Peace Corps psychologist who had driven down earlier that day and I got into the car to go to dinner. I sat in the back, slinking down low into my seat. I couldn't remember the last time I had eaten yet I didn't have an appetite.

David said that the majority of his time testifying was about the state of the Peace Corps, not about the assault committed against me.

"David, are you aware of the '20/20' episode and the accusations being made against the Peace Corps about the treatment of sexual assault victims."

"David, are you aware of the Congressional hearings that are going to occur on the issues of Peace Corps and sexual assault? Are you as an agency under a lot of pressure for prosecutions?"

"Did you receive conflicting reports from the victim and your CIRS system about this case?"

"Lt. Sullivan, the Peace Corps is not on trial, move on."

The defense lawyers were trying to make this about anything other than sexual assault.

Later, as I lay on my bed, I analyzed the day. I was just hoping to disappear.

How much longer would I have to feel like this?

A Game of Telephone

Day 183: Saturday, April 23 to May 8, 2011
Pader, Northern Uganda
26 weeks

Saturday morning, I was waiting to search the Norfolk newspaper to see what the journalist had written about the Article 32. I'd had articles written about my travels and work in the local paper in Indiana; my college alumni magazine did a two-page spread after I'd spent six months in Uganda. There had been stories published nationally and internationally about my work and the people I served. I was usually confident that whatever was written was done so in a positive and accurate manner.

Having a complete stranger who sat in listening to all the testimonies and then writing a piece about the Article 32 made me uneasy. I wouldn't be able to give input on what he covered. I had no control over what he put in writing for the world to see.

Typing "Norfolk Article 32 Uganda" in the search engine gave me what I was looking for. I took a long deep breath as I opened the page. My heart beat faster as I read it:

Sailor accused of raping teacher in Uganda

The Virginian-Pilot
© April 23, 2011
NORFOLK

A sailor working in a support role for Virginia Beach-based Navy SEALs has been accused of raping a Peace Corps volunteer in Uganda.

Petty Officer 2nd Class Dominik Jones faced a preliminary hearing Thursday and Friday to determine whether there is sufficient evidence to prosecute him in a court-martial. A decision is expected in a few weeks.

This week's proceeding at Norfolk Naval Station, called an Article 32 hearing, featured graphic and emotional testimony from Jones's accuser, a 26-year-old woman who teaches at a girls' school in a remote town in northern Uganda.

The Virginian-Pilot does not identify alleged victims of sexual assault.

The incident is alleged to have occurred in November in Kampala, the Ugandan capital, while Jones, a builder, was assigned to a construction project for a SEAL team.

Navy spokesmen would not say this week what the secretive sea-air-land commandos were doing in the African country.

Jones's accuser testified that what began as a consensual sexual encounter in Jones's hotel room turned violent after she insisted that he use a condom. He reluctantly did so, she said, but after it came off twice, she asked him to stop. Instead, he forced himself on her, she said.

"I tried to get away and could not," she said. "The next thing I know, there's a hand around my neck."

Jones was choking her, pinning her head to the mattress and making it difficult to breathe, she said.

"I was very fearful of my life," she said.

Jones forced himself on her three more times over the course of the night, each time without a condom, she testified. On one of those occasions, he followed her into the shower and again choked her during the sex act, pinning her head against the shower wall with his arm, she said.

"I did not want to be choked again, so I let him have his way," she said. "I silently took it. I just wanted him to be done."

Over three hours of testimony, the accuser avoided eye contact with Jones, who sat ramrod-straight at the defense table in a crisp white uniform. He did not testify.

The accuser met Jones while bar-hopping with three other young women, all Peace Corps volunteers, on a weekend visit to Kampala, according to testimony. The three other women testified for the defense, two of them by telephone from Uganda. They said the accuser flirted with Jones, seemed to enjoy his company, and went willingly with him to his hotel.

One of them described the accuser as conservative and very religious.

The accuser testified that she was active in a Christian club in college and later worked in Kolkata, India, as a volunteer for Mother Teresa's charity.

At one point during the evening in Kampala, the conversation turned to how long it had been since each of the four women had had sex. It was determined that Jones's accuser had been abstinent the longest — two years. That led to a consensus that she should pair up with him for the night.

"The girls decided I needed it the most," the accuser testified. "They kept pressuring me."

She now feels betrayed by her friends, she said.

"To them, this was just a game," she said. "To them, a one-night stand is something you do for fun. They saw it as this night of passion, and it was anything but that."

She acknowledged that for two days, she told no one she had been assaulted.

"I was in shock and denial," she said. "I had never been with an abusive man. I had never been traumatized like that before."

It was only when she went to a Peace Corps medical officer that the whole story came out, she testified. She was seeking the "morning after" contraceptive pill and a drug that reduces the risk of acquiring the AIDS virus.

After she had recounted the details of what she called her "night of hell," she said, the medical officer asked her: "Were you raped?"

Until that moment, "I had not thought of it that way," she said. "I thought rape is something that happens to someone else."

Jones's defense attorneys suggested that the Peace Corps pushed the accuser to bring charges because of political pressure.

An audit last year by the Peace Corps Office of Inspector General faulted the agency for multiple lapses in its safety and security procedures, and several media reports have focused on sexual assaults on volunteers. In January, a congressional oversight committee announced plans for hearings.

If Jones is court-martialed and convicted of the most serious charges, he faces a range of possible penalties up to life in prison and death.

Breathe.

Although the reporter wrote that the paper did not identify alleged victims, he made it awfully easy to figure out who I was.

There were 160 volunteers in-country, maybe 20 in northern Uganda, about six of them were females, two who taught at schools and only one who was 26, one who volunteered with Mother Teresa's charity in India before coming to Uganda.

I couldn't believe the details in the article—especially since I was not allowed to talk to any other witnesses about testimonies.

The part about me being conservative and very religious made me laugh. I was super-calm and non-judgmental—not a religious fanatic. Yes, sometimes I would go to the Christian club in college. They forgot to mention that I was also a senator in stud¬ent government, active member in student union board and a speech and debate competitor.

I was glad that in a non-military court rape shield laws prevent previous sexual history from being covered. Was my decision not to have sexual relations with men for two years really that newsworthy?

What the article did not report was the sick feeling I felt when Lt. Mayo asked me to demonstrate the chokehold. It did not report how Lt. Mayo kept asking me the same questions over and over again until I was so exhausted I slipped up.

The more I looked at shortened articles that have found their way on the internet, the more I remembered playing the game telephone as a kid. With each turn, certain details get left out, words get switched or changed depending on what the new author wants to emphasize, and I got less satisfied with what I read.

On May 8, on my first day back at work in my Ugandan village of Pader, I was sitting with my laptop answering emails, and the second in charge of the organization said he had a question for me.

As soon as he started saying something about the newspaper, I quickly tried to cut him off.

"Ah, so I read about this tragedy. Who did it happen to?"

I do not know if he was playing dumb or could tell how uncomfortable I felt. I thought this was ill-fated since he was in charge of the child-protective projects and yet he wanted the scoop on a rape that happened to a volunteer.

"It is very unfortunate that a man in the U.S. military would do that to a volunteer. This sexual assault makes Americans look bad!"

"Not all Americans choose to sexually assault others."

He kept asking questions and I kept deflecting him or only restating facts that were in the newspaper article. My privacy was more important than what little information was given to the public.

"Sandi, who was this? What volunteer was harmed?"

I shrugged my shoulders.

"I will have to ask Katherine when she gets back."

My hands shook as I hastily sent my site mate a text pleading with her not to say anything to him if he asked.

A few minutes later, I entered the director of my organization's office. Before leaving to testify in court, I had told Alice that I had been sexually assaulted. Her first question was if he was a Ugandan. She was shocked that my perpetrator was a U.S. military member, "one of my own."

She was glad that I was back although she knew it had to be difficult. She made sure to let me know to take my time getting back into things and to take care of myself. Since the school was for young women who had been rebel commanders' sex slaves/wives and now had children, or had gone through many sexual assaults, Alice was worried that I would be working out of emotion or out of a personal agenda, would have flashbacks and wouldn't be able to work with level-headedness.

But I had been interested in working with this type of population way before I was ever raped. Yes, hearing someone else's story reminded me of my own, which was difficult but still manageable.

As I was talking to Alice, my phone rang. It was Laura, the birthday lady that Bridgette, Gwen and Crystal had told Dominik to be her present for the night, the week after he assaulted me. I was concerned when I saw her name on my cellphone screen since I did not know her relationship with the other three volunteers.

I excused myself from talking with Alice and answered. None of the volunteers had directly called me up to this point about the newspaper article, so I braced myself for the first conversation.

"Hi Sandi. I wanted to talk to you about something sensitive," she said nervously. "I got really scared after reading the article. The night of my birthday, I gave Dominik the cold shoulder since I didn't want anything to do with him. While I was washing my hands at a sink in the hallway of a club, he came up behind me and whispered in my ear how he wanted to be in me; he wanted to take me back to his place; he wanted to strangle me."

"Did he really use those words?"

"Yes. When I read the article and saw that he had choked you, I couldn't believe it. If he was willing to say that to a complete stranger in a club, of what else is he capable?"

The newspaper article was the first she learned of what had happened. She had no idea I was going through a legal morass to get justice.

She continued, "Please know you have my support. I am so sorry this happened to you. I'm sorry that the others are testifying against you. If the information about what Dominik said to me that night would help, I'm willing to talk."

Dominik was a reckless danger to women and something had to be done. Unfortunately, the prosecutor didn't think her experience would be admissible as testimony. Yes, it sucked that other volunteers I was serving with were aware of the situation, but I hoped that, if nothing else, it would start honest dialogue about a difficult subject matter.

The New Article 120, U.C.M.J.
Day 200: Wednesday, May 25, 2011
28 weeks

The newspaper article had stated, "If Jones is court-martialed and convicted of the most serious charges, he faces a range of possible penalties up to life in prison and death." This made me curious about what penalties he might actually face.

A friend helped me find "Sex offenses in the military—the new Article 120, U.C.M.J.," which outlines definitions and charges used by military lawyers. The packet dissected what actions were done to or with the victim, went through how the actions were done and then the suspect's role in the actions done to or with the victim to determine the consequences.

From what I learned talking to the military lawyers, going over and over in my head the events of that night and this article, I determined what I thought would establish the "what" in my case:

Indecent Act B(11). The term 'indecent conduct' means that form of immorality relating to sexual impurity which is grossly vulgar, obscene, and repugnant to common property, and tends to excite sexual desire or deprave morals with respect to sexual relations.

Maximum penalty is five years. One count due to inappropriate conversations and behavior between Dominik and the other women while at the two bars in Kampala.

Indecent Exposure B(14). That the accused exposed his or her genitalia, anus, buttocks, or female areola or nipple; that the accused's exposure was in an indecent manner; that the exposure occurred in a place where the conduct involved could reasonably be expected to be viewed by people other than the accused family or household; and that the exposure was intentional.

Maximum penalty is one year. One count due to the penis exposure in the second bar.

Wrongful Sexual Contact. (T)he intentional touching, either directly or through the clothing, of the genitalia, anus, groin, breast, inner thigh, or buttocks of another person, or intentionally causing another person to touch, either directly or through the clothing, the genitalia, anus, groin, breast, inner thigh, or buttocks of any person, with an intent to abuse, humiliate, or degrade any person or to arouse or gratify the sexual desire of any person.

Maximum penalty is one year. One count due to his hand over my jeans before leaving the second bar.

"Sexual Act" was separated into two categories. The first was when there is force, causing grievous bodily harm; threat of death, grievous bodily harm, or kidnapping; rendering unconscious: drugging to impair; any of which concludes to be rape. If there is bodily harm, threat that is less than death, grievous bodily harm, kidnapping, and taking advantage of incapacitation, it's considered aggravated sexual assault.

> Rape: B(1)(a) By using force. That the accused caused another person, who is of any age, to engage in a sexual act by using force against that other person. B(1)(c) By using threats or placing in fear. That the accused caused another person, who is of any age, to engage in a sexual act by threatening or placing that other person in fear that any person will be subjected to death, grievous bodily harm, or kidnapping.

Maximum penalty is death or life in prison. Two counts due to strangulation in the bed and then again in the shower. If a jury member was in the position to judge the defendant and believed the person was guilty of the charges at hand, I wondered if the sentence of life in prison or death kept them from actually finding the individual guilty. Even if the juror thought the individual was guilty of rape, would they acquit the case due to not wanting to inflict what they deemed was too harsh of a punishment? When I pressed charges, I hadn't considered that the punishment might be death or life in prison; I had just wanted to make sure that Dominik wouldn't have the chance to assault another woman.

> Aggravated Sexual Assault: B(5)(c) By using threats or placing in fear. That the accused engaged in sexual contact with another person and that the accused did so by threatening or placing that other person in fear that any person will be subjected to death, grievous bodily harm, or kidnapping.

Maximum penalty is 30 years. Two counts due to the second time in the bed and also the "quickie" before being able to leave the hotel.

The second portion of the packet was about determining the how:
- By inflicting force—placing his hand around my throat to pin me to the mattress, putting my throat in the crook of his elbow while in the shower.
- By inflicting bodily harm—pressure on my trachea, which resulted in me not wanting to move out of fear of it being crushed.
- By threats or placing in fear—after the first time of trying to get away and him using force to pin me back down, getting away and then him putting me in a chokehold when I turned away, I was in fear of him repeating this or what else he might do when it came to the second bed incident when he aggressively pulled at the shorts I was wearing and then in the morning when he grabbed my side.

- Lack of permission—he never asked if it was OK to put his hand around my throat or push my neck into the shower wall. He asked if I liked it as if to justify his behavior, but that was 30 minutes after the fact; he had already broken the law by raping me.

Lastly, for this case, the packet emphasized determining the suspect's role in what was done to or with the victim.

- Perpetrator (engaged in the act or conduct)

After reading this, Dominik could have been facing six counts against him including indecent conduct, indecent exposure, wrongful sexual contact, aggravated sexual assault and rape. Technically, this could have led to the maximum sentence of death or life in prison, but I didn't think that was realistic. After reading over the JAGdefense.com website months ago outlining their pride and joy in getting perpetrators acquitted of all charges, who knew what the outcome might be.

Can't Say the Word
Day 215: Thursday, June 9, 2011
30 weeks

Dad's birthday. This was the first time I had spoken to just him since Christmas. I called him twice. First try, he was at the park with my niece. Second time, a few hours later when he was back at the house and everyone else was in bed, he answered.

I could not verbally tell him about what actually happened to me. I could not say the words rape, sex or forced, and instead gulped every time they should have been there. I chose cryptic words with vague meanings. I wasn't sure if I was doing it for his benefit or mine.

In December, my dad had told me about his friend who had been in prison a couple of years for attempted manslaughter. He had tried to kill the guy who raped his daughter.

I did not want my dad in prison on my behalf.

"Google 'sailor accused of,'" gulp, "and 'teacher in Uganda' and it should be in the Virginia Pilot or Norfolk paper."

We kept talking, slowly, not knowing how to fill the widening gap of silence with what we were unwilling and unable to say out loud.

He read the article.

"I told Mom I would ask permission before sharing anything with her. Do you want me to show her the article?" he asked.

Silent pause.

"Do you think that is wise? Do you think she can handle it?" I asked.

"No."

Dad deleted the search history.

He never told my mom.

I love my parents dearly and have never wanted them to hurt for me.

"Thanks!" But No Thanks
Day 248: Tuesday, July 12, 2011
Pader, Northern Uganda
35 weeks

July 12, 2011

Ms. Giver,

Good morning. My name is LN1 Carie Sharp and am a defense paralegal working with LT Lauren Mayo and LT Daniel Sullivan in the case of United States v. BU2 Dominik Jones. I just wanted to touch base with you after the Article 32. Have you returned to the States? If so, we'd like to schedule another interview with you. Also, you mentioned at the Article 32 that you would be willing to send us information on the case study that you put together regarding sexual assault. If you are able to forward it to us, that would be greatly appreciated. Thanks!

Sincerely,
LN1(SW) Carie L. Sharp
NLSO MIDLANT
Norfolk, VA
Defense Department LPO
Team 1 LPO/Paralegal

July 13, 2011

LN1 Sharp,

I am sorry to inform you that I am no longer in the States and I will not be able to meet with you for an interview. Also, I have no information to forward you.

Have a fantastic summer and we'll meet again in August.
Sandi

To (My Dear Friend Sandi)
Day 253: Sunday, July 17, 2011
Pader, Northern Uganda
36 weeks

Receiving love letters from random people was not uncommon in Uganda. They could see you walk to work every day or maybe be a server at the local restaurant. "Circle yes or no if you will be my friend." People fell in love with the idea of leaving Uganda with a rich white mzungu who would forever treat them with love and shower them with gifts.

I've known plenty of expats who have been received love letters. I've received a few myself.

Because of the school I worked in and the relationships of trust I built, the letters I received were of a different nature and content. They still had "I love you Sandi" written on them and a couple of song lyrics dedicated to me in the side margin. But they also included a line or two like, "It is a secret please! No one needs to know about it. It's for you and me only plz dear."

July 17, 2011

Dear Sandi,

First of all I would like to thank the Almighty Father for having given me this special time to communicate to you through this small sheet of paper. How are you? Back to the author, I am not all that fine because am missing your fantastic classes of encouragement. The main purpose of writing to you this letter is that I would love and like to be your friend. Just because of the following views, I am Pamela by name, Acholi by tribe. 17 years by age and a Ugandan by nationality. To go into details, I am an orphan. I lost my dad when I was still very young and by that time I was only 9 and half month. But I am staying with my stepmother. You may ask me why? The reason is I never saw my real mama. They told me that they divorced themselves after I was 7 month only and my granmum took care of me. But she has already died. She died on 3rd/7/2003 and by that time I was in primary three by then. I was then taken away by my stepmother who was living in Masindi District. I went there and always she mistreat me. I sat for my end of year paper in P.3, I passed very well. I was in position 4. But she told me that the position was not good and I have to repeat that class in 2004. In addition, you know women whom at first they were soldiers' wives, they like moving up and down. I was told my father was a soldier before he died and so she kept moving up and at times left us at home alone. One evening I was preparing dinner. There comes a very big man who came to me and asked me my name and then I respected him as a wise person and I told him my name. I asked him that who are you? He told me he is my uncle. I kept quiet went away and after some few minutes he came back while he was pretending that he was drunk and raped me. So by that time he ran away and the good thing I did is that I never kept quiet and I woke up very early in the morning I prepared my selves as I was going to school and I even put on my own school uniform and my friend were asking me if I was going to school. Because they saw me crying and I was taking other directions. I went straight to the hospital and I explained it to the nurses and they gave me some medicines and injected me. By then I cried very much because I had never wanted to break my virginity and since then up to now I have never had sex with any man only because of these reasons below. I promised to myself that I never wanted to disappoint my step mum because of getting pregnant and also I promised to study hard and get a white man who will marry me and take good care of me. And that's the promise I have up to now. So I wanna beg you that if possible you get me a friend who is a boy from your country there and give me his contact only that because I never wanted to suffer again in future. I also have to enjoy good life future. The greatest thing is that I want you during this holiday of the end of year, that is the holiday for Christmas, I would love to go with you to your country and I come just because I want to go and see your country. And we will live as you're my friend, sister, mother, and my everything because I never enjoyed the love of parents mostly for my mom. I hope if my request is put under your consideration, then I will enjoy the love of a mum from you as my friend because we will stay together as family with joy and happiness. I will give you my photo and for my stepmother next term if we come back for end of year studies.

May the good lord bless you Sandi

Pamela

Letters like this broke my heart. I wanted to cry and hold her in my arms. I wanted to tell her I was sorry for the man's behavior and that she had a good heart.

The young women I worked with had not had easy lives. As soon as they were able to pick a child up around age 3, they were in charge of carrying around the new 4-month-old. In my own compound, Apio was maybe 9 years old, an orphan and was living with her "aunt" who had a 2-year-old. Every day, I saw Apio hand-washing clothing, doing dishes, bathing the 2-year-old and completing other tasks. Some days she went to school, other days she didn't. She had a place to sleep and she seemed healthy but there didn't seem to be much freedom in her life. Yet compared to other children in the community, her life was a piece of cake.

During the insurgency, thousands of families were displaced. Rather than being in the place of action, families moved to the cramped camps or stayed with extended family. One girl around age 12 was orphaned and taken in by a family to be their house girl, someone who does the majority of chores and cooking.

She was not allowed to go to school and instead had to take care of all the household needs. In a developed country, there is no way to imagine life where you have to fetch your own water from a borehole and cook everything from scratch using four ingredients. Not only did the family treat her like free labor, the father also sexually abused her nightly. This went on for years until she was finally able to escape. Even with different surroundings, she felt the impact of the years of abuse. She tested positive for HIV. She had been taken out of the area where rebels killed and raped villagers only to find herself in the care of a family that enslaved and sexually assaulted her.

Even when we believe we are taking ourselves out of a dangerous situation, and that the new situation will be in our best interests, what's on the other side may be more dangerous than what we were facing before.

When I read Pamela's letter, I wanted to tell her that rapists abuse victims regardless of their location on a map. Rape and sexual assault are used as psychological warfare in conflict zones and, after there is "peace," there is a higher percentage of everyday citizens who sexually assault young children.[18]

Whether a man lives in an African village pretending to be your drunken uncle or an American military man who won't let his sexual ego be challenged, individuals who aren't afraid of taking what they want, who abuse others, are everywhere.

In 2010, my school hosted a weeklong workshop for teachers in the district. On the final day, there was an open question period. The men started complaining about the female students and how they would disrespect the teachers by not greeting them. The students would keep walking, ignoring the male teachers and would go on about their studies. Man after man started agreeing and the group became louder.

Finally, I couldn't stand what they were saying anymore, which seemed like they were entitled to respect. I timidly raised my hand, not knowing how what I was about to say would be received.

"Hello everyone. My name is Sandi and I have been in Uganda since August 2009. One of the workshops I attended was about speaking out and advocating for women's issues. While there, I learned about the high rates of students who are physically violated and the sexual abuse by male teachers. In 2008, 43,000 female students reported being sexually violated by their male teachers here in Uganda. These young female students aren't disrespecting you because they are stubborn or rebellious, but because the men here have created a reputation of abusing and disrespecting their young bodies. The men here have a reputation and it is not a good one. If you want these female students to respect you, you need to respect them. Even if you are not personally defiling them, keep the other male teachers you work with accountable for their actions. Change the reputation of sexually violating young women by being men of honor and integrity."

And then they clapped. There were "a-ha" faces all around the room. I had been shaking inside the whole time I was speaking but I knew the reality of the issue needed to be heard.

I wished I could have protected Pamela from hurt. I wished perpetrators would take responsibility for their actions and people would treat each other with respect.

Until that happened, more letters, more pleas for help would be written. How many more young women would want to escape? How many more letters would they write?

---

18 http://www.un.org/en/preventgenocide/rwanda/about/bgsexualviolence.shtml: Background Information on Sexual Violence used as a Tool of War

Living by Principle
Day 255: Tuesday, July 19, 2011
Pader, Northern Uganda
36 weeks

Days passed where I did not think anything good could happen. The defense wanted access to my Gmail account, all medical records since the incident, phone records, my Peace Corps personnel file dating back to my application and all I wanted to say was, "No."

Email was my main source of communication with friends and family. I lived in a village where the electricity would go out for hours at a time. What use would my personal emails have been? I felt sure they should have been able to make a case without delving into my personal email account.

Doctor–patient confidentiality was still in effect. There was a decent chance that the defense could get access, but only to the records that pertained to the incident.

I was fine with giving up my phone records but I bought the SIM card for less than $2 and had never gotten a receipt for any of the airtime. Texts were only saved for about a week so none of those from the time of the event would have been accessible.

I wasn't sure how my Peace Corps personnel file would help the defense but I was sure they'd be able to twist something to their favor. It simply detailed the work I had done prior to the Peace Corps.

There were other documents and questions the defense had. At this point, I had stopped trying to make sense of what they were asking for or why. I felt like I was lying on an operating table with my chest wide open, able to look down and see the different people poke and prod my exposed internal organs. If I said anything, my chest would move too much and my lungs would collapse.

I talked to David from Peace Corps safety and security. He asked how I was doing and I broke down. I cried so hard my eyelids felt raw and swollen.

"I don't want to be here," I struggled to say between deep breaths. "I don't have the passion for working with my students that I once had. Everything was going great and then this happened and nothing has been the same since. Having the students and teachers excited to see me is grand and all, but I don't have the energy to be excited back. I am depressed, unhappy, can't sleep at night and then, once I do fall asleep, I sleep for 10 hours. Bridgette and Crystal are running their mouths and I can't defend myself. I can't do anything."

"Have you talked to anyone there about how you are feeling?"

"How can I? The defense just called my site mate. People do not remember things correctly and can misquote me. Anything I say can and will be used against me. I hate how isolating this feels."

David reminded me that I had options, that I didn't have to stay in Uganda. I knew I could leave but I was so close to finishing. I do not quit. Plus, I didn't know how a job interviewer would react if I informed them, "I'll need a week off in August to testify against my rapist."

Sometimes what's best is coming to the realization that the current situation is not healthy and the time has come to take yourself out of the situation.

But I was just too stubborn to leave. I. Don't. Quit.

I had already been thinking about being done with Uganda once I left for the trial.

There are only three people in the States who called me and all three called in one night. My mother was the last one. At that point, I was tired from talking and thinking. All I remembered was that I seemed downtrodden and my mom wanted to know how to pray for me.

I honestly didn't know what to tell her.

A few days later, the prosecutor called to inform me that if the defense didn't get the personnel files and medical files, they would complain to the judge that they weren't allowed to properly defend their client. A subpoena for the files could take a long time and delay the trial—a delay so long that the case might never go to court and all the charges would be dropped. I didn't want the case to be ruined just because I didn't want the defense poking in my files.

I signed waivers to get around the time a subpoena would take. I also wanted to show that I was serious about the case and willing to work with the military.

The Peace Corps general counsel wrote up waivers to release the information relevant to the case. They were to be kept sealed and any information received could not be published or given to the general public.

By signing the waivers, the medical staff in Uganda would photocopy my files and overnight them to the States. In D.C., a member of the Peace Corps general counsel would sit with the prosecutor and select which papers were related to the incident. After this, the papers would be sealed and given to the judge for him to go through and see what was relevant as evidence and given to both trial counsels.

One of the benefits of giving them my medical file was while they wanted more information about my mental health to see if I had a split personality or had a habit of falsifying information, both the defense and prosecution would also get the reports made by the psychologist about the effects of being raped had had on my mental state since November.

A few months ago in March, counselor Lyla in Uganda emailed the Peace Corps medical staff about our session. I remembered sitting on the floor, crying, with my knees to my chest, dumbfounded about how "messed up" my life was.

To gain access to my email, the defense sent a request to Google for access to my account. Google denied them access, and sent me a notification about the request.

The defense said that because I sent an email to the JAG investigators about further information, sent an email to some other military employee working on the case with a revised statement and had sent the therapy letter to the three women that I must be sending other emails about the incident.

The defense had not brought to the judge any specifics on how they would filter my emails. I felt that the defense going in without a plan of action was ridiculous and I refused to let them openly search through my email.

At first, I told the prosecutor that the military would have to go through the legal system to get access to my emails. Then I reconsidered, not wanting the judge to think I was hiding something. After thinking about the possible consequences of the defense pushing even harder or threatening to drop the case, I decided to give them access with conditions.

If the defense could give their methodology of filtering emails, a list of words or phrases they would be searching for, and a detailed account of how they planned to use my email account, I would give my email username and password to the judge. He would go through and see what was relevant. As soon as he was finished, I would change my password. The judge would then hand the emails over to both prosecution and defense.

I sent an email to the prosecutor explaining what I would accept. During the Article 32, I had no idea what emails were going to be brought up. Lt. Mayo asked questions about something I had emailed in November. She would quote something, leave half of the sentence out and ask me to agree with what was said. I was not able to remember the second half of the line and it upset me that she was taking everything out of context. I requested that if my emails were accessed, that the prosecutor and I would sit and discuss whatever was brought forth so I could clarify the context and meaning.

During the Article 32, the defense had a copy of my therapy letter I'd sent to the three female volunteers. I wondered if Gwen had given their responses or any of the emails they had sent. I copied the ones out of Facebook and Gmail, created a Word document and sent them to the prosecutor.

Struggling With Justice
Day 272: Friday, August 5, 2011
Pader, Northern Uganda
38 weeks

On Friday, August 5, I walked 15 minutes to the school to see the senior-level students. The majority of them stayed in two side-by-side dorm rooms. I went inside the first and the students happily greeted me. We talked about sitting for exams next term and when they would go home for holiday.

They knew my time in Uganda was coming to an end. They didn't know that I might have to leave earlier because of the trial. This could have been the last time I saw them. I just didn't know. Juliet, our head girl, came out of her separate room and sat down beside me.

"Cindy"—she, and many Ugandans, had trouble pronouncing Sandi—"when are you leaving us?" she asked.

"In September, but I have to go back for a little over a week."

"Eh! You are always coming and going! Why must you go in August? Last time you left, they said you were sick."

"Well, I have to take care of some business." She was not very satisfied with my answer. I had not disclosed to any of the students what had happened but now that I would be leaving I thought the risk of sharing a small idea of what happened was not as high.

"I have to go testify in a trial."

"Cindy! What did you do!"

"I did not do anything, Juliet. I am going to testify against someone else."

"Eh! Sorry. I hope he did not hurt you!"

I quietly said that the man was violent during a bad incident. I said how he was looking at a possible 60 years in prison for his actions.

"You want him to rot in jail the rest of his life? Oh, Cindy, you must forgive him!" she insisted.

Juliet was a former "wife" of the infamous Joseph Kony. For her to say that I just needed to forgive him, knowing her experiences of abduction, forced sex slavery to a rebel commander and eventually having a stillborn child, intrigued and perplexed me.

I returned to the dorms to see Juliet a few days later, wanting to speak with her before the students went back to their villages.

I found her at the dorm and walked with her to the teacher's room. All the teachers had left so we sat alone at one of the large tables.

"Juliet, what is justice?" I posed.

"Justice is the fair treatment offered to a person after a wrongdoing."

"What about injustice—what is that?"

"Injustice is the unfair treatment given to a person."

"Dear Juliet, you know how I have been coming and going to the U.S.? I have been going there for reasons more complicated than only health reasons. A member of the United States military sexually assaulted me in November. I am seeking legal justice and it is very difficult. The pre-trial was challenging and draining. I know I must persevere through with the actual trial."

"Cindy! I am so sorry!"

"Justice is difficult to fully comprehend right now. The main reason why I am going through the legal justice system is because I cannot let my silence be the factor that left him unaccountable for his actions. What if he traumatizes someone else? What if I had the chance to have a role in preventing that but then I gave up? I am not as concerned about the amount of time he will potentially serve but rather that he doesn't force himself on another woman like this again."

"You just let them know you only want him to serve two years then."

"It doesn't work that way in the States; you can have a say, but ultimately the verdict is up to the acting judge or jury," I explained.

Traditionally in northern Uganda, there were ceremonies that must be completed after someone has killed a family member. The breaking of the egg and drinking a bitter root are a couple of traditional reconciliation methods. Once the ceremony is over, the perpetrator is accepted back into the village and people live side by side. It's not that there isn't resentment or distrust of the person, but ultimately the ceremonies are supposed to be a way of putting the past in the past and moving forward.

"Cindy, the first time I saw the man who abducted me from my village, I was at the Gulu reception center. People would go there for physical and psychological support after escaping captivity. I saw him standing across the room and I knew who he was right away. He was still a young man, like I was a young girl. There was no way that he understood what he was being forced to do when he abducted me for the rebels. I had to forgive him."

I could understand her acceptance to forgive someone who was threatened with death if they did not obey a command. What was difficult for me was the fact that the man who chose to sexually assault me was not a rebel soldier, did not act out of fear for his life, but was a fellow American who had sworn to protect our nation. He made a choice to act on his own.

"Juliet, about how much prison time do you think would be legal justice for the man who abducted you into the bush?"

"One year. It is good for a man to understand what he did was wrong. I do not believe that too much time would be needed."

"Only one year?

"Yes. I have visited the prisons, ah, and they are not good places. After a year or two, he will change his behavior."

"What if he doesn't change his behavior? We can't control what they learn or if they change. What should happen if they do it again?" I asked.

"If he has not learned, he should go back for 10 years."

"Now, Juliet, I know a small amount about your past. What about Kony?"

"Kony should get 10 years," she stated flatly.

Somehow, I did not believe that a man responsible for giving the command for abduction and murder of thousands of people should only receive 10 years' punishment. But in Juliet's mind, this was the most he should be punished. To her, that was justice. After everything he did to her, she was resilient and strong and remarkably forgiving of the man who was responsible for the majority of her pain. I couldn't imagine how 10 years could be enough to make up for what he had done.

Then again, I was still confused by what justice even meant. To me, there was no simple definition to the word. It was a confusing, intangible and objective word—situational and culturally defined.

What would be my justice? Which of the thousands of definitions of justice applied to me? What had happened that night would never be erased or cleared from my mind, no matter how many years Dominik spent in prison or what titles were stripped from his name. A price tag could be placed on an actual therapy session but not the psychological and emotional damage. That price, to me, was inestimable.

How do you quantify justice for destroying a life?

Technically, there were quite a few actual events that Dominik was charged with: lewd behavior because of the conversation in the taxi (one year), indecent exposure for revealing his penis at the club (one year), forcible rape/aggravated sexual assault with threat of life in the bed (30 years), same in the shower (30 years), sexual assault on the bed the second time (one year), sexual assault in the bathroom the final time (one year). If found guilty, the sentences would not be served at the same time but rather consecutively, equating to 64 years in a military prison.

The last two charges were only weighted as 1 year rather than 30 because I said I was not fearful for my life. Semantics. They were in the same classification as sexual harassment or groping. He had already conditioned me that submitting to him was the path to the least physical harm to my body. Unfortunately, the court did not see it that way.

Retributive justice is similar to the military theory and law of retaliation: an emphasis on finding some legal "truth" of what already happened and then presenting an equal punishment. I was interested in seeing if the military would actually keep the offender accountable for his actions.

Restorative justice, on the other hand, is concerned less with retribution and punishment for the offender but more concerned about taking the proper steps to reintegrate the offender into society. Restorative justice puts emphasis on the aftermath of an incident and focuses on making the victim whole: counseling, providing appropriate services to the victim to live out a positive life. Although these services are provided in the States, they can be rather costly and difficult to actually obtain. This approach brings an offender and a victim together so that the offender can better understand the effect of their offense on the victim.

I wondered if I could successfully communicate to Dominik the effect of his assault on me. Anxiety and stress filled me as I thought about the week of trial and him staring at me as I spoke about the rapes.

I was in no need of a courtroom with a judge and jury to validate what happened to me was sexual assault. I already knew the truth. I was in that hotel room. I lived through it. The legal system was set in place for retributive justice and keeping lawbreakers accountable for their actions.

If he admitted his actions against me were legally and morally wrong, sought counseling to better understand his issues and his behavior was kept accountable, that would feel like justice to me.

I didn't want him to rot in jail. I wanted him to never traumatize another woman again and to be held accountable for what he did to me.

Preparing for Lift Off
Day 272: Friday, August 5, 2011
Pader, Northern Uganda
38 weeks

The week before had been full of ups and downs. I had accepted the fact that I couldn't control what went on with the court. I didn't know when I was leaving and when—or if—I was coming back. I prepared myself for many different scenarios in regards to the rest of my service and traveling afterward, letting the trip to the States decide which one would actually play out. I knew my time in Uganda was coming to a close but I had no idea how many more days I would be able to enjoy the presence of people I had grown to love there.

I was living as though it was my last week in Uganda before the trial was supposed to take place the week of August 15. I gave away coloring books and a squirt gun, just random things to random people. I took photos and had a bittersweet day. I packed everything I owned since I didn't know if I would come back. Sunday, I traveled 10 hours to Kampala. Monday, I went to the office and filled out paperwork. Theoretically, Tuesday, I would fly out of Uganda and arrive on Wednesday afternoon in D.C. Thursday, I would sleep. Friday, David and I would drive to Norfolk. Saturday and Sunday we would prep with Lt. Riggio. Monday morning, jury members would be chosen and the trial start Monday afternoon. Monday through Friday, I just wait and prepare for testifying. After the last witness, the jury would discuss, and I should be asked to come back to the courtroom to hear the verdict.

If the hypothetical situation went smoothly, after all of that, I planned to leave as soon as possible to get back to Uganda for Peace Camp. I hated that I hadn't been able to make any of the prep meetings and that I wouldn't be there to chaperone my student from the school to where the camp was. The week after Peace Camp was an All-Volunteer Conference. Then, the first week of September, school started and I would say my goodbyes and finish my volunteer service in mid-September.

Much of my life, I'd felt like I was constantly coming and going. Growing up, we moved often and I never felt rooted. I'd sit down, then immediately have to get up. As much as I've had to do it, I've always hated saying goodbye. Leaving Uganda, there was a real chance I wouldn't ever see these friends again. I went to see

Brenda, the teacher I'd worked with on the handbags, and was filled with sadness sitting there on her floor. There was so much more I wanted to learn from her, to develop a deeper friendship with her, but there was no time.

The fruition of the hypothetical situation would have to wait. As expected, the defense asked for a continuance of the trial. At 10 p.m. Friday, August 5, thankfully while still in my village before traveling 10 hours to Kampala, the prosecutor called to say the trial had been moved to September 6-9. Even with the waivers and being able to get the files next week, the defense did not feel they would have the time to prepare their case. Also, they weren't happy with how the emails were playing out.

On one hand, I really wanted to get this over with. On the other, I would have a little more time to spend with people in my community, attend the full week of Peace Camp and attend the first part of our All-Volunteer Conference. I'd miss my training class's close-of-service party, but that wouldn't be the end of the world.

Both Gwen and Bridgette had terminated their service early. Crystal was the only one left in Uganda who I would have the chance to run into. Crystal's last day was supposed to be October 3. I only hoped that she would leave Uganda before the All-Volunteer Conference.

As the days in Uganda dwindled down, I had a recurring dream. I was with a group of people at a restaurant and one person hadn't shown up yet. I decided to go outside and wait so I could show them where we were seated. I bent down to tie my shoe and the security guy walked over to where I was. He smashed my head and I went down with a thump and blacked out.

I woke up with staggered, short, shallow breaths.

Repeat.

Only one more month to go.

I Have a Secret
Written on Saturday, August 6, 2011
Pader, Northern Uganda
39 weeks

I have been a statistic since I was 5 years old.

His name was Andrew and I liked going over to his house down the street. My mother wouldn't let me play Teenage Mutant Ninja Turtles on Nintendo because it was too "violent," but Andrew's mom would let us play and would even make us tasty chocolate chip cookies.

I was supposed to go with the family across the street to a Vacation Bible School but somehow lost track of time. For being 5, that was not a surprise. I remembered being sad I was not able to go but then got over missing the ride once I got Leonardo to the surfing level.

There was a rule at Andrew's house that the door always had to be open. He left to go talk to his brother Kevin and when he came back, he closed the door. I noticed it was closed because his mother had the rule but did not think anything of it. I just kept playing, trying to dodge sewer rats.

I needed to get home before it got too late. It was still light out but the Alaskan sun lingers in the sky long after "bedtime." I rose to leave and Andrew quickly moved to stand between me and the door.

"I need to go home. Does your mom have any of the tasty chocolate cookies left?"

"Before you can have any, you have to do what I say," he said.

"OK," I said, unsure and not thinking that he would ask me anything difficult but rather to put away the toys or something.

"Let me see," he said as he pointed to my vagina.

"No." If there was one thing my mother had taught me, it was that bathing suit areas are private and aren't shown to others.

"If you don't, you can't come over again. You won't be able to come over again to play videogames or have snacks."

I don't remember exactly what happened right after that. I remember feeling overwhelmed and doing what he said.

"Don't tell anyone. You'll get in trouble if you do."

I quietly left the house, not making eye contact with anyone. I felt horrible as I walked home.

Afterward, I tried avoiding Andrew on the street. Kevin, his older brother who was probably 12 years old, would ride his bike over to my house and tease me, asking what happened with Andrew. I would run inside and hide in my bed.

I would draw bodies with crayons and scribble on them. If there was a paper that said "Sex:_____" I'd say "No" instead of "Female." In my mind, I knew sex was not allowed yet and truthfully did not even know what the word meant. I clearly remembered sitting on the toilet looking down and waiting for a tiny baby to slip into the water once I was finished peeing.

A simple "Show me yours and I'll show you mine" and I felt guilty and shameful.

I was also 5 when my biological parents got divorced. I didn't remember my biological father being home much anyhow so it was not a big change in my life. My oldest sister would babysit us while my mom worked a couple of jobs to support the family. My oldest sister moved away for college a couple of years later. When I was 8, the rest of us moved to a town three hours away for a fresh start.

I had to have been 11 when she came back for a visit. We went to Dairy Queen because she wanted to have a serious talk over Blizzards. She asked about what happened between Andrew and me. Squirming in my seat, I told her what I remembered of that day.

Somehow, she knew something within me had changed after that day of innocently wanting to play Nintendo. I wouldn't realize until later how much that small incident had changed how I viewed myself and others.

I was an average kid, overachiever with my grades, involved with all sorts of activities and, from the outside, I was like everyone else. In high school, I learned that some of my friends had been abused by fathers, uncles, boyfriends, random guys, and noticed how some of them had similar behaviors.

For some, they started turning toward males for the "love" and affection that they craved. They thought they needed to sexually please someone to be cared for and to be found appealing. Some thought that being aggressively in control of their sexuality at a young age meant that no one else would be able to take advantage of them. People who did not know their stories saw them as sexually promiscuous; I saw them as friends who needed control over a variable in their life that others had exploited.

For others like me, we turned inward instead. Rather than become overtly sexual, we hid in silent fear of betrayal and never uttered a word of what happened. We prayed and hoped that no one else would take advantage of us and avoided relationships because we didn't know if we could trust someone not to break our trust.

I never put my lack of romantic relationships in this framework. I had plenty of other reasons for not engaging in relationships: massive amounts of change, instability, and very strict dating rules all seemed to lead to me being single.

My mom got remarried to my dad, technically my stepdad but more of a father than my biological dad ever was, when I was in fourth grade. Before moving to Indiana, we had the Biological sign adoption papers on a Wednesday, went to court on Friday, and left Alaska without telling many people on Saturday.

With a new last name and eight different schools on my transcript, forgetting the past was easy. What happened with Andrew was thousands of miles and several states away. With each new school, I was able to start fresh and learn more about life.

I had wanted to live in Africa since the sixth grade when I learned about a missionary named Mary Slessor. She moved from her quaint Scottish town to a Nigerian village to live "amongst the people." While there, she learned that any time twins were born, one would be deemed to have a good spirit and the other child an evil spirit. Because you could not tell which was which, the parents would put the twins in the jungle to be eaten by lions or other predators. She would go in the middle of the night, risk her life and save the children. She'd bring them back home with her and raise the rejected and abandoned kids as her own.

I wanted to be like this woman. I wanted to help give life to those who were destined to die. I wanted to work with children so I became the youngest volunteer with an organization doing after-school and weekend programs in villages across Alaska. When we moved to Indiana, I helped with children's church until eventually I led it. I decided to study elementary education in college so I could have a tangible skill to take to Africa.

The more I learned about orphaned children, the more I learned about the factors that placed them in vulnerable situations. High HIV rates left children parentless or with parents who could not care for their kids, creating a growing number of child-headed households. Sometimes the older female children— middle-school age—would leave their families behind to "work" the streets. Because of all the ports in southern Africa, there were a lot of men coming and going who would look for "a good time."

During an American Education class in college, I decided I did not want to teach writing and math, and changed my major to social and behavioral studies. I wanted to understand the societal influencers in which we make decisions and live our lives. I took all the classes that were available about anything family related. I wanted to understand my own family. I wanted to understand how to create a family when you have no biological relations close by.

During these and other gender-related classes, I became intrigued by prostitution, power and control issues and women's empowerment. In fall 2006, while at a young adults church meeting, a young woman spoke about her life in Kolkata, India. She lived and worked with women who were either still sex workers or were now employed with their business making bags out of old saris. She had such passion and talked with such intensity that I wanted to learn more.

India had never been on my radar. I had always been stuck on South Africa. On the organization's website, they stated that before you could work for them, you had to complete a four-month servant team assignment. While having coffee with the speaker, she had said the organization was interested in starting a site in South Africa. Perfect. I'd do a servant team now and then have my prerequisite completed so I could start with them possibly when they opened in South Africa. I applied to this organization and the Peace Corps in the same week, anticipating the Peace Corps application process would last a while.

Everything worked out perfectly. After college graduation, I worked at a camp for the summer, traveled and worked around Alaska for a couple of months, went back in Indiana to complete medical forms and raise support for India, and off I went to Kolkata for four months.

I had a love/hate relationship with India. There was such beauty in the culture and people, yet such perversion and ugliness too. Our group was made up of three females and one male, ranging from age 19 to me at 24. We volunteered at Missionaries of Charity; had book discussions; learned about poverty, injustice and prostitution; visited women in brothels; and hand-stitched bags and quilts next to women who had been liberated from the sex industry.

We read "Bitter Chocolate," a book about child sexual abuse in India. The others thought it was disgusting and questioned why we had to read the examples of child abuse. I was intrigued. I made notes. Never before had I made the connections between what happened when I was 5 and how I was living my life almost 20 years later.

I wasn't lashing out at anyone. I didn't avoid men. But there were subtle signs of child sexual abuse in my own life. I never thought I was worthy of someone who would actually be really good to me. I never dated anyone abusive, but instead chose those who were safe, almost to the point where I thought I could fight them and beat them if I needed to. In conversations, I would sneak in intense things from my past to see if the person could handle what I had gone through, to see if they could truly handle who I was. I held back from having a truly loving relationship in fear of being pressured into something that would hurt me or become attached to someone who would just leave me.

I realized then, sitting on a tiled floor in sweltering 48 degrees Celsius heat in India, how much even a simple small incident can affect someone.

Sexual abuse has deep roots no matter the form. Not until years later after the incident did I learn that Kevin, Andrew's older brother, had done something similar to the neighbor girl across the street from me. How many other little girls did this brother duo "play" with? Where did they learn it?

My mom and I had a very interesting conversation one night when I was waiting for the trial.

It all started when my mom said she could relate with going to trial. I thought she was referring to her divorce. She wasn't.

My mom and her sister, who was a couple of years younger, weren't allowed to date when they were younger. When their mother tried explaining why they could not, my aunt responded by saying, "It's because he wants us all to himself."

My grandmother asked for an explanation. She had no idea what her husband was doing to their little daughters.

This was the start of their legal proceedings and divorce. My mom was bitter toward her mother since she and her sister were the ones who had to testify and not her. My mom felt bad because her father, who was the man who chose to sexually abuse her, was only a couple of years away from receiving a great retirement package from the military and she now felt responsible for taking it away.

"I never knew that my little sister was getting abused and our rooms were across the hall. I let my father continue with me because I was trying to protect my sister. If I was so close and yet was unaware, I can't blame a mother who doesn't know her husband is abusing their child."

That last statement struck me. My mother tried to protect her sister but, at the end of the day, despite her efforts, their father abused both of them. My mother couldn't blame herself for his actions and for not knowing that he was abusing her sister, his daughter. My mother later married my biological father. A husband she couldn't blame herself for not knowing he was abusing their child, her daughter, my sister.

I don't believe anything legal ever happened to my biological father. Maybe my mom thought it was more of a family issue after 20 years of marriage, with dismay and guilt coinciding. Maybe she didn't want to put my sister in the same position of testifying at trial that she had gone through. I can't imagine the look on my mom's face when she first realized that the man she married to get out of an abusive home was now repeating her nightmares in her home.

I never knew any of that as a kid. The Biological used to call me his "Little Princess." He would take us to the Renaissance fair and buy us tiaras made out of flowers. He never seemed like he wanted to hurt me. He was my father—who I later found out had molested his own daughter, my sister.

I have only one vivid memory of him as a child. My mother had the mindset of "spare the rod, spoil the child." I was a rowdy kid and every time I disobeyed and was about to get a spanking, she would say, "This is going to hurt me more than it will hurt you."

I remembered the Biological was supposed to be working but came home early. He walked into their bedroom and started yelling how dare she spank his Little Princess. My mom frantically whispered to go to the other side of the bed to hide.

I sat crouched in the shadow of the bed with my arms over my head as I could hear him yelling at her. I flinched each time I heard videotape after videotape hit the ceiling and then crash to the floor. I didn't look up to see if he was throwing them at her or just throwing things in anger. I don't remember anything else from that day. Other times when I felt threatened, I would get into as small of a ball as I could, hiding underneath what I could find and go blank.

During the divorce, he tried to get custody of me. My mom fought and won.

The day we went over to his house to get the adoption papers signed was the first time I'd seen him in three years. He had married a Filipino woman, the daughter of his boss, only two years older than my oldest sister (who was 10 years older than me). We left Alaska not telling him we were leaving. We didn't contact him again.

In 2008, I'd been curious about the biological father who never once tried to contact us. He had missed all of these important events of my life and I wondered if he even cared. I decided to take a couple of months off work and head back to Alaska. My goal was to explore and live an adventure. Seeing a rare possibility of connecting with the Biological, I sent him an email.

Within an hour, he replied.

I sat staring at the screen, amazed at the small amount of effort it had taken to contact him.

While visiting Anchorage, I stayed with family friends who happened to live two doors down from him. One day, I sent him an email and asked about coming over to see him. He said yes and we planned on a Saturday morning.

In my mind, he was a monster. He had wanted to bring other women to bed with my mother, sexually abused his own daughter, abandoned us and all I could remember about him was his tantrum about his "Little Princess" and throwing videotapes at my mom.

The door opened and there stood a man only a couple of inches taller than me. He looked normal. Almost timid. He gave a tour of the cars he had collected over the years for an hour and a half. He had no idea what to say.

His second wife was nice and made a pasta dish for lunch. She said he didn't tell her about the email until a few days later after he received it. I couldn't get over the fact that he didn't look like the monster that took up residence in my head whenever I pictured him. He looked like an average Joe, working and supporting his new wife and their young son.

He didn't ask much about my life. I sat there and thought that even though I was his flesh and blood, I was nothing like him. After that, I was content with not having him as part of my life.

I am a statistic. This time, I was choosing to be a statistic who was proactive about her life and who was making the hard decision to follow through on prosecuting a rapist. I chose the difficult path to try to protect other women from becoming a rape statistic.

A Mother of Sorts

Days 287-294: Saturday, August 20-Saturday, August 27, 2011
Gulu, Northern Uganda
41-42 weeks

Over the years I have "mothered" many. Heck, my title while working with pregnant teens in the States was house mother. I was the proud "mother" of six Acholi young ladies who attended the school I was partnered with as a volunteer. Never before had I been so proud of my students.

We spent the week at Peace Camp, an initiative to peacefully bring together different tribes affected by the Lord's Resistance Army's 21 years of insurgency. The six of them were attentive, accepting, helpful, active and brilliant. They even learned basic sign language in a day to communicate to the four youth who were hearing impaired.

I knew the week would be difficult for them. This was also a huge opportunity for them to gain knowledge, strength and support from one another. These young women, aged 15 through 17, were the leaders of our Peace Club at the school and leaders at our school in general.

There was much to learn. Each day was focused on a different topic such as peaceful living, positive communication, forgiveness and reconciliation and a peaceful future.

All but one of the students had been chosen to attend Camp GLOW the previous December but were unable to attend since I wasn't in country to chaperone them. Sharon was especially eager to attend Peace Camp and asked me daily what she needed to do and if I had heard back about nomination acceptance. Each time, her eyes were huge and she wouldn't breathe until I answered.

Sharon had a sweet heart and put extra effort toward getting to know the hearing-impaired students and making them feel part of the group. While practicing Acholi traditional dancing the first day, her head bobbed with enthusiasm.

While in a logistical meeting on Sunday night, I saw that same head walking across the dark compound and knew something was wrong. All day, Sharon had been happy meeting new people and enjoying the opening ceremony. After dinner, the youth watched the 2005 film "War Dance," a true story that took place about an hour from where we lived.

The film follows the stories of three students affected by the war in different ways. Hearing their stories at the beginning of the film is difficult, since the atrocities that they either had to partake of or saw are horrific.

While seated with the logistical staff on the other side of the compound, I heard deep crying coming from the film. In it, the female student's father had been killed by LRA rebels and this was the first time she had visited the ground where his body was buried. She goes with her mother, who tells her to be quiet otherwise the rebels might hear her crying. She lies on the grave, her father's body underneath, filled with deep sorrow.

As soon as I saw Sharon across the compound, I left the meeting and walked over to find her.

"Ah, Cindy, the film is not good. It is not good," she said shaking her head and looking at the floor.

We talked outside the large room where everyone else was seated. The scene of the young woman mourning her father's murder struck a chord with Sharon. I didn't ask questions. I held her hand and told her the film got better, that there is hope for the female student. I asked if it would be OK if I sat with her until the end. We walked back into the room, hand in hand, and sat on the reed mat.

For the next hour, we sat there, even though our legs fell asleep. I held her hand and grounded her, reminding her I was there for her.

I'll never forget the day I almost had a panic attack in the market from seeing a light-skinned African who reminded me of Dominik. Or the day a friend and I were being silly and rough housing, and he jokingly put his hands around my neck, no pressure or anything, and my whole body went hot and uneasy. Or how whenever the showerhead is large and points directly down, I feel the discomfort of not being able to breathe from Dominik's arm around my throat, gasping for air and my mouth filling with water. Any time I think back to the night of November 5, the morning of November 6, I feel uneasy.

Sharon carried on. She stayed in the moment, held my hand and her countenance lightened.

By the end of the film, Sharon was smiling again. I later asked her what she thought of it.

"Watching the film was not easy but I am glad to have watched the ending where everyone was happy."

Monday was a full day for all the campers. Rafiki Theater, a drama group from Kampala, performed and facilitated conversations with the campers. The main topics were domestic violence and bullying.

Uganda is a very male-dominated society, where a wife is expected to produce children and tend to her husband's every need without a will of her own. In the drama, there were two married couples and at one point, one husband came home drunk, unhappy with his wife's desire to continue her studies. Although there was no physical contact, their tone, facial expressions and then the despair in the woman's face as her husband beat her and then portrayed marital rape was overwhelming.

This was rather mature material for an audience of 15- to 19-year-olds. Then again, early marriages of 15-year-old females, especially in the smaller villages, were common. They did not have the option to get an education. They did not have the option to choose who they married. They were told what to do and how to do it and were married off so their families would gain wealth or materials through the bride price.

One of the youth asked why women did not stand up to their husbands.

"I believe it is because we have low self-esteem," replied Sharon. My Sharon.

During the previous school year, we had spent time focused on personal awareness and self-esteem. We had talked about knowing and understanding who we are, our potential, our feelings and emotions, where we were in life and our strengths and weaknesses.

For Sharon to say that women did not speak out because of low self-esteem may seem very simple to a Westerner, but to those who have had their whole lives destroyed and controlled by others, it was a huge statement. These were youth who had been abused and violated, who had been told they were worthless killers, who were rejected by their families and society.

At my school, I worked with students who had lived through traumatic experiences, shattering their self-esteem. In class, we talked about what influences our self-esteem and how who we are surrounded by is a large factor. If a mother tells her daughter daily, "Anyaka marach, amaro pe, maleng pe" ("Girl, you are bad, I do not love you, you are not beautiful") and then hits her daughter, she will most likely have poor self-esteem.

If a mother tells her daughter daily, "Anyaka maber, amaro anyaka, tye maleng" ("Girl, you are good, I love you girl, you are beautiful") with a hug and warm smile, she will most likely grow up with good self-esteem.

Knowing that my students didn't have much emotional support, I "adopted" these young women and tried to be the best mother figure I could be.

When I said, "Anyaka maber, amaro anyaka, tye maleng" in class, the students started hooting and hollering because they thought it was funny that the white lady was learning their language. Students still greeted me with "Anyaka maleng, amaro anyaka." I smiled every time, knowing that, even though they were laughing, they recognized its significance.

At school, I never really knew what the students understood or remembered from class. During camp, I realized that the lessons had gotten through. When Sharon answered the question about self-esteem, I knew I had played a part in her understanding of the concept. Hopefully, I had played a part in improving her self-esteem as well.

At the end of the day, I smiled a very proud "mother" smile.

• • •

On the trial side of my life, at 7 p.m. on Tuesday, when all the youth went off into their tribal groups to practice traditional dancing, I went to the lightpost on top of a hill. This was one of the only locations on the campus I could get phone service.

The prosecutor had emailed earlier in the day requesting to discuss a few things. There was a "wrinkle" that needed to be worked out.

I called him first to see if I was standing in the right location next to the lightpost. He called back with another lieutenant in the room when they were ready.

Out of all the files that I had previously signed a waiver agreeing to give access to, they picked out a physical medical form that had to do with the rape, the résumé I had sent the Peace Corps in 2009 when I applied, a signed paper that I assumed was a rules or regulations agreement and a safety and security notice that went to Peace Corps directly after the incident was reported.

Apparently, this report said we (the other three women and I) met him, I went back to his hotel, was raped, got away and took a taxi at 3 a.m. back to where the other volunteers were. In so many ways, this report was wrong. I had not talked directly to whoever wrote and sent it to Peace Corps headquarters in D.C. I was disappointed in the report's lack of accuracy and confused as to where it originated.

I stood there, clutching my phone, answering questions and clarifying the details of my own assault as young students, who each had their own personal traumas, walked by. I tried to keep my voice down or told them to quiet down if they got too close in their language, Acholi, but it was not lost on me how very surreal the situation was. I switched back to English to discuss my rape any time the coast was clear.

The judge was still not happy with Google for not complying with the subpoena to access my Gmail account and so the military was trying to use a search warrant to gain access. The judge could choose to forget about the emails or push further with them, which could delay the trial (again). This time, the delay would be because of the judge's decision and not the defense, which was apparently allowed.

As for the actual trial, I would do some trial prep two hours on Saturday and Sunday. Jurors would be selected in the morning and I would be the first to testify in the afternoon. The whole trial wouldn't last longer than five days and we'd be done by Friday morning.

. . .

Thursday's topic at the camp was forgiveness and reconciliation—not an easy topic when you are dealing with a group of traumatized young students. They also learned ways to manage their anger over what happened. I didn't know the majority of their experiences, but I had gotten a glimpse a month prior.

Over the course of the week, I had kept an extra eye out for Pamela. She was the student at my school who had given me the letter about her rape and wanting to escape. Pamela had a special place in my heart, partially because of my own personal experience.

The closing ritual that night was intense. Each student was given a strip of paper to write down a message of anything they wanted: a fear, a blessing, a prayer, a statement, anything. Afterward, each paper would be placed in the fire as a symbolic way to release the anger and pain and to forgive. They were told that the universe and God accepts their message to try and lift the burden off their shoulders. Then, each individual was given a purple string representing peace. As a group, they said aloud, "I am a peacemaker."

As the night went on, youth started opening up in their groups about their past tragedies.

I had left the main room partway through the session to work on a few things and to give the student I was sitting next to privacy. Everyone was dispersing as I came back to the large room.

I searched around to find the female staff member who was staying with the youth in the dorm.

"How is Pamela?" I asked.

"Eh, she is OK."

"No, how is she really doing?" I pressed.

"OK, to be honest, not so well. She was somehow struggling through."

I went up to the girls' dorm and she wasn't there. I came back down and had just entered the compound when I saw her coming my way with a few others.

"Pamela."

She slowly walked away from the others. I opened my arms and her down-trodden face fit right into my shoulder. We stood there for at least five minutes while she gasped in small breaths.

"I am sorry, Pamela. I am so sorry."

I whispered to her that the real reason I had been leaving so often was because I had been raped as well.

"We did not deserve this pain. We did not deserve what they did to us. This is not easy, but we will get through."

We stood there in our grief and sadness. Only a few other words were spoken.

Margaret, an older Acholi lady helping with the camp, came over and saw

Pamela and me. She took Pamela in her arms and started speaking in the local language. An older, wiser woman who knew the culture, knew the situation of the north from firsthand experience, was speaking truth into Pamela's young mind in a way that I never could. I could see the love and support pouring out and wrapping itself around Pamela in only a way someone from the same culture could do.

I had no idea what she said, but Pamela would nod and Margaret kept speaking. Once they were finished, I asked if Pamela would feel safer down in the compound with me and a few others in one of the extra rooms or if she would rather go back to the girl's dorm. I did not want her to have a night terror without one of the staff close by.

Pamela chose to stay with me and I grabbed the mattress off my staff bed and put it in the extra room next door. I also brought my sleeping bag and inflatable pillow. There were a few other mattresses in the room already.

A group of staff gathered outside the room and were discussing the intensity of the night. After I checked on the other campers, and on Pamela again, I joined the staff of about six and their discussion.

"Sandi, I do not know how you do it," said the leader of the nightly ritual, still with a few tears in her eyes. "Hearing these stories. This is what you do."

I wasn't really sure how I did it either.

"For me, this is my reality. For the last two years, I've been living in this environment. I work at a school where every single student has a story. I don't ask them their stories, but rather accept them and go forward."

I looked back toward the room where Pamela lay.

"I only know about a few of my students' experiences. One was sexually assaulted by a man who said he was her uncle. You probably don't know this, but I am dealing with my own sexual assault case right now. Actually, I was supposed to leave a couple of weeks ago and the trial should have been over last Friday. Tonight's topic is not an easy one. With something traumatic, a part of you is gone and will never be the same. Everything irritates you, upsets you, people make stupid comments and you are forever reminded by the smallest things of what happened. You have to grieve the person you were and somehow go forth and live a normal life. For one of my students, I know today was hard and the task of forgiveness is not something that happens overnight but is rather a process, like so much of the healing process."

After more discussion, we eventually all went to bed. Pamela had the pillow awkwardly underneath her head and was very sleepy at this point. I crawled under the other half of the sleeping bag with much on my mind.

It hurt. It hurt to know the pain of others and to also have my own pain. I could only hope that through my pain that I would be more empathetic toward others and give them the care and acceptance I either received—or wished I had.

Another night of silent tears. This time, for someone else.

• • •

Friday was the final full day of Peace Camp. After Pamela got up to prepare for the day in the dorms, I checked in with my other students before breakfast. Something was not quite right with Monica. She was one tough cookie, yet this morning she looked downtrodden. Since all the students were right there, I asked if I could speak to her after morning assembly.

We walked into the middle of the compound, away from everyone else, and sat on the cement ledges. Something was truly bothering her.

The day before, forgiveness and reconciliation was the main topic. Monica could not quite forgive her father for abandoning her family. He would have nothing to do with Monica or her mother. He would pay school fees for his other children, visit them, be a dad for them, but not her. She could not understand why he didn't love her and why he had chosen to abandon her, why he decided to put his effort into a family other than Monica's.

We talked about the difficulty of knowing an individual should love and care for us yet they choose not to. We talked about the pain of rejection and how that affects our perceived self-worth. How we may never have a conversation with them for an affirmative interpersonal resolution and how sometimes we must release it simply for ourselves. That was the case for Monica. No interpersonal resolution seemed to be on the horizon.

On Saturday morning, as we prepared to leave camp, the students made their action plans for the next term. They wanted to teach other about peaceful living, how to forgive and about controlling their emotions. Excitement grew as they brainstormed ideas they could bring back the information to their fellow students and share their knowledge.

I listened, observing their interactions. Originally, because of the trial, I would have missed the beginning of the week. Although I would have been happy to have that part of my life over with, I was thankful I was able to experience this week with my students.

A Sad Ugandan Ending
Day 315: Saturday, September 17, 2011
Pader, Northern Uganda
45 weeks

Although the last year had been rather tough, Uganda and the people I met in it would always be a part of me. Saying goodbye when I knew that in all likelihood I would never see them again was heartbreaking.

My Ugandan friends told me to never forget them and I told them they would forever be in my heart. The female teachers told me that I should have married someone in the village and stayed forever. I told them they had had two whole years to find me a good one but they were all married and I was no side dish. I said I would try my luck with men in America and if God willed it I'd bring that husband and kid back with me next time.

I'd spent the last year going back and forth to America, not really confident when or if I would return to Uganda. I did return though. This time around, leaving would be absolute.

This final time, I slowly took down the pictures, sold my furniture and ate what was left of my food. My last week in my village was full of finishing projects at the school, doing paperwork for the end of Peace Corps service, taking photos around town with friends and having some meaningful last conversations.

The last morning, one of the students from my first community-based organization came over to help with the final cleaning of my place. I went to lunch with an American short-term volunteer who had been in Pader when I arrived back in 2009 and had just returned the night before.

I took her out to the school to meet the Peace Camp ladies so they could work on recording some of the songs they had written. A few of the students came back to my house to pick up a few items I was donating to the teachers at the school.

Along the way, the students held my hands and kept saying how I would have to return to teach and help with the Peace Club. They knew this was my last full day in town but it had not sunk in fully.

As we were leaving the compound, Janet, the landlord's wife, screamed at me, "Hey! We need to talk about the rent!"

The last few weeks, we could not seem to be in the same place at the same time so I could pay her. She was in the deep village tilling her garden; I was at a Peace Corps conference.

Earlier in the week, I had received a text saying she was hurting for money and asked for rent money. Then on my last morning, she came around when I was trying to say goodbye to my students and on my way back to the school compound.

"I will be back later, I have to get back to the school for now," I explained but she started getting angry and followed us out of the housing compound.

"I have to get the students back to the school but I'll be back later," I said again.

"Fine, leave! I'll call the police!" She yelled as she stormed back to the compound.

I tried to shake her reaction off and enjoy the last few hours with my students. The time was filled with funny stories and then moments of silent contemplation. I found Brenda, the tailoring teacher, finishing a couple of dresses for me.

After leaving the school, I went to dinner in town with the fellow staff and teachers. There were heartfelt speeches, silly group photos and goodbyes. A rainstorm had knocked out the power, so we finished by candlelight. I was going to miss these friends who had welcomed me into their homes and accepted me as one of them.

Brenda came with me to say one final goodbye to the students at the school.

While walking down the rows of bunk beds, I said farewell and gave many, many hugs.

Toward the entrance of the large room, I found Josephine who had gone to Peace Camp.

"This is goodbye, my friend," I said, holding her hand.

"Ah, this is not good!" she wailed and she took her hand out of mine.

A group of students I had been closer with followed outside. Monica suggested they say a traveling prayer before my journey home. With sincere faces, they prayed for traveling safety, that I wouldn't forget them and that I would return.

"Ah, and I want to thank you for Sandi who has shown us the love and acceptance that no one else has ever shown us before. I thank you for Sandi who has loved us as Jesus truly would in the flesh. We thank her for teaching us good skills and for her time here."

She kept going but at that point I couldn't see or hear anything through my tears and the rushing blood in my ears. I truly hoped that I was able to convey love and acceptance to these young women. My Peace Corps journey was full of challenges out of my control that left me feeling like I had failed in different ways, but I did not fail.

Because there were so many international donors that came to the school for field visits, my arrival the first day was nothing special. I walked onto the compound and no one seemed to notice or stop what he or she was doing. But for my departure, it was different. I may have entered the first day on my own, but that day I left, I was surrounded by my students with whom I had built real relationships.

As we took a few last photos by the school entrance gate, I had them get into a group. They waved goodbye in one. They "pretended" to be sad about my leaving in another. While looking at the photos later, Pamela's face had the same sad expression in all.

I didn't want to leave. I wanted to finagle a way to I could come back and spend more time with them, to see them become dignified young women taking care of their families. But, it was my time to leave.

Brenda and I walked together until we reached the main road. I would miss her the most. The street was quiet. Everyone went to bed early because of the rain and because the power was out.

When I reached the front main gate of my compound, someone had locked the middle section of the gate I had to get through. I could not open it from the outside and tried getting someone from inside to come out and open it. I could see the candlelight from the closest room as I loudly banged and kicked the metal door but no one answered.

By then it was only 9 p.m. Usually, people were up until 10 or 11 on a Saturday. I walked around to the other street entrance, populated with bars and loitering drunks, then to the inner compound to find a board nailed across my screen door. What on earth did Janet think she was doing? Was she seriously going to board up my place on my final night? I had a few last things I wanted to organize and then had to get up at 6 a.m. to get on a bus. I tried to calm myself.

Janet finally walked over and screamed at me, "Pay me! Pay me 240,000 UGX, or I don't unblock your door! You owe me money!" I told her that of course I would pay her, but that I only owed her one month, 100,000 UGX. But she insisted, "There is a balance of 20,000 each for May, June and July. All of August for 120,000. Half of September for 60,000."

In mid-January 2010, my first organization signed a lease with the landlord for my unit, costing 100,000 UGX a month, which was less than $40. Technically, my name was on nothing. Since the organization didn't give us a monthly salary, they "invested" in the volunteer's housing. In my case, the organization signed the lease, but I received a housing stipend to pay the rent. If my host organization had been paying for rent, I wouldn't be dealing with Janet at 9 p.m. on my final night.

When I first arrived, I had dealt with her husband, but he had been arrested for tax evasion. At times, the compound would be locked because the landlord refused to pay taxes. His wife took over the compound some time later.

I had never signed a contract increasing rent by 20,000, and I had paid through mid-August. I told her then that my rent was still only 100,000 and she blew me off. And, this being a rural village, I had no proof of receipt that I'd paid her. She said once again she wouldn't let me in until I paid her 240,000; I showed her the 100,000 and said that was all I was going to pay her. She stood at the door angrily and I decided to stubbornly sit on the ground.

Agitated, she eventually went back to her hut at the back of the compound. I lay on the cement veranda, shivering in my new dress that Brenda had made, trying to keep out the chill with my wraparound skirt and a large piece of fabric I'd received as a going-away gift.

I may have been able to hold back tears while hugging my students, but now, lying on the cement as it began to lightly rain, I began to silently weep.

I tried sleeping but could not. I texted my site mate Katherine around 11:30 p.m. for help.

Katherine called, concerned, and reminded me how part of the screen door was out of the frame. If I pulled back the screen a little more, I'd be able to unlock the door and duck in. It worked.

At 6:45 the next morning, I left the room with a large backpack with all my clothes and living needs, a box of electronics and books to return to the Peace Corps office and my purse with my laptop and more electronics. I left the 100,000 UGX in the boarded door so Janet could get it when she woke up.

I could see why I couldn't get in the main gate the night before. Janet had locked the front gate so I went around to the back of the compound to leave. As I passed her hut, Janet came out of the door and started asking for her money again.

I told her I'd left the money in the door.

Instead of picking up the money, she quickly walked beside me and then grabbed my arm with a death grip to prevent me from leaving. With my backpack on my back, a heavy box in my right arm and my purse with the laptop on my left arm, I was having difficulty walking. It became nearly impossible when Janet started tugging on me with all her strength.

"Let me go, please!" I pleaded.

"Not until you pay!" she yelled.

She called the local chairman, the traditional leader for that part of the village, still holding on to me. I tried pulling my arm away but she tightened her grip. I started yelling at her to let go of me.

I didn't want her—or anyone—touching me. She wouldn't let go.

I backed up as far as I could, and my large backpack hit the compound door with a thud. I tried pushing her away, but she wouldn't budge. My arms were still full of my belongings and bags making it difficult to get away. She grabbed my purse while I tried balancing the box and gave it to her 8-year-old son, who then ran away with it. She had just stolen my laptop.

As I juggled the box under my arm, she started to attack me. She punched my head and my glasses flew off. Then she grabbed my right forearm with her hands, lowered her mouth to my skin and bit down.

She bit me.

What the hell was she doing?

She looked up at me with crazy eyes as I looked down to see the indentations of her front upper teeth in my skin.

She kept biting and punching me all over. I kept yelling at her to stop and trying to back away, but I was as far back as I could go, still laden down with my backpack.

I started screaming in hopes that others would hear and she would stop. People started coming into the compound as she kept assaulting me, but they just watched. She punched me everywhere, bombarding the sides of my head and chest with her fists.

I kept walking along the gate, trying to break her grip, but she wouldn't let go of my bitten arm.

I could feel her hot breath on my neck as she tried to bite down.

She missed but continued to beat my head with her fist. I stumbled with my large backpack still on into the side of a covered structure that had a short wall. She had me cornered and I could not get away. I leaned against it, tired and unable to leave.

At that point, a crowd of people had gathered on the other side of the puddle to watch Janet punch my head.

I yelled for help, but they ignored my pleas. I tried to focus on one person to ask for help, but that didn't work either.

She pounded on me again as a couple of women said something in the local language, waving their hands but doing nothing physically to stop her from assaulting me.

Finally, the local chairman and a few other men appeared and my landlady stopped beating me. Finally, someone she respected and needed to impress. I unsteadily walked over to the inside of the pavilion.

I tried to explain that I was a U.S. government volunteer and that the embassy would be called, but they didn't believe me or care.

"Oh, sure you do! We'll call the president of Uganda on you!"

"Eh! You dodged my phone calls!" said Janet. "I would stand outside your room and hear you turn off the phone. Do you think I am stupid?"

"You wanna know why I silenced the phone? You call at 7 a.m.! You wanna know the real reason I do not answer at 7 a.m.? Because I was raped in your country and now I do not sleep until after 2 a.m.! Are you happy now?"

Janet was silent. That may have quieted her down for a minute. With the last of my energy, I made my way over to the ledge to sit and propped my giant hiking backpack next to me against the pole.

Someone found my glasses and returned them to me.

I looked down at my arms and could see white and red teeth impressions on my skin. I was not sure about the order in which they happened—one clear circle on my right forearm, one just a little further around the right arm, one on my upper left arm.

The skin was slightly broken from the swelling that had started to stretch the skin. Spots of blood were on my shirt where I must have raised my arm to try to get away. The bite wounds started to throb. The pain was settling in as my breathing returned to normal and the adrenalin made its way out of my system.

My box was placed on the corner ledge of the pavilion. As I started to move it, Janet and a couple of men got closer to look inside.

I yelled for them to get away.

A group of six men surrounded me as I sat on the ledge staring at my wounds. They listened to her share her story in Acholi. They believed her and didn't care what I had to say.

"You give her her money!" they yelled at me.

They demanded I pay her over and over again. I tried explaining but it was useless. They did not listen or understand.

I called Fred, the Peace Corps safety and security manager, so that he could try to talk sense into them. Even though Fred explained that he would come up to investigate the situation, they didn't believe him. They wanted the money right then and there. He talked to a couple of people and then talked to me a final time. He told them to let me leave the compound.

They still wouldn't let me leave.

When I tried re-explaining and that they were to let me leave, they refused and gathered closer. I called my site mate who was waiting for me at the bus station.

"Katherine, will you come to the back of my compound?"

"Sandi, are you OK?"

"Umm... Not really. Please come."

A few minutes later she walked through the red door that Janet would not let me leave through. Katherine looked at my swollen arms, bewildered by the distorted flesh.

"Who did this to you?!" she asked me. I pointed toward Janet. Katherine's mouth gaped open. "You do not treat people like this! Why did you bite her? Assaulting another person is not acceptable!"

Katherine and I both tried talking to the people but they wouldn't listen. When Katherine said we would now be leaving, Janet aggressively grabbed Katherine's arm. Janet ran away and got a lock to put on the door so we could not leave. Suddenly, we were hostages.

We called Fred again, and he wasn't happy. He said he'd call the regional security officer at the U.S. embassy and the local police chief, and get back to us.

The local chairman decided to leave the compound and Janet unlocked the door for him. Katherine walked over and stood in the door way explaining how they needed to leave the door unlocked but the local chairman pushed Katherine further into the compound.

When a plainclothes policeman finally arrived, he didn't help the matter at all. We called Fred again, who called a higher-up policeman to check the situation. The new Peace Corps/Uganda country director called and talked to me, Katherine and the landlady.

Almost three hours after Janet bit me, I received another call from the country director. Even though I was standing firm on not being cheated, I was instructed to pay the 130,000 UGX for health and safety concerns. After I paid her and as we left the compound, a policeman in uniform finally showed up in a vehicle.

At this point I just wanted to leave. I was tired and wanted to get away from Pader and the insanity there.

The policeman wanted us to make statements but he didn't have any paper. He wanted us to go back into the compound, but we refused. We walked down the street to the bus station so I could write my statement.

I had to hold out my throbbing arms because they hurt any time they touched my body. People stared.

Eventually, we went to the police station to complete our statements. The big police boss came in and apologized for the delay. He looked at my arms and asked what had happened. Finally, someone listened and confirmed that it made sense that I shouldn't pay the extra money.

He was rather upset with the policeman who had initially arrived and told the uniformed officer to go get statements from witnesses. When they tried looking for Janet, she had fled the area. Eventually, they were able to find her and bring her in.

It was surreal to make a statement in Uganda for a second time for a totally different incident. The policeman who took the statement was much less dramatic and very to the point. His wording was very Ugandan and made me chuckle, even though the incident was not funny at all. We took photos of each page of the statements and my bite marks.

In the car as we left Pader, I sat staring out at the huts and buildings that I had called home for the last two years. I loved this place. I hated it too.

As I looked out the window into the fields, my forehead pressed against the glass, occasionally a small tear would fall down my cheek. Katherine would notice and rub my shoulder.

I didn't know how I could have deserved such an awful year. I thought about my students and how much we loved each other. Then I thought about the people who clearly did not share the same beliefs, and willingly chose to abuse another person.

My time in Uganda was coming to a close.

Taking a Bite(r) Out of Crime
Day 317: Monday, September 19, 2011
Kampala, Uganda
45 weeks

This is going to be a week.

I had completed my 27 months of Peace Corps Volunteer service and then I got to begin the close-of-service process with medical examinations and paperwork. Bloodwork, stool samples, teeth cleaning, closing bank accounts, exit interviews, health insurance information meetings—all the joys of making sure we were ready to leave Uganda and enter America (somewhat) healthy.

Right after getting to the hotel in Kampala, I stopped to buy a long-sleeved hoodie. I didn't want anyone in the office to get grossed out by my bruised, swollen arms or ask too many questions. I wanted to have a joyful last few days, not filled with glares and probing questions.

One of the nurses asked how I was and if she could see the bite marks. Slowly and carefully, I slid the sleeves up over the marks. My right arm was so swollen that the fabric was tight.

She took one look at my arms and said she didn't realize the bites were that bad.

My right forearm was swollen with what now seemed like a golf ball-sized lump under the skin from the first bite. Bite marks and bruises nearly covered my arms. The largest bruise was about eight inches long by four inches wide and the others were just a tad bit smaller. I also could not feel the skin when she touched them.

Nerve damage, giant bite marks and bruises, sore spots along my shoulders and skull. Three fist-sized bruises on my right upper arm and shoulder, one on the left. One bruise behind my left ear. Bruises on my upper right chest.

All the other volunteers got to be happy and stick around the office, filling out paperwork and hanging out. Me? I got to go to the forensic doctor. Again. This started to feel like a less-serious repeat of November. Other volunteers took care of normal business, and I got to combine a different business on top of it.

And, the Peace Corps staff and I had to think about the legal implications. We had the option to press charges or to let it go. Not pressing charges meant I would get to leave and go to Kenya on vacation as planned. But if we didn't press charges, did that mean I was saying what happened to me was OK? That she could do it again?

The embassy did not know if pressing charges was a good idea or not. The regional security officer did not pick up his duty phone while the incident was being handled in the village but Peace Corps staff were finally able to get a hold of him the next day.

Day 318: Tuesday, September 20, 2011

As soon as I arrived in the Peace Corps compound, I was needed in the main office area. The safety and security officer and I decided to speak with a Ugandan lawyer who had worked with the Peace Corps before.

The lawyer told us the difference between a criminal and civil court: Criminal is the government pressing charges and results in less financial compensation but more jail time, whereas civil court is one independent party pressing charges against another independent party resulting in more financial compensation but less prison time.

He explained some timing factors with a typical case, such as delaying as much as possible. The Peace Corps safety and security manager, Fred, asked about the reasoning behind that.

"That way, the events aren't as fresh, resulting in forgotten details, disparities between the original statements and the ones presented in court," I explained. I knew this was what the defense was trying to do in Dominik's case.

"Sounds like you are familiar with the law," the lawyer said quizzically.

At the end of the meeting, we decided to go forward with pressing charges and that my presence in court was pertinent. The problem was that I was supposed to leave the country in a few days. I offhandedly mentioned that they could keep me as a Peace Corps volunteer until this was taken care of but we didn't discuss it in any detail.

We arrived back at the Peace Corps office later and I still had a lot to do with medical and with exit interviews. For the second day in a row, I didn't eat lunch.

Later that day, I went with some volunteers to dinner at a rooftop restaurant. We had just reached the top when we heard a commotion down below on the sidewalk. Looking over the edge, we saw what looked like one man being beaten by a group of men. They were shouting, pointing to a bag and then kicking his ribs, punching his skull, each taking a turn. Each punch seemed louder than the one before. A large crowd had formed.

Anxiety filled my chest as I heard each punch land and the men hitting him over and over again.

I shouted for them to stop, feeling it was the only thing I could really do as an outsider.

Mob justice. Maybe he had taken a bag, maybe he crossed someone and they weren't happy. But the needless beating? I didn't understand. This wasn't something the police would deal with so people took "justice" into their own hands. Thankfully, within a few minutes he was able to escape and ran away. What happened after that I do not know.

On Wednesday, I completed all the paperwork and medical tests to finish my service to become a returned Peace Corps volunteer, and join the alum. My Peace Corps ID card was whole punched around 5 p.m.; my Peace Corps volunteer service was finished.

Around 7 p.m., I received a call from a familiar D.C. safety and security friend, to discuss the option of extending my service until the incident with my ex-landlady was resolved legally.

My freedom was short-lived: I was back to being a Peace Corps volunteer.

Day 325: Tuesday, September 27, 2011
Pader, Northern Uganda
46 weeks

We were headed to the trial for the physical assault in Uganda. Trial for the rapes in the States was scheduled for November.

Fred from safety and security, a female Peace Corps programming staff, the driver and I arrived a little after 9 a.m. The prosecutor asked us to come into his office, where a policeman and Landlady Janet sat. One person sat between us.

"How about you tell us what happened," the prosecutor said.

"What do you mean?"

"Tell us what the problem is and what happened that day."

"I do not understand. I wrote a statement, which you should have reviewed. Janet is sitting in the room. Wouldn't me sharing in her presence tamper with statement evidence? I am confused on what is going on."

"What do you want to happen?"

"I want the correct legal procedures and for this to end fair and justly."

"Sounds like you want to go to court," he said, as if I was a bad person for my response.

"I did not say that. I want this to be taken care of fairly and with legal justice."

"So tell me what happened that day."

"I am sorry, but I do not feel comfortable in doing so with Janet here."

He seemed upset that I was not complying with his tactics. I was not going to let him push me around, but I didn't understand what was happening. We were told to leave and wait for the trial.

• • •

We sat in the courtroom waiting for the judge. The prosecutor skimmed the six-page statement, reading partial sentences aloud and not including the fact that I had actually paid the money she demanded.

When asked about the charges, Janet pleaded guilty. A few of the highlights included her responding that the judge should take into consideration that she was the sole provider for her kids and family.

"Where is your husband?"

"He is not around."

"Where is he?"

"He is out of town."

"You are unwilling to share where your husband is?"

"He is in prison. If I am sent to jail, there will be no one to pay government fees for our compound."

"If you are also sent, you will only have to walk across the street to pay your dues."

She did not seem happy about this. Janet was extremely upset when he explained the punishment had the possibility of sentencing for up to five years.

"What would you like to happen?" the judge asked her.

"I would like Sandi to forgive me," she said in a small voice still looking at the judge.

"It's a little too late for that," the judge said.

The prosecutor kept sliding back in his chair as if at any moment he would fall off. He rubbed his forehead repeatedly and looked like a combined ball of anxiety and worry.

I wonder if she had paid him.

After I showed the judge the marks I still had on my arms and made a quick statement about how I wanted a fair and just trial, he decided to give a verdict. The final sentencing was the maximum under the circumstances. A 200,000 UGX fine or eight months in jail for court fees, which had to be paid before she could leave the building. A 200,000 UGX fine or eight months in jail paid to me to cover medical expenses. She looked nervous as she sat in the back of the room unable to leave until she paid.

I was frustrated. I was frustrated because this was a woman I knew. I was frustrated because of how hateful she was that day. I was also frustrated because I knew that as soon as she grabbed onto my arm, I reacted more forcefully because I was still healing from when I felt helpless with Dominik's hand around my throat. I was frustrated because something in my reaction triggered this usually sane woman, who had potentially seen family members hacked to death in front of her, to use violence against me.

I was frustrated because the cycle of one violated and hurt person violating and hurting another was vicious and felt never-ending.

I wondered how long the bite marks would stain my skin. How long would I be reminded of the day I was bit by Janet, my landlady? My flesh was still numb to the touch. I wondered how long she would remember me and if the unit I lived in would be a daily reminder of the American woman who played with her children and who she also bit that one time.

Confidential? Think Again.
Day 347: Wednesday, October 19, 2011
49 weeks

Goodness, Google—you failed me. For the longest time, you ignored the military search warrant and I was OK with that.

How exactly would this unfold? I had no idea.

Without knowing what the search warrant stated, I had no idea to what extent they would comb through my emails. Were they going to read each and every email I had received since November 2010?

Peace Corps emails.

Delta membership emails.

Emails from my mom.

Emails to my friends.

Emails to my old friends I hadn't seen in years.

I would have rather not gotten people who I hadn't seen in years and who didn't know what was going on involved, but the defense loved checking in with anyone who might possibly say something to their benefit.

To some degree, this whole process made me question confidentiality with any communication method or conversation with particular individuals. Once upon a time, I thought counseling sessions were confidential since they are communications between a psychotherapist and patient.

Not only had the military gained access to my email account, but I also signed waivers allowing access to my personnel file and medical records—after I was told the case may not move forward unless I did—which included "confidential" communications between myself and the counselor. I signed waivers because I was willing to sacrifice my personal privacy and go through this hell so that other women would be protected from Dominik Jones.

When I was medically evacuated from Uganda and headed to the States, I had no idea that the notes from therapy would later be reviewed for evidence. I spoke to the psychologist honestly and didn't hold anything back. I shared everything so that he would be better informed on how to direct my healing. Looking back, had I known his notes would be looked over, maybe I would have stayed silent, harboring my thoughts.

At what cost was the judicial system willing to undermine the healing process of an individual for the sake of "evidence" for the perpetrator? Was getting help from an outside professional source, trying to moving forward with life, worth the risk of your pain getting thrown in your face by a brutal and unprofessional defense lawyer?

I still didn't know what they were looking for. I didn't understand why they kept pressing for access to every little thing about my life.

What upset me was thinking about other women who were dealing with this. I hated how there was (and is) a stigma that women "ask for this" by the way they dress or how they act.

Fact: If a woman does not consent, forcible or coerced sex is rape. Period. End of sentence.

One life is not more valuable than another. It does not matter if you are a sex worker or the mayor's daughter, shame on the person who violates another.

Knowledge of sexual assault doesn't make someone immune to having an incident. Just because I had worked with individuals who had been raped, it didn't mean that I was immune to falling in the trap of a rapist. Working with a population is far different than being a part of that population.

If I could have stopped the violation of my privacy from the government, I would have. Too bad the military judge believed combing through my email was more important than keeping a rapist off the streets. The longer this military judge waited and succumbed to the defense, the longer Dominick had to traumatize others.

If my emails, as the victim of the crime, continued to be a factor for delays, that would be insane. Especially since Lt. Riggio was denied the request of Dominik's emails. It was very one-sided and another example of sex discrimination in this case.

So thanks, Google. Thanks for sharing my personal emails with the defense lawyers. Thanks for nothing.

A Breathtaking Encounter With Gwen

Day 356: Friday, October 28, 2011
Kampala, Uganda
50 weeks

"Gwen!"

Whoomph.

Thump.

It had been a good week. I traveled with some friends to the coast, relaxed and had a splendid time. I was about to head north for the Invisible Children's Halloween party for the third year in a row. Sunday, I was going to go on my one and only safari in the two years that I had been there. I would be leaving at the end of next week on a plane to the States. Life was good.

It didn't last. Before I left for the North, I saw Gwen's boyfriend at a restaurant. Six of us were having lunch, and he rode over on his bike to meet some of his friends. He mentioned that Gwen was back in Uganda for a couple of weeks.

I was a little nervous when I heard this. Out of the three from that night, Gwen was the one who had been the slightest bit supportive. The prosecutor had said she had stated when she testified for the pre-trial that she regretted some things from the night. Out of the three, Gwen would be the one I could talk to and try to make sense of what happened with them.

Or not.

A few of my Turkish friends and I went to a pub later that night. As I was leaving the ladies' room, I saw Gwen on the dance floor, doing her usual loud foot stomping, with a neutral look on her face.

I called her name and went to give her a hug. She had other plans.

Before I knew it, she slammed her hands into my ribs, pushing upward. The force lifted me off my feet and I flew back a yard or so. I landed on my butt and my right elbow, which started to ache immediately. I sat on the floor for a few seconds and shook my head as I caught my breath.

The bathroom attendant stood and gave a glaring look toward the door. Gwen got me right where she would block people from the restaurant from seeing, though a man came over and asked if I was OK.

"Yes, I am fine. Don't worry about it," I assured him.

I was pissed. Gwen was not worth my effort. But I could feel my blood go hot and my body tense. Pursuing it would not be worth it.

My friends didn't see what happened. After a couple of minutes of deep breathing and a bottle of water, I found them and explained what was going on.

They tossed out the idea of kicking her ass, her boyfriend's ass and her boyfriend's friends.

They also wanted to buy me a beer, but that wasn't going to help either. I caught my breath and focused on something other than her.

Before she left, she walked by again and gave me the middle finger.

I stayed calm and tried to let it go.

A Year in the Making
Day 364: Friday, November 4, 2011
Somewhere Over the Atlantic Ocean
52 weeks

The time came when I had to say my final goodbye to Uganda as a Peace Corps volunteer.

Fifty-two weeks ago, exactly a year earlier, I had traveled from my village in northern Uganda down to Kampala. Traveled to the city where later that night I would be sexually assaulted by a member of the United States Navy. I had traveled many amazing journeys during my 26 years but that particular journey had forever changed my life.

This flight was the bridge between my beloved Ugandan life and the transition back to America to deal with the complicated military long-distance relationship and the trial scheduled for the following week.

America. I had no job, no confirmed place to live. The next few months were going to be a challenge. I had a lot of catching up to do.

My clothes, the majority of which were over two years old, showed serious wear and tear and needed to be replaced. I was going to need to get an American cellphone. I was clueless as to what cereal I would buy and I knew I would spend at least 10 minutes looking at toothpaste trying to figure out which of the 100 types I should buy. Figuring out my place back in America was going to be stressful, but in an exciting new way.

The long-distance relationship with the military was stressful on a whole different level. The good part was that in just over a week we would begin our last dance. After that week, I would be free of that abusive relationship.

Just after I was assaulted, all I wanted was to avoid life—that was my coping mechanism. I deliberately avoided stimuli like thoughts, feelings, people, conversations, situations and activities that led to remembering the trauma of the assault. I didn't want to talk about the incident. I wanted as few people to know as possible and I wanted my story to be told on my terms.

To some degree, I felt like I'd missed out on creating the long-term friendships that often happen during Peace Corps service because my focus had been somewhere else. Hell, I had been physically back in the States dealing with issues surrounding the sexual assault more than physically around other volunteers during the last year. I would never be able to have the friendships I wished I could have had with other Peace Corps/Uganda volunteers. There would always be an underlying uncomfortable feeling.

Slowly, I had gained the strength to stop avoiding, to stop letting the incident control and debilitate my life and to confront my pain. I struggled with being emotionally numb. I felt like I was in isolated turmoil. My lifelong cheerfulness had been replaced by a constant sadness I couldn't shake.

Realizing I was not alone and that many of the women I deeply respected had gone through their own trauma of sexual assault was huge. Knowing we shared this common bond, that someone else understood my turmoil, was comforting.

I know there are women and men who are forging a new movement against gender-based violence—one where victims place their undeserved shame upon perpetrators and enablers who are held accountable for their actions.

I realized I wanted to take my personal experience and further my work with women who have lived through tragedies as well. Though I still struggled, and I still cried sometimes, I knew I couldn't give up.

And the Plot Thickens...
Day 368: Tuesday, November 9, 2010
Washington, DC
52 weeks

The first phone call I had with the prosecutor when I got back in the States was rather unexpected. I had seen an email from him the Thursday before asking when I was available to talk. That was my last day in Uganda, and I figured whatever news could wait until I got back and had a proper phone, so I delayed talking to him for a few days.

Oh. My. Goodness.

Last Wednesday, a father called the prosecutor on behalf of his daughter. Somehow, they had seen the newspaper article about my case, contacted the journalist who wrote it—who included so many personal identifiers—and he put them in touch with the prosecutor.

Apparently, three years ago a similar incident happened to his daughter involving the one and only Dominik Jones while he was stationed Stateside. She had never pressed charges. Lt. Riggio said it sounded like the incident was still fresh to her. If she had never spoken to anyone about the incident, had never reported, I couldn't imagine the personal and mental torment she had felt for those three years—especially once she knew he raped another woman.

I couldn't fathom how many other women in other parts of the world were also sexually assaulted by him.

It also made a pretty damn good case against Jones.

The prosecutor called this "damning evidence" for Dominik. Because it was evidence of similar conduct, the prosecutor could bring the new evidence into the trial. Because he was on active duty, they could press separate charges in another court hearing.

If she never reported before, it was doubtful she would want to be the single victim/witness of her own brand-new case now.

Lt. Riggio was able to speak to her. She hadn't responded to the defense asking if she would speak to them.

"Does she have the same options as I did? Where she technically doesn't have to speak to the defense?"

She did, but then the defense could pull the whole "we did not have time to prepare because this unruly witness refused to cooperate" bullshit.

"Can you get her in touch with a victim advocate? And I do not mean someone who is just passing time while they are on trash duty or until they get discharged after having a kid. Someone who is smart and knows law and is not afraid to speak up to the defense? The whole process is overwhelming and there is no way I would have been able to do this without support from individuals within Peace Corps," I told him.

"Yes, they were trying to get her connected to someone in California," he said. He mentioned something about a support network.

"If this is the first time she has spoken out about what Jones did to her, I doubt she has a strong support network. There is no way on earth I would let Lt. Mayo speak to her the way she spoke to me. She needs a good victim advocate who won't let Mayo bully her."

"We are trying to be...smarter, about protecting victims."

Good. Hopefully, her experience would be better than mine. At that point, she was considering the idea of testifying in court and would give a more solid answer later. For the time being, she would be placed on the witness list and was told that she could back out at any time.

Both the defense and prosecution asked for a continuance to gather more information after this new development.

The prosecution had also asked to allow an expert witness on rape trauma syndrome.

The Peace Corps had contacted Dr. Connie Best, who was an expert in rape trauma syndrome and had experience working with the Secretary of Defense Advisory Committee on Women in the Services. Her work focused on criminal victimization and psychological trauma. Best was retired from the Navy Reserve after over 20 years of service. She had personal research and expertise directly related to both the military and the type of crime. Dr. Best even received a presidential award for outstanding service on behalf of victims of crime.

Despite her credentials, the judge elected not to approve Dr. Best.

The judge also released my emails deemed "relevant" to the case. Lt. Riggio mentioned there was one from a name that I did not recognize until I asked for the last name since I had forgotten writing the email. It was my sister who is a counselor back in the States—the only family member I had emailed directly afterward.

November 9, 2010
Dear Sister,

So, don't be too alarmed.

I was sexually assaulted this last weekend. It's really complicated and a mess now since we found out that he is here with the American military. I do not necessarily want to press charges, but we are acting as though we are going to. I hate attention. I hate drama. Our medical people have been super good and I am doing fine. One interesting thing is that I have the option to go to Washington for counseling and whatnot. Learning more about that option and will probably take it depending on timing and work here. Not telling mom. Not something she needs to be overly stressed about. I am honestly doing fine and actually one of my friends is taking it harder than me (which her man-hating and bitterness is not the most supportive way to act right now). K, I need to eat. :-)

How are you doing today?

Love,
Sandi

November 10, 2010

Dear Sandi,

I am so sorry. What do you mean you were sexually assaulted? That can mean a lot of things. I understand if you are not ready to divulge the full details, but you need to at some point. Are you physically OK? What medical treatment are you getting? Too many questions running through my mind...

I am OK. Suddenly busy after being bored for so long. Exhausting, but good. I need to get my notes done, but will write you more later.

I love you and let me know if there is anything I can do.

Your Sister

November 11, 2010

Dear Sister,

Glad to hear that you are busy now! It's nice to be busy after being bored. I've been working on Maleng Designs and learning and it's been quite exciting. Can't exactly work on anything right now due to being in Kampala though...

So, I have to give my testimony to NCIS investigators in about 15 minutes. I am physically OK. I've been treated for anything that could possibly be wrong. I had a physical checkup on Monday, Tuesday we found out that he was U.S. Navy, Wednesday we went to the police to report as well as the forensic doctor (who just looked at the former report, asked more questions and signed the papers), Thursday I got news that the NCIS were coming, this is the first ever particular type of case between   the embassy and D.C. and Peace Corps, today I get to be interviewed, as well as another PCV, two of our medical people and the country director. Hopefully this will all be finished soon but it is doubtful. I am writing the story out to help process so I can send you that when I am done. Bah. This has become complicated and a huge deal. OK, I think the people are here now for the interview. I keep thinking of all the CSI, SVU, NCIS, Law and Order shows I've watched and how I never thought in a million years I would ever be caught in something of that sort. I am going to be OK...

Sandi

Oh, goodness.

Putting on the tough front and downplaying the seriousness of what happened was something I did to make myself feel more in control of the situation.

Everything was out of my control. Thankfully, I knew that pursuing legal justice was vital to potentially preventing other women from being sexually assaulted by Dominik since he was not a onetime offender. I hadn't been able to control the feelings of violation of my emails being read by the presiding judge. I had no say in anything.

And my life was going to be delayed even more. It gave me a headache just thinking about it.

Continuance granted until December 5.

Pillow Talk
Day 375: Thursday, November 16, 2011
Washington, DC
53 weeks

November 15, 2011 - 1:43 p.m.

Afternoon LT Riggio,

I was just wondering what the judge decided about approving the expert witness on rape trauma syndrome?

Also, I was wondering if it would be possible to have a professionally made board with the correct dimensions of the hotel room created by someone else rather than me go up front and dazzle the jury members with my ability to draw pillows and oversized closets. I like to be a perfectionist and not getting things perfect in marker that can't be erased is discouraging. This would alleviate a lot of unneeded anxiety since my drawing abilities aren't what should be judged but rather the atrocities which happened within those squiggly lines. Plus, I do not want to look like a 5-year-old and feel smaller than I already do when LT Mayo is annoying and heartless.

Alright, let me know if that is possible and what the judge says.

Thanks!

Sandi

November 16, 2011 - 12:36 p.m.

Sandi,

The judge has allowed us to present expert testimony, but has limited it somewhat on the timing of presenting the evidence and the manner in which we do so. Neither of the limitations particularly hinder our ability to go forward, so I am happy with the ruling.

As for the diagram, I was planning on making one anyway. I had not decided whether or not to use it, but thought we would have it just in case. If the defense wants to use something like that, they will likely make one as well (or potentially use the same one). Trial is very different than the Article 32, for many reasons. If they want to use a diagram, it is very unlikely that they would ask you to draw it off the cuff like they did at the hearing.

No other updates right now. We will plan to talk again before Thanksgiving. When do you head to OR?

Very respectfully,

LT Aaron M. Riggio

November 16, 2011 - 1:15 p.m.

LT Riggio,

Well, I am glad the judge is at least letting you present the expert witness. I am sure you guys will make it work within the guidelines presented.

I am really glad the Article 32 is not the same as the actual trial. Honestly though, if I did not have the right support from key people—my self-worth was at a record low—I probably would have given up right about then. And then at each time of a continuance dragging my life into a longer limbo. You were right about the Article 32 being a free for all. That is horrible for someone who is faced with testifying yet another time and would never want to do so under the same conditions. In my perspective of being the victim of a crime, LT Mayo was extremely disrespectful and unprofessional and it's a shame if that is typically how defense lawyers treat victims. I had been warned that she was bitchy in the courtroom. I do not understand how in such serious matters someone can treat someone else with less than basic human dignity. I haven't researched the model rules of professional ethics to know enough but I plan to.

Anyways, I would really appreciate a pre-made diagram. Thank you so much for your diligent work and for thinking about small details.

I leave next Monday, the 21, for the West Coast and will be back Thursday, December 1.

Thanks again,

Sandi

What NOT to Wear

Day 384: Friday, November 25, 2011
Portland, Oregon
54 Weeks

November 25, 2011

Good day,

Two questions and I would really like the help of LT Galentine with the second one:

1) What is the proper spelling and title of the judge overseeing United States vs BU2 Dominik Jones? What other rape cases has he overseen?

2) I want to be respectful to the military professional standards of dress and appearance. What advice can you give when it comes to appearance in court as a victim? Hair up or down? Glasses or contacts? Suit with pants or skirt? Or dress pants and a nice shirt? Black, blue or a different color? As silly as this might seem, I believe that first impressions can make a huge difference on how people judge you. Since I am not too familiar with the military, I want to give a respectful good impression.

I hope you are enjoying the weekend with your families!

Thanks,
Sandi

Monday, November 28, 2011

Sandi,

The judge's name is Commander Douglas Barber. I could not tell you how many rape cases he has heard. This is his second tour as a judge, and since he has been here he has heard at least five or six (three that I have been involved on). I do not know how many he heard at his last tour.

I have cc'd LTjg Genevieve Loutinsky, the assistant trial counsel. LN1 Galentine is on leave for a couple weeks, and Genevieve can give you all the dress/appearance advice you need.

Hope your Thanksgiving was restful. Let's talk today or tomorrow to catch up and discuss when you're coming to Norfolk.

Very respectfully,
LT Riggio

Monday, November 28, 2011

Hi Sandi,

I am more than happy to help you out on the clothing front. As a former civilian prosecutor, I definitely know how tough a balancing act dressing for court can be. This is a bit long, but I tried to break it down by outfit component.

Suits: I suggest that you start off with a well-tailored, nice suit, dark colored, in tropical wool or something similar. (The fabric type should be the least of your worry, but if you have the choice, go with the natural fabric). I encourage you to wear something with feminine (but not super-girly) tailoring—you do not want to look like you threw on a men's suit, or a very boxy woman's suit, since those tend not to fit well. Try Ann Taylor if you're looking to buy a new one.

I do not suggest a straight-up plain black suit. They can look very nice, but they can also be boring. You do not want to be boring, believe it or not—not that you want to be a party girl, but you can't appear like a kid playing dress up with her parents' clothing. If you have something in a charcoal, or a dark dove, that would be great as a plain solid. Blue is not my favorite for solid suiting, it somehow always looks dated. You want to look together and professional—not prudish and out of date. Pin striping or herringbone is also great, provided it is well done. I'd avoid houndstooth as a pattern for anything.

Suit Jacket: Do not go for one of the cropped jackets, or one with ruffled or rounded lapels. They tend to look less formal, and more "girl on her way to her first job at a magazine." I suggest more traditional peaked lapels, and a longer jacket. They'll be sleeker looking and more professional in court. Your lapels should be moderate in width, tending slightly toward more narrow than more wide. Do not get a jacket that's too tight. A lot of women buy these tight, cropped suit jackets, and it just looks like they shrunk their suit in the wash.

Suit Pants: Wear a pants suit, not a skirt suit. With a skirt suit, you'd need to have the skirt go below your knees (and remain below your knees while you are sitting), wear panty hose and be sure that you are hyper-vigilant every time you cross your legs or move at all. Pants are just going to be easier. Nothing too tight or low rise.

Shoes: Shoes should be nice, fairly plain, well shined and neither superhigh in heel, nor superpointy in toe (or superboxy. Please do not go and buy a pair of, for want of a better term, old lady shoes. A two-inch heel, something between a chunky heel and a stiletto, almond toed, is what I am picturing. Patent leather if possible.) Also, wear socks or hose with them.

Shirts: I wouldn't wear a white shirt, or a pastel colored shirt—unless either happens to look better on you than any alternative. I would look for a saturated color that looks good on you without being obnoxious. If you have a collared button-down shirt, that's ideal. If not, a plain long-sleeve T-shirt should do the job (J. Crew sells good ones, if you're looking to buy). Definitely long sleeves. Just do not wear anything low-cut, clingy, sheer, or stained (I know this sounds obvious, and I am not worried about you, but I have seen some horror stories). If you have tattoos, do not let them show.

Jewelry: A conservative, understated wristwatch is fine. Earrings are fine. I wouldn't wear more than one pair, if you have multiple piercings. I'd go for simple studs, not dangling earrings. You can wear a necklace if you wish, but none of those big statement necklaces. Something very simple, on a chain. If you normally wear a ring, as long as it is not a huge cocktail ring, that should be OK, but if you do not—the rule about looking in the mirror and removing one accessory before leaving the house is just as true for court as anywhere else.

Hair: Some will say you need a bun. I am not sure what your hair looks like, or if your face type is one that looks good in a bun. Frankly, it's more important that you look pulled together than that you hit a checklist of things someone else tells you to wear. I would do a low ponytail, a low bun, just nothing too messy. I wouldn't let it out, I would tie it back in some way. Do not worry about trying to do a military bun.

Makeup: Minimal. Powder or foundation to keep off the shine (even if you normally do not get shiny, I am assuming you'll be nervous which will up that shine factor). Light mascara, light matte lipstick or stain. Skip eye shadow and liner. Maybe some blush if you're worried about looking pale. No gloss!

Glasses or contacts: Wear whichever makes you feel more comfortable—if you try something too new on the stand, you'll feel awkward and the members will pick up on it, but will assume a different reason than the fact that, for example, you usually wear glasses but today you're wearing contacts.

Purse: Do not worry about your bag; you won't take it to the stand with you, so the members won't see it.

That was long, but I hope it helped. Please feel free to email me or call my office if you have any questions.

V/r,

LTJG Genevieve Loutinsky

Well then. I printed this email, highlighted the key points and went shopping for the most important "interview" outfit of my life. Here's the rundown:

Simple earrings: $14

Suit jacket and pants: Originally $368 but half off at $184

Three shirts: All on sale totaling $75

Pantyhose: On sale at $15

Shoes: Half off at $35

$323 for a single outfit. I could have lived off of that for two months in the village. Thank goodness for my Peace Corps readjustment allowance.

No one had any idea how much pressing charges had cost me in time, energy and actual money. If I weren't serious about seeking legal justice keeping Dominik accountable for his actions and preventing him from raping other women, I would have dropped out of this months ago.

Headache and a Twitching Left Eye
Day 389: Wednesday, November 30, 2011
Portland, Oregon
55 weeks

She wasn't coming.

The young lady from California who was sexually assaulted by my rapist was not flying to Norfolk next week for trial.

The prosecutor had asked if we could speak about updates and travel arrangements. I called earlier in the day but had left a message on his voicemail. My mom and I continued the day by running errands and doing last-minute things since it was my last full day with them for the unforeseeable future.

As we drove to the airport terminal so I could say goodbye to a friend, the prosecutor called back. I was sitting in the car with my mom, fidgeting around for a pen to take notes, searching for the familiar face of my friend about to leave. I was disappointed about the woman backing out of testifying and more issues with Google. He kept throwing technical terms around. Too much was going on.

"Riggio, I am super-distracted and can't concentrate. Can we continue this in an hour?" I asked as calmly as possible.

I was too distracted. My everyday life and the long-distance relationship with the legal issues were, not surprisingly, not meshing well. Nothing about this whole trial was convenient. Being committed to the trial was like being forced into a horrible job you don't want without any pay or benefits. It felt like a nonprofit job I was doing because I was committed to the greater good.

I agreed to talk to Lt. Riggio an hour or so later and stood inside the airport while mom drove around, and around, and around again as I waited for my friend. I couldn't help but be sad at the latest news.

The woman was willing to testify over the phone, safe in her home far, far away. Being in the same room and facing her rapist from three years ago while giving intimate details of his violation of her body was going to be too difficult.

His face was the one I saw in my nightmares. I was sure his face haunted her as well.

No one willingly wants the face of their nightmares, which have mercifully blurred with time, to become clear and crisp again.

I had looked away while Bridgette happily chatted with Dominik 24 hours after he sexually assaulted me. I purposefully didn't look at him during the Article 32.

I couldn't blame her for not wanting to testify in court.

I finally met up with my friend to bid her farewell and safe journey. She was so excited yet nervous about her journey overseas. Although she had been extremely supportive about my situation, I didn't want to dampen her mood by telling her about the latest setback.

My mom and I left the airport some time later to finish the last few errands. The time was getting close to when Lt. Riggio and I agreed upon talking again. My mom asked a few questions regarding where to go next and I answered in a short, aggravated tone.

"I am sorry, Mom, but these calls put me in an instant off mood. I have a headache and my left eye is twitching now. Please don't take this personally. I just need to get somewhere I can sit and you can go inside so I can take this call," I explained.

We parked and my mom left me in the car with a little pad of paper and pen ready to go. I sat for about 30 minutes doing Sudoku waiting for the call. Lt. Riggio mentioned that he had a meeting to attend. Maybe it went over and he wasn't able to call?

Sometime later I got an email from David at the Peace Corps saying Lt. Riggio had tried calling but my phone was "not accepting calls at the time." I had no idea how that happened. David wanted me to teach him how to get the phone to say that, but I was clueless.

By the time I got a voicemail from Lt. Riggio, it was late on the East Coast. The next day, I'd try calling while at the airport waiting for my flight back to D.C. If that didn't work, we'd talk on Friday.

Spending time with the family would be a lot more enjoyable if I didn't have this hanging over my head like a dark ugly cloud.

I couldn't wait for this to be over.

Resolution

Day 420: Saturday, December 31, 2011
New York City, New York
60 weeks

When a new year approaches, many people make lists of New Year's resolutions: spend more time with family and friends, fit fitness into their busy schedule, quit drinking, get out of debt. Those types of resolutions would have been dandy, but I had to focus on resolutions of a different sort.

I kept waiting and waiting and hoping that the resolution would come soon.

I had no job. I had no stable place to live. Both of these are common circumstances when you finish your Peace Corps service. But my added unknown—the legal case—made transitioning back to the States even more stressful.

I would be sitting with friends at dinner, and my mind would begin to wander. I would inevitably end up thinking about the court case and I would excuse myself from the table, walk quietly to the bathroom and cry.

The prosecutor's legal assistant called on Wednesday to give me a brief update. My friend Kat, who had been a photojournalist in my village, and I were driving and she commented about how relaxed and nonchalant I was on the phone.

"Basically, the legal team is prepping for the appellate court, which is an appeals court, hoping that you won't be forced to present any more emails. You are reaching out to the other rape victim having given her a victim's advocate and making sure she gets the therapy she needs. We can't have trial the week the prosecutor's wife is due to have their second kid in March, so most likely we won't go to trial until April at the earliest," I summarized for the legal assistant.

I only talked about the phone conversation for a few minutes with my friend before looking at the New York City skyline at sunset. Quickly, I pushed the trial to the back of my mind. I wanted to enjoy the road trip rather than worry about what I couldn't control with the trial.

Later that night, thoughts I had put on pause started to play again. One of Kat's friends asked me if I was OK. My eyes had gone out of focus as I stared off over their heads. I shook my head no and walked to the bedroom.

I needed to cry, to release my tangled emotions. Kat came in and laid beside me as my knees touched my forehead in the fetal position.

"I want this to be over. I want to fall asleep in a basement until this is all over. I try so hard to ignore the way the trial affects me, making me depressed, constantly in the back of my mind. I am tired of waiting. I want this to be settled."

There was only so much I could do as I played this waiting game. In my personal life, I had no energy to put the effort toward gaining stability. I tried to establish myself in Washington, D.C., but there was an emphasis in the city on meeting people and social gatherings. In my current state, I found those events truly draining, to an extent they never had been before, so I tended to avoid them.

I knew severe depression was lurking inside me. I knew that I needed to stop staying in the basement all day wanting to hide. I made myself commit to some realistic and vital resolutions.

My resolutions:

1. With the New Year, I would make a firm determination to get out of the house more.

2. I would allow myself to have meltdowns, even when that meant my eyes would be swollen the next morning, knowing that it was healthy and needed to happen occasionally.

3. I was determined to support other victims of crime. In the job realm, I had to take myself out of consideration for a job supporting victims of military crimes because my case was still active. I would have been passionate about doing what I could to give them the resources they needed.

4. Stability. So many times I had to change plans at the last moment because of the trial. It was chaos. I was determined to have stability.

My plan of action:

1. When I got back to D.C., I would set up coffee dates with people in the field I was interested in and I would push through. For the time being, I would stick close with the few friends I trusted and ask them to keep me accountable.

2. In the next month, I was determined to work on my mental health and to become involved with a support group. The DC Rape Crisis Center lists support groups on their resources and information page and I would call and see which one fit.

3. For however long it took, I would continue to look for jobs supporting women and children in some capacity. I would love to work with young women who have been trafficked and are in the States but wanted to work with anyone who had gone through adversity—homelessness, refugees, at-risk youth. I would continue working on cover letters. I would be more active in reaching out to others in the field and gain their wisdom.

4. That year, I promised myself I would slowly, slowly have stability. I couldn't control what happened with the trial but I was seriously hoping it would be settled in April. I would make a schedule of weekly activities even if it looked boring. I would nurture friendships and would reconnect with friends and family I had

postponed because I kept waiting for the incident to be resolved.

I would make this next year work for me. I was determined to evaluate all that had happened and to use it to the benefit of others and myself.

Resolution for me was on its way.

Everything Will Work Out
Day 431: Wednesday, January 11, 2012
Washington, D.C.
61 weeks

Life was starting to work out. I had a good feeling.

I finally had enough energy to push myself to get my life in order.

My good friend Kelly, whom I was staying with in D.C., was helping me stay accountable in getting up and out of the house. I was starting to not feel like the new kid and was able to invite others out.

I was a little nervous about the individual counseling session that was scheduled for next week; I felt like a lot had happened in the last year, and to fill someone in on even a synopsis would take forever. If only I was able to stick with my Peace Corps psychologist since he'd been there since the beginning. I tried finding a group therapy to join, but the one I found didn't start again until June.

A few coffee conversations had gone really well and I was learning more about what was happening in D.C. in regard to trafficking in persons and also speaking out about sexual assault. I started to see that I wouldn't be unemployed forever.

Stability was slowly coming.

The trial. I hadn't heard from Lt. Riggio in a while so I randomly called him while sitting at a bookstore. It was after 5 p.m. and I was shocked when he answered.

"Did the legal assistant update you on the status of Google producing the rest of the emails while I was away?" He asked when he answered.

"Wait, what?" I had not heard of any of that.

Google said they had produced everything Judge Barber requested and he had received a disk, which he was not allowed to open. The judge must first ask permission of the appellate court if he could review the information to see if it was correct. Progress of a trial for my case had been put on pause due to the defense making the argument that my emails needed to be subpoenaed for their need to make a case against me. Previously, the prosecutor had argued that legally Google did not have to comply and the judge was not allowing the case to move forward, not allowing due process, therefore the prosecutor filed a complaint against the judge. The appellate courts are part of the judicial system that is responsible for hearing and reviewing appeals from a legal case that have already been heard in a trial level or other lower court. In this case, the complaint about the judge was still with the appellate court and they had to dismiss the complaint to move forward with my trial.

If the judge was satisfied with what he saw from Google, he would request that the case be given back to him so we could move forward with trial. The appellate court had the option to refuse his request and to hear the case anyhow. Although the prosecutor thought there was a very slim chance that would actually happen.

The judge seemed hopeful and asked everyone to keep the week of February 27 clear for trial. The prosecutor was extremely doubtful everything would be cleared by then. I certainly wasn't holding my breath.

I asked about the other victim. They were still waiting to reach out to her. They had given her the holidays to be with her family, the first she'd shared with them since revealing the incident from three years ago. I hoped they got a gentle move on this. The prosecution team was working with their superiors on the best way forward to balance getting her help and also reaching out. At the end of the day, they could subpoena her to testify.

If I were having a hard time processing the violation of sexual assault after years of repressing it, I wouldn't want a call to force me to discuss details I'd held hidden silently or dealt with years ago.

As the person who was willingly participating in this, I did want stability and to get this over. And I wanted to prevent assault or help individuals who had gone through this too.

Back in December, I had emailed a contact at RAINN asking about volunteer and job opportunities with them. The only one she knew of was working with the Department of Defense Safe Hotline. I didn't know how the defense lawyers would respond. I emailed her back saying that, with my current situation, I should probably abstain from interacting with the military population.

"How do you think the defense would twist me working with the military population? I can't keep waiting for this to be over and postpone finding a job when supporting traumatized individuals has been the field I've been working in for years and want to continue supporting others. For me, because of what happened, I am even more passionate about helping others going through their own rape or incident. I would find this to be even more proof of a crime," I said.

"Right and you shouldn't postpone living your life. If you feel comfortable doing the work, say exactly that if the defense tries to twist it," they counseled.

If the defense chose to twist the way I was living, feeling empowered enough now to help others, this would only show how they expected me to stay the victim, to stay feeling broken and useless, to feel incapable of working through the traumatic experience Dominik inflicted on me.

I couldn't continue life in the victim mode and I needed to start doing things for myself.

There's a quote that applied to me: Everything will be OK in the end. If it is not

OK, it's not the end.

I wouldn't let the defense scare me into crawling further in a cave.

Day 433: Friday, January 13, 2012

"Hey Sandi, it's Aaron Riggio, in Norfolk, almost 4 o'clock on Friday calling with an update. I think when I talked to you yesterday or the day before I said some stupid number like 90-95 percent sure that trial would not be February 27, which was stupid because of course the appeal has been lifted by the appellate court and the judge is telling us that he wants us to go to trial on February 27.

"So I can't say for sure and guarantee that day because obviously we haven't checked the availability of anybody to be here then but as of right now that's what the judge's plan is.

"I'd love to talk to you more. Obviously need to see if this time works for you.

"You know, another ping-pong back and forth. Sorry about this here, and then not here, and now it's back.

"We will work with you to try and find, you know, if that week is going to work for you and if not when the next best option would be.

"I'll be in for a little bit yet this afternoon and all then next week. So, just give me a call back when you get the chance."

The 3 "C"s
Day 469: Saturday, February 18, 2012
Washington, DC
66 weeks

"You are the prettiest crier I have ever seen," the young man said. I couldn't help the tears from flowing after feeling overwhelmed once again.

"Why, thank you," I said before random concerned young man bought champagne for me and my friends after learning the Prettiest Crier was celebrating her 27th birthday.

Happy birthday to me.

I started the night well enough. We went to a local show, met up with friends. I wanted to have a fun night, filled with good people but the variables I couldn't control were eating away at me.

What a week. Valentine's Day was Tuesday, my birthday on Saturday and I got to look forward to trial in a week: Three interwoven issues at hand and I was barely holding on.

To begin, let's talk about the first "C"—the case. Specifically, the case calls. Since I finally had a job, I wasn't as flexible to go into the Peace Corps office so David and I could call the defense together. Calling with David was not as stressful as doing it alone since he asked the questions, leaving me to sit back, process information and write notes.

After our calls about trial issues, I usually became pretty depressed and was fairly useless for the rest of the day. This was not useful in life when you had a job where you were expected to be productive. Thankfully, my job was flexible with hours and I was able to work from home. If I had a full-time office job, I could have seen myself having a breakdown in the coffee room.

On Thursday, Lt. Riggio said the other young woman who Dominik sexually assaulted in California had decided to testify again.

The defense was not happy about this and requested seven motions, including another continuance. The defense of course wanted to completely exclude the other victim's testimony because they felt it wasn't similar enough to our case. This was the opposite of how the prosecution felt as her incident had similar variables, showing Dominik's aggression and violence and how his intensity had increased.

The defense said she was not cooperating with them, when in reality they were trying to do what they'd done to me before the Article 32. They would bully and intimidate victims within the context of the law on behalf of their client, the accused rapist.

The other victim would speak to the defense only as long as Lt. Riggio was also on the phone. Of course the defense would rather blindside her or trigger her so she would back out from testifying. If they really wanted to know the details of what happened, they would talk to Dominik and see what he had to say.

The defense also wanted to get Lt. Riggio thrown off the case. Since Lt. Riggio was her main point of contact, the defense believed he was acting more like an investigator than a lawyer. To me, it just sounded like he was building his case. The defense wanted to see his notes, and filed another motion.

The prosecution could appeal if the judge excused her testimony, but that would result in another delay.

Friday morning, Lt. Riggio called me to prepare for trial. I had decided to work from home, and prepared for the call while sitting on my bed.

The other woman had backed out again.

She wasn't doing well. Her family explained how this hadn't been good for her. She'd had increasing panic attacks. She was incapable of functioning properly.

I saw how her family was concerned for her. This was a difficult process to go through. Riggio could technically subpoena her, but wanted to respect the fact that he had agreed with her father that she could back out.

The horror of being sexually assaulted often prevents victims from pressing charges and holding an attacker accountable. Sometimes it's just too hard to relive the event over and over again during the legal process. Thus, he was never held accountable. And who knows how many women he sexually assaulted before her, in between our incidents or after me?

She was having panic attacks and not able to properly function. Who was to say that I was functioning properly?

I wasn't.

I wanted to be understanding; I wanted to be empathetic. But I also needed her to testify.

After I let Lt. Riggio know what I thought of her backing out and him not subpoenaing her, we talked about my testimony. We reviewed basic information about how I decided to apply to the Peace Corps and chose Africa, my work, trainings related to health and safety.

"How have you assimilated to being back in the States?" he asked.

A simple question with such a complex answer. Thinking about all the difficulties I'd had in the last year was depressing.

"All of the different things you've said have happened to you are part of 'victim impact,'" he said. "If he's found guilty by the jury, you will be given the opportunity to share your story on all of these events and it will help determine his sentencing. Sandi, you are far more prepared than you think for this trial."

I still feared that I would fail. I feared that I wouldn't be able to clearly explain what happened. I feared that if I wasn't well prepared for this trial he would be acquitted. I feared something bad would happen and I would be at fault when he sexually assaulted his next victim.

The prosecutor and I agreed that I would make an outline of impacts and he would help direct the conversation in case I forgot any while testifying. The key was to stay genuine, show raw emotion and attempt to let the jury understand what life had been like since the incident.

At the end of the phone call, I was still trying to hold back tears. I was unsuccessful. Next Tuesday, we would talk to discuss more details of the actual incident. That would probably have to be another day that I worked from home in hopes that no one heard me discussing the details of my rape.

I ended the call feeling depressed and sad about the way life had turned out. I called David at the Peace Corps and reached his voicemail. I was doubtful he'd be able to understand my crying and blabbering.

This brings us to the second "C"—counseling.

Lying in bed in the fetal position could have lasted longer but I had to get dressed for my counseling session. Last time, I looked put together with a nice shirt and my hair well done. This time, I threw on a hoodie and jeans with Toms, pulled up my hair and wore glasses. I did not have enough energy to properly get ready for the day.

My first session with my new counselor was more about what I was hoping to get out of our time together and what I wanted to work on. Because of the trial, we decided ways to cope during trial and my victim's impact speech were top priority.

We went over basic grounding techniques, ways to sit that would allow constant blood flow to decrease the possibility of becoming lightheaded, how to deal with emotionally jarring questions and how to calmly handle the defense lawyer while sitting in a box.

With my therapist, the trial was the most gripping and timely issue to work on.

Even more than the trial, I wanted to discuss with her my issues with the final "C"—coitus.

Before I left to go overseas, I didn't get invested in relationships because I always knew I would be leaving the country and I knew I didn't want to pursue anything long distance. Now that I was planning to stay in the States for some time, I was so confused by everything I didn't know where to start.

Over the summer 2011, I hung out with a new male friend while I was on medevac again in the U.S. Because of lingering trial dates and not wanting to get someone else involved with my intense life, I kept him in the dark about a lot of things going on in my life. He was completely respectful, good-natured, really thoughtful and I felt bad that, while I truly enjoyed hanging out with him, I was still going to keep my distance until the trial was over.

The first time we hung out by ourselves, he tried to hold my hand while walking down a path.

"I am sorry but I can't," I said quietly as I extricated my hand from his.

This led to him taking the reins and a sit-down talk. Awkwardly, I vaguely explained some aspects of my situation, while not going into actual details. I remembered him holding his hands out saying, "The left hand is point A, right hand is point B—what are the boundaries?" To verbally and frankly discuss what I was able to do in the open was beautiful.

"Sandi, I think you are really great and if hanging out is all you can do, that's fine with me," he told me.

So we kept hanging out.

Somehow, when I returned to the States in November, dating became more confusing.

In November, I simply hung out with this really attractive guy, testing the American waters. He was adventurous and had traveled for work as a ski instructor. I had stayed slightly distant for the first few weeks and, at some point, I decided I would let myself begin to like him. I left for Portland for 10 days and somehow "We should see each other sooner rather than later" wasn't followed through. It wasn't a big deal since he was leaving for law school. I didn't give him much more thought.

During a New Year's celebration at a friend of a friend's house, I was warned to be careful about a certain guy; apparently, an ex had treated him badly years ago and now he continued to return the favor.

So I chatted with him with caution. But our interaction was fun. We played Tetris on the arcade game console he built. He was smart and had designed a roller coaster. He was coy, and we both agreed that we should be standing next to each other as the New Year began.

A couple of hours later my friend came back and pulled me aside.

"Sandi, I told you be careful. He doesn't feel anything for women," she reiterated.

"It's OK. I don't feel anything either," I replied simply.

This was the point where I decided I needed to get back into counseling. My emotions were either unhealthy extremes or non-existent.

In mid-January during a friend's birthday night out, a guy approached me because he saw my amazing robot dance moves. I became filled with anxiety simply because we were at a bar and a guy came up to talk to me. My nervous system went on high alert and I felt threatened.

But he was amused. He said someone doing the robot could not be pretentious and joined my robot dancing with some of his own. I thought about the interaction a couple of days later and decided that he was probably a good guy rather than a guy looking for his next victim. So after deciding to risk the unknown, we hung out for the next month.

February was a complicated month for me in general. My birthday is four days after Valentine's Day so it could be an awkward week.

On Valentine's Day, I sent him a text saying "happy 45th day of the year." The next day, a friend and I went down to where he lived and grabbed a drink with him and his friend. Saturday was my 27th birthday. His friend sent me a text but he did not.

Between the trial, this non-fling and all the other stressors of life, I found myself being declared "The Prettiest Crier I Have Ever Seen."

It wasn't until Monday that I got a call asking if I had a minute to talk.

"Sandi, you are really cool. It seems like you want something more serious and I didn't want to say anything on your birthday..."

"Are you finished yet?" I asked after he kept talking for a few minutes too many.

I didn't know what was going on. I felt like my dating life was going the opposite direction I wanted. I didn't know how to explain why things were happening the way they were. I was trying not to let what happened in Uganda affect my interactions with men, but ultimately I knew it was.

The 3 "C"s—

Case.

Counseling.

Coitus.

Anxiously Awaiting
Day 478: Monday, February 27, 2012
Norfolk, Virginia

Though a mighty army surrounds me,
My heart will not be afraid.
Even if I am attacked,
I will remain confident.

Psalm 27:3

The trial was happening. No more delays. No more questions of when.

I sat at the hotel, only hours before I would testify, trying to remember all the details of that night and trying to prepare for the questions I would be asked. My hair was in a side bun, foundation and lipstick was applied. My suit was hanging in the closet, ready for me to put it on for the most important interview of my life to date.

I had seen the courtroom. It was at least twice the size of the Article 32 room. There were chairs on both sides for more observers. A chair for the Associated Press reporter, a couple of other journalists, David, Dominik's mom and whoever else would be there waiting to hear each testimony. I wouldn't be able to see them though because the prosecution and defense tables and the stage platform was raised six inches above the floor.

The judge would be to my left, sitting above me.

The jury would be to my right. The jury was originally seven men and three women. Because the military was required to have sexual assault response officers and, those are typically females, two of the women had been trained in identifying sexual assaults. They were dismissed. The defense didn't approve any jurors who were knowledgeable about sexual assault trauma and impact, disallowing anyone who knew the definitions and legal implications from being on the jury.

At most, the jury was going to have one woman. It would be mostly men who were officers or Dominik's peers. Given society's casual sexism of phrases like, "That's what she said" and "I'd do her," I was uncomfortable sharing the details of Dominik's violation of my body. While I sat there sharing painful details about the worst night of my life, would any of these men be thinking, "I'd do this girl; I'd like to see how she ran." What worth would they give me and my words describing how one of their comrades sexually assaulted me?

The lawyers would ask the questions, but it was the jury I had to convince of the horror of that night.

It was unsettling how this seemed to be a dramatic performance of convincing people. I wished this was more factual. If my life had to be an episode of "NCIS," this one-hour episode had about a year and a half of overexaggerated drama and too many surprises for my liking.

Even when the defense lawyer upset me, I had to stay calm, yet vulnerable, yet strong, trying to explain to the jury members how Dominik traumatized me and how important their decision to keep him accountable and to prevent this from happening to other women was so important.

I had been trained to repeat part of a question when replying in interviews. Unfortunately, here a witness who does that will be suspected of lying, hiding information and untrustworthy. I had to keep this awkward interaction (read: interrogation) as much like a conversation as possible.

I did not enjoy talking about being strangled. I did not enjoy talking about how I was fearful that my life would end. I had to find strength in vulnerability and present my fear as raw as it had been. Beyond my fear for my immediate safety had been my fear for my health—HIV, STDs. My one requirement of safer sex was disregarded. Dominik had put my life in danger in multiple ways.

I told him to stop. I did not consent to sex without a condom. I never consented to having his hand around my throat strangling me on his bed. I never even saw his muscled arm as he wrapped it around my neck in a chokehold while water rushed down my face. I wouldn't have given him permission even if he had asked.

I had found him on Facebook before the Article 32. Just before the trial, in early February, he posted that there was some sort of Crush Fest happening in Virginia Beach and that he would be working the door. The event was in April. He also posted that this was his "last weekend—time to make it count." I wondered what he did to "make it count."

It was time to change into my suit.

No more waiting. No more preparing. I would do my best. I let go of my expectations and responsibility for the outcome, leaving it to the military justice system.

A Peace Corps Trial Begins
Day 478: Monday, February 27, 2012
Norfolk, Virginia

I walked slowly through the doors to the courtroom. There were more people in the audience than I had expected. People in military uniforms, people in business attire. Two male reporters and one female reporter who all seemed to be in their early 30s. One for the military and two for civilian papers.

Dominik sat facing the judge in his dress whites.

I remember thinking, Why were there so many binders, so many papers on the defense assistant's table? The prosecution has one medium black file folder holder and a binder. The defense has a cart and over 10 times more material. Good God, are we not as prepared?

I walked past them up onto the platform. Turned and raised my hand. I sat. Stated my name, and where I lived.

The 10 jury members were down to five.

Four males, one female.

Four Caucasians and one African American who looked like he was about to fall asleep.

The older male had a stern face with salt-and-pepper hair. One of them had a higher ranking than the judge. The only woman, who was not an officer and was one of the lower-ranked individuals out of the five, looked concerned as I began to speak.

Ted, the former country director, testified first so they knew the safety and security issues of Uganda.

I looked at the prosecutor when he asked the questions. I spoke to the jury when I answered. I looked at their faces; they were the ones who needed to hear what happened.

I tried to look at Dominik but I couldn't. I didn't want to. Was he wearing glasses? Was he trying to look more mature by doing that? His Facebook photos had him showing off his tattoos in board shorts surrounded by women or him wearing goggles for snowboarding or skydiving. I wondered if the tactic of him wearing glasses was similar in the reasoning for why Lt. Mayo colored her hair from blonde to brunette. Was it so she would be taken more seriously in court?

I reminded myself not to cross my legs so that blood circulation was not cut off. I always took a breath before answering.

I answered questions as honestly as I could. If I didn't remember something, I said so.

Three news reporters were in the audience. I had to be careful of what I said, what identifying information I gave. Who knew what details they would decide to publish for the world to see? I kept my answers simple and realized that, most likely, my words would be put out of context and twisted to get the "best" story out to the public.

Answer this, answer that.

"And the scariest moment was when I turned away from him in the shower and he put his arm around my throat. I didn't even see it coming. The pressure, the water, I wasn't sure what was going to happen."

Victims who don't cry might not be believed because the judge and jury expect some tears. Expressive witnesses who cry "too much" may be dismissed as hysterical. Expressive victims who respond with anger might not be believed because our culture is extremely uncomfortable with angry women. In a Queens, New York, case involving a sexual assault by several members of a university lacrosse team, the jurors said that among the reasons they didn't believe the victim was that, on the witness stand, she was angry and argumentative during cross-examination.[19] One juror said the victim wasn't believed because her demeanor "just did not coincide with what we felt a victim should behave like."

I hated testifying. I hated sitting there and feeling weak. I hated sitting there trying to be exactly what the jury needed me to be. I couldn't be too sad, too angry or too calm.

This was going to be OK. I was doing exactly what I needed to without any nervous laughter, staying serious without faltering. Just a little longer and then the prosecution would be over.

I hated the defense lawyer. I hated how she started with a snide remark. My body physically became tense while she talked. She did this on purpose. She wanted me to fight back. She wanted me to come off as a bitch with an agenda. I was so tired of people disrespecting me and always feeling like I was being attacked. I just wanted this to be over.

She asked questions that left no room for explanation. I tried to explain and she cut me off. I could feel the blood rushing to my head, making the room too hot to bear. I wasn't taking breaths before I answered. She was gaining control of this game of hers. She had to make this as dramatic as she could.

She knew if she hit on the right issue or topic or phrase or incident throughout the night that I would automatically regress into flashbacks, making it difficult for me to answer because I couldn't focus, couldn't breathe and all I wanted to do was escape those feelings. She knew how to trigger a PTSD episode

---

19 http://www.ok.ngb.army.mil/j1/sarc/sarc_documents/Training/Other_Misc_Training/Barriers_to_Credibility.pdf

and she was doing her best to trigger one in me. I was trying to stay level but my body remembered being attacked that night. I could feel his arm snake around my neck as I sat there on the stand. I could smell his sticky skin close to my face. His breath was hot on my cheek as I heard her ask another question. I was drowning again.

What was she asking now? I said I could not recollect to the best of my knowledge—why was she getting that binder out? Why was she dramatically flipping page by page? Slowly. I filled my glass of water and took a drink to try and steady myself. What was she doing? I was told that the Article 32 transcripts weren't going to be used during the general court-martial and now she was pulling statements from that? I tried to shake the feeling of Dominik's hands strangling me.

"As I said, I do not recollect." It was a minor detail from before the sexual assault, not even relevant to anything he was being charged with, but she was pounding on it to make me seem unreliable.

Wait, what was she trying to get impeached? What does that mean with this scenario? I didn't say anything conflicting from last year's statement. Why was she dragging this out? I was confused why they were still talking about getting something impeached.

This was not going well. I was not responding how I wanted to, how I had mentally prepared.

The prosecution did not have the same paper she was reading from. The judge called a short recess. We stood while the jurors left. I was allowed to go to the bathroom but I did not want to run into him. The man who sat by the door escorted me to a restroom down a different hall. I could breathe again, but I was unsettled.

The prosecution did not have the same papers as the defense and the judge suggested they needed an overnight recess to put things in order. Take two would start the next day.

• • •

I was later told that during the break, some of Dominik's Navy friends were talking to his mother, saying how he was a good soldier. Dominik walked up to his mom and put his arms around her for a hug.

She kept her arms at her sides.

Day 479: Tuesday, February 28, 2012
Norfolk, Virginia

I was tired. Exhausted, I had slept deeper than usual the night before. Rather than watch TV in the waiting room, I chose to read a book about death, brutality and survival. At least I was still alive.

I was tired. I didn't want to be there. I didn't want to fight with the defense lawyer.

Too much was going on. I was being pulled in every direction.

Walking into the courtroom, there were not as many people as yesterday. The defense lawyer started off exactly where we stopped the day before. She read the line from the Article 32. I responded with quick "yes" or "no" answers. Composed and weary, I answered apathetically to her snide remarks. I had to trust that Lt. Riggio would cover the main important points that needed to be explained.

I wanted to clarify her questions with explanations, but I was too exhausted to fight her with my words. She tried to get me impeached—holding me in contempt for lying to the jury. I was only confused at what was going on yesterday rather than upset. But I didn't say a straight "yes" or "no," so she couldn't say that I was purposely lying.

She was trying to make me look flaky and wishy-washy. She was trying to make it look like I was tampering with Bridgette and Crystal's testimony. She was asking about my earrings. She was making it sound like I wanted the others to go hang out with Dominik, and that I was pushing them to go and get my earrings that I had left behind.

Lt. Riggio began to cross-examine me and asked about the sentimental value of my earrings. I explained how I didn't tell them to go to his hotel for the purpose of getting my earrings but rather asked multiple times if they were seriously going to his hotel. I wanted to say that my earrings didn't sexually assault me, he did, and how I didn't understand why they had become a big issue.

How I didn't know Gwen or Crystal well and how the weekend of the incident was the first time Bridgette and I tried mending our friendship after seven months of not speaking. Did I trust these women?

No, not at all.

Then I was done. Other witnesses were still to come, including the medical officer from Peace Corps/Uganda and Dr. Best, the expert in rape trauma syndrome who the judge reluctantly allowed to testify and only within a very limited scope. But for the time being, I was finished.

I could see the finish line of this awful, grueling race.

The Public Speaks

The Associated Press reporter sat in the first row to my right on the first day of trial and, within a couple of hours of recessing for the day, he had uploaded his story on the day's findings. After reading his article, I wanted more facts and less focus on the defense's opening statement, which had nothing factual or proven in it, but rather assumptions that reinforced victim blaming and rape culture.

Here are a few of the headlines:

Military trial in Peace Corps rape case begins — Fox News

Rape trial begins for special warfare sailor accused of raping Peace Corps worker in Uganda — Washington Post

Ex-Peace Corps worker claims sailor raped her as Norfolk trial opens — WVEC

Rape trial begins for special warfare sailor accused of raping Peace Corps worker in Uganda
By Associated Press, Published: February 27

NORFOLK, Va. — A former Peace Corps worker who taught at a girl's school in rural Uganda told a military jury in Virginia on Monday that a special warfare sailor who does construction work for Navy SEALs raped her multiple times in his hotel room in the East African country's capital.

The trial comes months after Congress responded to complaints that the Peace Corps hasn't done enough to protect its volunteers from sexual assaults with legislation requiring the agency to better train participants in how to avoid such attacks.

The 27-year-old woman, who was born in Anchorage, Alaska, and now lives in Washington, testified in a courtroom at Naval Station Norfolk that her sexual encounter with Petty Officer 2nd Class Dominik Jones in November 2010 started out as consensual.

But after his condom came off twice, she said she wanted him to stop.

She said she tried to push Jones off her, but that he grabbed her throat and held her against the bed. She said he later raped her in the shower when he put her in a choke hold and that she feared she might drown. She said he did not have to force himself on her the next two times — including once when his roommate was in the next bed — because she was afraid for her life.

Jones's military attorney said the case was simply about a woman who regretted her decision to have sex because she was embarrassed by her behavior. As part of her job, the woman, who graduated from Indiana University, taught girls to avoid peer pressure and to use condoms.

"This is not a case about rape. This is a case about regret," said Lt. Lauren Mayo.

The accuser said that she and Jones had met in an Irish pub in Kampala while she was out with three other Peace Corps volunteers who were in town for a conference. She said she voluntarily went back to his hotel room with him and that she had no idea he was in the Navy at the time. She said she did not learn more about him until after she had been assaulted and she had mentioned that she was not on birth control. That's when he told her his full name so she could find him on Facebook because he wanted to keep the child if she was pregnant, according to her courtroom testimony.

Mayo said she did not mention to any of her friends the next day that she had been assaulted. One of her friends said she thought it was "kinky" that the sex was rough and that he had choked her.

"That was my night of hell," the woman later recalled thinking during the exchange.

The Associated Press does not generally identify alleged victims of sexual assault.

It was not until days later when she saw a medical worker about emergency contraception that the word rape came up, and only when the medical worker mentioned it, according to courtroom testimony.

Mayo also said that the woman did not do anything to stop Jones, such as scream, slap him or try to leave the hotel room.

"You did not do anything to stop him, did you?" Mayo said to the woman, who simply responded "No."

At other times during her testimony, the woman said she did not scream because it was too difficult to breathe while she was being choked. She also said she did not leave the hotel room until the morning because Uganda is too dangerous of a country for a foreign woman to wander alone during the early morning hours.

In April, during a procedure that is similar to a preliminary hearing in civilian court, Jones's attorneys had suggested that charges were only being brought forward due to political pressure. The Peace Corps had been under criticism for not doing enough to protect is volunteers from crime, particularly sexual assault. In May, Peace Corps Director Aaron S. Williams appeared before a Foreign Affairs Committee hearing to apologize for the agency's shortcomings on volunteer safety issues.

In November, Congress passed a bill requiring the Peace Corps to develop sexual assault risk-education and response training. The legislation also requires the agency to establish a victim's support office.

Jones's trial is scheduled to resume Tuesday.

By Tuesday morning, there are already 220 media outlets who'd published an article about the trial. Over 200 news sites with an article about a rape victim, 27 years old, born in Anchorage, Alaska, graduated from Indiana University, returned Peace Corps volunteer, now lives in Washington, taught girls in rural Uganda. For the Associated Press stating they do not generally identify alleged victims of sexual assault, they may as well have. Short of printing my actual name, they clearly identified me.

When I first learned that an organization such as the Associated Press would be covering the case, I was excited. I thought this would be a great opportunity for people to read about the reality of overseas incidents with the military or the challenges that victims face. Instead, the author evenly weighted the defense lawyer's unproven assertions and characterizations against my testimony—an unfair pairing.

Rather than stating facts about rape and sexual assault or even just focusing on the incident, the article instead served to excuse sexual violence and, in the article, contributed to the perpetuation of a rape culture with victim blaming and rape myths.

Clearly, the reporter was not concerned with media sexism when he published—much less the journalistic responsibility of not doing harm to the victim. Newspaper articles such as this one can play a part in supporting rape culture—in which prevalent attitudes, norms, practices and the media normalize, excuse, tolerate or even condone sexual violence.[20] Far too often, sexual violence and exploitation is seen as the norm and victims are blamed for the behaviors of the person who assaulted them. Instead of focusing on the perpetrator's actions, the focus is on the victim.

Far too often, the victim of a crime, an accident or any type of abusive treatment is held entirely or partially responsible for the transgressions committed against them. This is regardless of whether the victim actually had any responsibility for the incident.

With my interaction with Dominik, sex did not start as an illegal activity. It wasn't until Dominik decided to change the type of engagement into rape was it illegal.

Let's say Dominik and I had gone to a basketball court to shoot hoops in his neighborhood. Half-way through, he started smacking the ball out of my hand and trying to trip me. I ask him to stop and to play fair; he does for a minute, but then goes right back to foul play. I decide to sit out since I do not agree with the way he plays and walk over to the sideline. No harm done. I agreed to play a civil game and chose to leave when I didn't like the circumstances.

If he had started strangling me after I wanted to stop shooting hoops, most people would identify this as a normal legal activity that shifted into an illegal incident.

Yet, this case is about the taboo subject of sex and somehow society says that, as individuals, we do not have the choice to quit or there's "proper" reaction to someone forcing another person to continue.

I take responsibility for my actions that night, but I also recognize that I didn't do anything illegal. I didn't make the wisest decision, going back to his hotel, but that's not illegal. Dominik was the one who chose to change the type of engagement and take illegal actions.

Reading the articles was discouraging but even more discouraging was reading the comments of readers across the country. Some individuals said there was not enough information in the article to make an educated evaluation of the situation. (And really, I'm not sure how anyone could make sense or determine the legality of a whole night and the next year and a half from a one-page newspaper article.)

---

20 http://www.wgac.colostate.edu/what-is-rape-supportive-culture

There were other comments, though, that got under my skin and reinforced how society holds rape and rape victims to a different standard.

> "This woman should be ashamed...You can bet today with all the liberal women beating the date rape drum this is not surprising. Give this woman a dose of truth serum otherwise do not buy anything she says. I am sure most real rape women wait days to report it to authorities. I hope the sailor gets acquitted."

I'd never had anyone insinuate that I was a liar.

I was learning firsthand how society's "rape myths" are misbeliefs about sexual assault. Because of inherited structural conditions, gender role expectations and the fundamental exercise of power in a patriarchal society, misconceptions around rape and sexual assault are unknowingly passed down and perpetrated.

Lt. Mayo played into the societal myths that there is a "right way" to respond to a sexual assault situation implying that, because I did not "fight back" in a particular way, I was not really sexually assaulted. She implied to the jury that I could have prevented being sexually assaulted had I put in the effort to stop him. I was being blamed for the incident because I didn't do enough to protect myself rather than him having to take responsibility and ownership of his behavior.

In reality, sexual assault can be life-threatening and each incident is unique; the best thing a victim can do is to follow their instincts to make it out alive and with as minimal harm as possible. Individuals may choose not to fight back violently because they are socialized from birth to be polite, to smile, to not offend and to not say "no." By the time they realize they are in danger, it may be too late to get away. If the perpetrator is bigger and stronger, that in and of itself may be threatening enough to intimidate or overcome the victim's resistance. Some individuals respond with disassociation and frozen fright—terror-induced altered states of consciousness.[21]

Lt. Mayo implied that because I wasn't outwardly hysterical that I wasn't really assaulted. But, individuals who have been raped and sexually assaulted display an array of emotional responses, including, but not limited to, hysteria, laughter, anger, apathy and shock.[22]

Lt. Mayo insinuated that because I didn't directly say that I was assaulted by Dominik the following day when talking to the other three volunteers that I was not truly sexually assaulted. I did however say that he choked me. In a National Institute of Mental Health study, only 57 percent of women who had been forced to engage in sexual activity that met the legal definition actually labeled their experience as rape. The other 43 percent didn't recognize that it was rape or sexual assault.[23]

Lt. Mayo insinuated that because I didn't report immediately after I left Dominik's hotel room that I was not truly assaulted. Fact is, in America, only 16 percent of rapes are ever reported to the police.[24] If a victim is raped by a complete

---

21 http://www.ok.ngb.army.mil/j1/sarc/sarc_documents/Training/Other_Misc_Training/Barriers_to_Credibility.pdf

22 http://www.tipnational.org/images/tRape_Reactions_of_the_Victim.pdf

23 Mary P. Koss et al., Stranger and Acquaintance Rape, 1 PSYCHOLOGY OF WOMEN Q. (1988).

24 Id. at 6.

stranger, 90 percent of the time it's reported within 24 hours; but for rapes among individuals who were familiar with the rapist, such as a family member, family friend, neighbor, "good friend," someone they trusted or a stranger acquaintance, 90 percent reported after one week or more.[25] My reporting time frame was completely normal.

Lt. Mayo insinuated that regret and embarrassment propelled me into reporting and not that I was truly assaulted. Statistically, about 2 percent of rape allegations are false, even less frequent than false allegations in other types of crimes. As Lt. Riggio said in conversation before the trial, rape is an extremely difficult crime to charge and the easiest to defend.

Many people aren't aware of the difference between false allegations and cases that are "unfounded," in which police or prosecutors determine the evidence in the case to be unverifiable, non-serious or not prosecutable. This becomes problematic when they evaluate victim credibility within the context of rape myths. Police are more likely to believe a victim if it is stranger rape, if there was more than one offender, if weapons were used, if the victim made a prompt report or if the victim had a reputation for chastity.[26] If police and prosecutors aren't familiar with actual rape reporting statistics, these key players let societal myths around rape and sexual assault affect the viability of prosecutions tremendously.

Lt. Mayo also insinuated multiple times that political pressure on the Peace Corps was the reason I reported and pursued the case. I, Sandi Giver, as an individual, was sexually assaulted by another individual, Dominik Jones, and I chose to press charges. The Peace Corps' political situation had nothing to do with it.

Not until after reporting did I find out that Dominik was with the U.S. Navy. The year after my incident, the Peace Corps faced criticism for not doing enough to protect or support volunteers, but that was far from my experience. And not once did newspaper articles mention the military's abysmal history of creating reasons for "unfounding" cases, not taking them seriously and covering up incidents. Surely, I was not the only one in the courtroom who read reporters' accounts of the trial. I wondered how the media coverage had affected the jury. I wondered if the coverage supported beliefs they already held.

In the article, "When Will We Be Believed? Rape Myths and the Idea of Fair Trial in Rape Prosecutions," Morrison Torrey argued that jurors have trouble giving credibility evidence that is contrary to their personal beliefs.

> Jurors will even distort and twist evidence until it becomes consistent with their attitudes. These fundamental premises that jurors bring with them to the courtroom are what psychologists call "cognitive structures." While cognitive structures allow individuals to learn new information, they tend to perpetuate themselves by screening out information that is inconsistent with what is already

25 Daniel C. Silverman et al., Blitz Rape and Confidence Rape: A Typology Applied to 100 Consecutive Cases, 145 AM J. PSYCHIATRY 1440 at Table I, (1988).

26 KATZ & MAZUR, supra note 54 at 10; MacKeller, supra note 117 at 87 (if victim had friendly relationship with offender before incident, case has little chance in court); Pamela L. Wood, The Victim in a Forcible Rape Case: A Feminist View, in RAPE VICTIMOLOGY 194, 205-12 (George Schultz ed. 1975) (historically, lack of chastity, failure to resist, and waiting to report rape have adversely affected likelihood that woman will be believed); Berger, supra note 122 at 15-20 (courts consider a woman's virtue in evaluating whether she consented); See also, e.g., People v. Collins, 186 N.E.2d 30, 33 (Ill. 1962) (considering prior sexual conduct in evaluating issue of consent).

believed. Cognitive inflexibility is what prosecutors face in trying to convict rapists when jurors have cognitive structures based on rape myths. Jurors will strive to reach a verdict in a rape case that will not conflict strongly with the rape myth cognitions they hold at the beginning of the trial.[27]

27   Morrison Torrey, When Will We Be Believed? Rape Myths and the Idea of Fair Trial in Rape Prosecutions, 24 U.C. DAVIS L.REV. 1013, 1050 (1991)

That's It?
Day 480: Wednesday, February 29, 2012
Norfolk, Virginia

We waited five hours for the jury to deliberate. If it was too short, that wasn't a good sign. Three hours was more typical. Five hours could mean that they were having serious discussions. Five hours for five jury members made of four men and one woman. The jury had a lot to consider. They were told to consider Dominik's service history and deemed it as evidence. A couple of items the jury were told not to consider were my service record with the Peace Corps and the testimony of the rape trauma syndrome expert.

I was told that while Dr. Best was on the stand, the judge was not happy with Lt. Riggio. The prosecutor had started by asking about studies that had previously been submitted to the judge. When Lt. Riggio started to make the connections from the studies, her 20-plus years of experience and the actual case at hand, the judge threatened Lt. Riggio. The judge was reluctant to have the expert testimony to begin with and then silenced her when asked about my behavior based on her experience while working with sexual assault victims. The judge had the jury leave the courtroom so he could yell at Lt. Riggio, saying he would dismiss the case if Lt. Riggio continued to ask questions on those lines. "You know her testimony is damning to this case!" The judge was concerned about the damning testimony and scientific research and experience that could hold one of his military men accountable. Before the jury left to deliberate, the judge told them to dismiss Dr. Best's testimony altogether. Now, we were waiting for the jury to make a decision.

Waiting, waiting. When we first arrived on base and into the legal building, we walked down the prosecution hall like usual. I was about to go into the waiting room to my right, when I saw Crystal out on the couch in jeans looking very tanned. I looked to my left, and saw Bridgette sitting in a chair.

Bridgette. Neither the defense nor the prosecution could call her to stand because it was so apparent she was lying when they were doing trial prep in person. I wasn't angry at her, but I was sad about how all of it turned out. Because of her, people knew her one-sided self-interested version of what happened. Because of the pending trial, I wasn't able to tell my version of what happened. Bridgette didn't know the details of the sexual assault and she didn't know the complications and the events since.

After the two women left, David and I went into the waiting room to watch the news. Around 4 p.m. we decided to go to a coffee shop on base. In the back of my head, I still worried that someone was going to sneak up behind me and bash in my head, but I really shouldn't have been worried on base. The walk was short and Dominik had to wait somewhere else.

It was 8 p.m. when we finally got a call to go back upstairs.

I sat with David from the Peace Corps to my left and the assistant lawyer from the Article 32 on my right. We were in the first audience row on the left side, waiting for everyone else to come back. I wanted to look around but I was too nervous.

We rose for the jury and sat back down when told. None of them looked at me but rather straight at the judge. Dominik sat between Lt. Mayo and the male defense lawyer.

"And how do you find the defendant?"

The male jury member closest to the judge spoke. This was the moment that had consumed a year and a half of my life. His next words would determine if Dominik Jones was held accountable for raping me.

"We find the defendant, Dominik Jones, on all six charges, not guilty."

Did I hear that correctly? Was that it? Twelve words? Twelve words instead of 11? I looked straight ahead, not wanting anyone to see my distress. I saw Dominik do a fist pump before his lawyers patted him on the back. A fist pump, as if his football team had just won a game and his coaches were saying "good game."

It was over. For the past year and a half I had worked up to this one single point in time and then there was nothing.

How anticlimactic.

I wanted to cry but my heart had dropped so far into my chest that I didn't think I could feel anything anymore.

Dominik's assault had cost me so much and he wasn't even being held accountable for his actions. I had sacrificed so much in pursuit of justice. He knew he had raped before. He and I both knew the truth of November 5, 2010. I wished the court would have allowed me to share how his assault impacted my life.

I had done all that I could. I had no control over the legal system and I knew that it wasn't my fault he was found not guilty. But it still tasted bitter in my mouth.

It struck me as darkly humorous that the verdict was decided on February 29. A day that doesn't normally exist. It was almost as if the universe was giving me an out. I would only have to remember this failure every four years. I wouldn't have a yearly anniversary of this.

What a complete failure of legal justice.

Simply a Human Rights Violation
Friday, April 13, 2012
Washington, DC

First Name: Sandi

Last Name: Giver

User: Victim/Survivor

Service Affiliation: Other

Status/Position: Other

Installation/Base: Kampala, Uganda, East Africa

Date of Incident: 2/29/2012

Name and/or Office of Military Personnel: Judge Barbara

What is this person's title or position?: General Court Martial Judge in Norfolk, VA.

Comments:

On November 5th, 2010, I was sexually assaulted by a member of the United States Navy in Kampala, Uganda, where I served as a Peace Corps Volunteer. You may have read about my incident in any number of news sources...

I filled out a military feedback form on the SafeHelpline.org website, which is designed for military personnel to provide feedback. I wasn't enlisted or active duty but I wanted the military to hear about my experience as a civilian. I sent a letter detailing the entire incident and court case.

April 14, 2012

Good Afternoon, Ms. Giver,

Thank you so very much for taking the time to share your experience with us, as described below.

I am so sorry about everything you have gone through. Please know that we are taking action to bring your comments below to the attention of the appropriate people in the Department of Defense that can affect change in the areas you highlight.

You have been so brave to go through so much in order to try and bring the perpetrator to justice and, while the trial may have had a negative outcome, we will do our best to correct the deficiencies in the military justice process that caused you undue harm.

We all know that the criminal justice system is an adversarial system, but victims of crime have rights and we strive to treat each and every victim with dignity and respect and to provide all with a fair justice process. I am so sorry that we failed you.

I sincerely hope you will be able to recover soon, and just want to convey our deepest appreciation for your participation in the military justice process as well as sharing your comments below with us.

Please do not hesitate to contact me if I can be of assistance to you in anyway.

V/r,

Bette

Bette Stebbins, MSCP, CA
Senior Victim Assistance Advisor
OSD, Sexual Assault Prevention and Response Office

Interestingly enough, I had met Bette in December 2010 while I was in D.C. receiving counseling after the assault. I knew she was someone who had worked with the Peace Corps. I decided to send a response, detailing the ways my basic human rights had been violated according to the Universal Declaration of Human Rights—by my rapist and by the military justice system.[28]

The Universal Declaration of Human Rights is a declaration adopted by the United Nations General Assembly on December 10, 1948. It was a reaction to World War II and represents the first global expression of the rights to which all human beings are inherently entitled. There are 30 different articles and for my case, I chose to focus on five different ones.

Article 1 says that all human beings are born free and equal in dignity and rights. Dominik chose to act toward me in a violent way; the military judicial system chose to put his military dignity and rights above mine as a civilian.

Article 2 says that everyone is entitled to all the rights and freedoms set forth in this declaration, without distinction of any kind, including sex. Dominik's rights and freedoms as a male and as the perpetrator were upheld but mine were not. Was this sexual discrimination in the law? During the trial, Dominik's service with the military was brought forth as evidence as if to say this distinct sailor serving our country was too good of a soldier to be held accountable. My service to my country or marginalized populations in the states and abroad was never allowed.

Article 5 says that no one shall be subjected to torture or to cruel, inhuman or degrading treatment or punishment. Clearly Dominik violated this article. During trial, I was given degrading treatment by the defense lawyer LT Mayo in such a way that the newspaper journalist decided to include some of this treatment in national news.

Article 7 says that all are equal before the law and are entitled without any discrimination to equal protection of the law. Yet, I as the civilian, was not treated as an equal. Dominik was protected by the military law and the judge presiding over the case. Judge Barbara would not allow the prosecution to fully present their case for a fair and just trial resulting in Dominik Jones walking away a free man.

28 ???

Article 12 states that no one shall be subjected to arbitrary interference with his privacy, family, home or correspondence, nor to attacks upon his honor and reputation. Everyone has the right to the protection of the law against such interference or attacks. There was definitely not enough evidence to violate my privacy or electronic email correspondence.

On December 9, 1948, Eleanor Roosevelt gave a speech on the importance of adopting the Universal Declaration of Human Rights. "This declaration is based on the spiritual fact that man must have freedom in which to develop his full stature and through common effort to raise the level of human dignity. We have much to do to fully achieve and to assure the rights set forth in this declaration." Over 50 years later, and as a country we still have much to do to indeed.

Something to Be Proud Of
Tuesday, May 8, 2012
Washington, DC

Scrolling the Women's Information Network listserve, a Democratic organization for women, I saw that a one-day conference needed volunteers. The Truth and Justice Summit held by Service Women's Action Network (SWAN) for survivors of military sexual assault and rape was coming to D.C. to lobby lawmakers. Although I did not serve in the military, I was sexually assaulted by one of their members and had been through the military's legal process.

I arrived right before lunch, and listened to keynote speaker Senator John Kerry address the group of over 100 military sexual-trauma survivors representing 27 states. One panel discussed the brutal reality servicemembers face after being assaulted, another comprised service providers.

During lunch, the women, and a few men, were given basic instruction on how to present their stories to their representatives and senators in Congress. As a volunteer, my job was to provide emotional and logistical support for the survivors. As we walked to Capitol Hill, I could feel their energy and how determined they were to be heard.

As groups broke off to speak to their congressmembers, I stayed with the largest one with 15 members. As a group, we went to one lawmaker's office where survivors, male and female, talked about how they were raped and sexually assaulted by fellow soldiers, the lack of accountability of male soldiers, how they were treated during and after the legal process and issues veterans with military sexual trauma faced.

I listened as they shared their stories: a victim was raped by someone in their command, they aren't able to leave, victim is unable to function and gains weight, the perpetrator is not held accountable with charges dismissed and then promoted, victim is discharged due to gaining weight rather than a proper documentation of military sexual trauma; a victim was raped by an opposite-sex perpetrator, victim was told by perpetrator that because of the rank difference no one would believe the 18-year-old victim, victim was born homosexual and was always homosexual and had never had intercourse with the opposite sex, victim was told that because there was an incident of child sexual abuse in their past that they must have liked what happened and all charges were dropped by the court; victim was raped by a superior in the 1960s, no charges, no financial or mental health support once a veteran for the victim because of the cultural belief that rape is about sexual desire rather than power and control.

I listened as the representative asked questions about procedures and standards that simply did not support or honor the integrity of victims. I watched as one of the younger survivors in the room never spoke, yet would wipe away tears as others shared their stories.

There seemed to be no code of ethics or rule of law when dealing with rape and sexual assaults in the military population. I had no clue the injustice was this grotesque.

It was as if the military was sending out a message that victims of rape and sexual assault were inferior. In many cases, the victims were shunned, abandoned or discharged without any support, while the perpetrators faced no consequences, the equivalent to a slap on the wrist or were even promoted. It perpetuated a pattern of abuse, that let perpetrators walk free and violated others' basic human rights.

These brave servicemembers had chosen to serve our country with full knowledge of the risks of being wounded and traumatized by enemy forces. Even while listening to their stories, I couldn't imagine the betrayal by fellow soldiers who had abused their power and rank.

The next meetings were individual district representatives. I accompanied a woman who was passionate about supporting veterans in her community, helping them gain the services and benefits they deserved. She knew intimately the difficulties veterans faced with homelessness and how educational benefits were not being fully utilized because the veterans who needed them most didn't know about them. She was confident, logical and knowledgeable.

We introduced ourselves to the representative, she with her name and branch of service and me with my connection.

"I actually never served with the military but am volunteering today since, while I was serving as a Peace Corps volunteer in Uganda, I was raped by a member of the Navy who we later found out raped another young woman in your state while he was stationed there. I went through the military justice system but he was still acquitted of all six charges against him," I explained.

I had only spoken for a moment but the look of concern on the representative's face lingered. Another military survivor came in at this point and shared their story as well. Afterward, the four of us posed for a picture outside the office, and the representative gave me a sincere hug and a hopeful look.

An hour later, a larger group assembled in another office. Someone asked which branch of service each individual was from. Army. Marines. Air Force.

"I was only in the Peace Corps," I said.

"You say that as if that's not something to be proud of! Sandi, you are one of us!" someone declared.

They were right.

I served my country through the Peace Corps. It was a lot to be proud of.

During my service, living in a post-conflict area was intense. I heard gunshots from far away, but also saw the flickers of shots across the street. I saw how individuals in my community were affected by war and I shared a blanket comforting my student while she slept, afraid of the night terrors. I struggled with secondary trauma from the atrocities, and did my best to help others through. And then had my own emotional healing to work through.

After being sexually assaulted, there were some days where I wished I wasn't alive, so that the pain and aching in my chest would end. Listening to the servicemen and women share their stories of despair, I knew that I wasn't alone in my struggles.

Throughout the military legal process, I had struggled with being in a separate, limbo category. There was a conflict between who I was as an individual Peace Corps volunteer and the military entity I was up against.

But there in front of me was another individual, a veteran, saying, "You are one of us!"

She was right. I was not alone. I was and am "one of us."

What happened on the night of November 5, 2010, was much larger than my rapist and me.

The issue of rape and sexual assault is much larger than the women and men directly involved—the individual victims and perpetrators.

The issue of victim support is much larger than the Peace Corps or the military. The issue of accountability is much larger than the military justice system, just one legal system in a world of many.

At the end of the day, I am "one of us." One of the many who have been traumatized and betrayed by justice. One of us.

And it's time for all of us to take the issue of rape and sexual assault seriously.

One of Us

"We rejoice in our suffering,
knowing that suffering produces endurance,
and endurance produces character,
and character produces hope,
and hope does not put us to shame."
Romans 5:3-5

Defense lawyer Lt. Mayo asserted repeatedly that this case was not about rape, but rather about regret, insinuating that I was ashamed of my behavior and had falsely accused Dominik. She questioned me repeatedly about fighting back, running away, screaming and using force, provoking the victim's psychological feelings of post-traumatic stress disorder and shame. Her questioning was the second-most belittling and dehumanizing incident I have faced in my life—second to the actual sexual assault and physical violation by the man she was defending.

In the years following my assault, I have struggled greatly. But I have also grown tremendously in my resilience and my desire to stand for truth and justice. I have found nonjudgmental, accepting individuals who have supported me along the way, including individuals at the Peace Corps, fellow survivors and the few friends and family members I have told about this treacherous journey.

In November 2010, I was unaware how my life would change after a single incident. Now, I am a resilient survivor, passionate about respecting and taking care of others, our families, our communities and keeping accountable individuals who choose not to do so.

I am only one of the many who have been sexually assaulted. A data point in a long data set of individuals who have been sexually assaulted. Like so many, when I started this journey, I felt alone and misunderstood. I was hazily going through what I needed to feel safe and start the healing process. I did not want people to judge me as I struggled. I wasn't strong enough from the actual event to handle their judgment.

I've accepted the fact that I was sexually assaulted. But I refuse to let that night dictate who I am today and in the future.

In America alone, there are over 17.7 million women and 2.78 million men who have their own unique stories of rape and sexual assault.[29]

Sexual assault is a societal problem, a social issue that affects all of us. We need to stop being in a state of denial and face the fact that rape and sexual assault occurs much more in our society than we want to acknowledge. We need to stop isolating and re-victimizing individuals who have already been traumatized and provide them with compassionate and nonjudgmental medical and legal resources.

We need to focus on restorative justice making the victim whole and holding perpetrators accountable for their actions.

We must place the shame of rape and sexual assault on those to whom it belongs—the perpetrators.

We need to shift the blame to the individuals who abuse power and control, who traumatize others, who sexually exploit individuals, who choose to sexually assault others. We need to judge the societal norms accommodating rape culture and the systems enabling this injustice to continue.

We need to protect those of us who are survivors, our families and our communities, for the injustice of sexual assault affects us all—directly and indirectly.

I have faith that we, as survivors, can heal. I have hope for the future for I have seen the diligence and impact of men and women within our society who, through their work and personal lives, are taking action against violence against others, to prosecute offenders, to train and raise a new generation changing cultural norms.

There is a future where sexual exploitation and violence against others is unacceptable.

That future begins with each and every single one of us, survivors and allies alike, playing our part to end sexual assault.

---

29 National Institute of Justice & Centers for Disease Control & Prevention. Prevalence, Incidence and Conse-quences of Violence Against Women Survey. 1998.

Sandi Giver has over 10 years of experience working in youth development, anti-trafficking in persons and women's health issues directly with survivors of sexual assault as well as community organizing and policy reform around sexual assault. Her experience is mostly with nonprofit organizations in the United States, Southeast Asia and East Africa. As a Peace Corps volunteer from 2009-11, Ms. Giver worked with war-affected youth and adults who were formerly abducted child soldiers, sex slaves, child mothers, orphans and vulnerable children, facilitating classes dealing with the psychosocial effects of PTSD in a post-conflict area. She is currently pursuing a master in social work at the University of Maryland, Baltimore, and resides in the Washington, D.C., area.

Visit oneofusmovement.com.

Made in the USA
Middletown, DE
24 December 2016